MAIN LINE STEAM

25 GLORIOUS YEARS OF PRESERVATION

BILL SHARMAN

Atlantic

Ex GWR 'Castle' class 4-6-0 No 5051 Drysllwyn Castle *was built in 1936 and with-drawn from service by BR in 1963. After languishing for seven years in Barry scrap-yard, the engine was restored at Didcot, and returned to the main line on the 26th January 1980 hauling the Great Western Society's rake of preserved GWR coaches between Didcot and Stratford-upon-Avon. The sun's dying rays catch the train as it powers through Fenny Compton on the return leg of the tour.*

MAIN LINE STEAM

25 GLORIOUS YEARS OF PRESERVATION

BILL SHARMAN

5051

Power personified as Stanier 'Princess Coronation' 4-6-2 No 46229 Duchess of Hamilton *storms up towards Blea Moor tunnel at Blea Moor sidings with the northbound "Cumbrian Mountain Express" of the 29th October 1983.*

Atlantic Publishers,
Trevithick House, West End, Penryn, Cornwall, TR10 8HE

First published 1997
© Bill Sharman, 1997
ISBN: 0 906899 76 1
Design and layout: Barry C. Lane, Sutton-in-Craven
Reproduction and printing by The Amadeus Press Ltd,
Huddersfield, West Yorkshire

British Cataloguing in Publication Data
A catalogue record for this book is available
from the British Library

Please note that all photographs NOT credited are by Bill Sharman.

Other contributors are:- Hugh & Toni Ballantyne, John Cooper-Smith, Brian Dobbs, Tom Heavyside, Brian Morrison.

CONTENTS

'King' No 6000 King George V *begins the return to Hereford on the ground-breaking round tour of October 1971 with the first "Return to Steam" special. In this shot it is seen between Goring and Cholsey, working from Kensington to Swindon on the 7th October 1971.*

(John Cooper-Smith)

There is an ancient Chinese curse which reads "May you live in interesting times." I think anyone who has been involved in the return of steam to the main line over the past 25 years would appreciate the irony of that malediction. It is difficult to transport oneself back to 1971; to remember how one felt in the absence of steam on the main line, and how grateful we were for the little we were allowed in the early years. The running of a steam hauled train on the main line was something to be looked forward to, something to be savoured, and something to be remembered. We lived from month to month and year to year, never knowing when the privilege of watching these magnificent machines in full flight might be withdrawn. It is difficult to quantify how much we all owe those early enthusiasts who beavered away for three long years and eventually not only managed to effect the return of steam to the main line, but kept it there against all the odds.

I am in the age group which grew up with steam railways after the war. Like so many others of my age I was a schoolboy trainspotter, mainly in the north-west round Manchester, but later in Edinburgh. I can still remember actually seeing a streamlined 'Coronation' class locomotive. With the return of preserved steam my personal interest lay as much in the techniques of steam railway photography as with the steam engines themselves. Often over the years I have asked myself why I do it, as this example will show.

On the 23rd March 1986 I, along with many other enthusiasts, travelled down to Andover in Hampshire where the Salisbury Area Management team of British Rail were organising a "Rail Event '86" as a follow-up to the GW150 exhibition and display at Salisbury in August 1985. The highlight of the "Rail Event" was the appearance of 4930 *Hagley Hall* hauling a 6-coach train to Ludgershall.

It was a typical March day with the usual pattern of weather that one associates with steam photography. The day started with clear blue skies, but as the time for the first train approached, so did the clouds. A biting north-westerly wind swept across the land and conditions were mostly cloudy for the rest of the day. I was standing on the road bridge to the west of the station — actually waiting for a service train to arrive, which I wanted to photograph whilst waiting for the next departure of the steam train — when I was approached by four teenage lads who wanted to know what I was doing. I told them that a steam train was running and that I had travelled down from the Midlands to photograph it. "When would it come?" they wanted to know. "In about an hour from now", I told them. They looked at me almost unbelievingly. "You're going to stand there for an hour just to take a photograph?" one lad asked. "Well", I replied rather defensively, "I'll take a photograph of anything else that comes along." They were incredulous. "You mean ordinary trains?" "Yes", I replied. This seemed to be stretching things too far. They looked me over carefully with obvious disbelief until one of the lads, with a burst of inspiration, asked "Are you an American?" — as if that would clear up the whole puzzle. When I replied that I was not, they left in puzzled bewilderment.

Photographing trains, particularly steam trains, is an incurable disease. Whilst it is quite difficult to explain to a non-believer why one would want to photograph diesels, it is a little easier to convince the sceptic about the pleasures to be had photographing steam engines. There is something alive about a steam locomotive — it snorts and coughs, and billows great gouts of smoke and steam. It has personality. However, even having said all that, it is still difficult to explain why one is prepared to stand on a freezing cold day in a gale-force wind for an hour or more waiting to photograph a steam locomotive.

25 years is a long time. The story of how preserved steam on the main line has arrived at its present position is a fascinating one, often like a good detective story with sudden, unexpected, and often unwelcome, twists and turns. It has never been all plain sailing, but rather a bizarre contrasting of fortunes. Behind it all has been the driving force of countless dedicated enthusiasts who have refused to give up even when the odds have appeared stacked against them — and that has happened regularly in the past two years!

I have tried not to let the story of 25 years of preserved steam on the main line degenerate into a series of lists of excursions year-by-year — though this is obviously the background to the story — but rather to try and show how things evolved. At the end of 1996, which happens to coincide with the 25th anniversary of the return of steam to the main line, we have reached a time when, I believe, we should reflect on the past and consider the future. Even two years earlier, anyone connected with the movement would have agreed that progress had been unbelievable. During the past two years boundaries have been pushed even further with mould-breaking developments, not always for the good of the steam movement. There were also some appalling problems. Now is the time to stand back, pause, reflect and take stock.

Come with me back to the exciting days of 1971, and trace the development of preserved steam on the main line through the years. It is a tale well worth the telling.

The End and the Beginning — 1971–1973

When British Railways let the curtain fall on its steam operations on August 11th 1968, and it was decreed that no preserved steam locomotive would be allowed to run over British Rail metals — other than the few excursions already agreed for *Flying Scotsman* — it seemed to enthusiasts that a new 'Dark Ages' had arrived. Steam retreated to the confines of a few preserved lines, kept alive by a handful of hard-working and dedicated enthusiasts, whilst the average middle-of-the-road enthusiast like me allowed his interest to drift away from the railways into new hobbies.

At that time, had someone forecast that in 1985 BR would sponsor no less than 180 steam-hauled main-line excursions and that a further 55 would be promoted by the Steam Locomotive Operators' Association, or that in 1996 we would see regular steam departures from the London termini or steam 'time trials' over Shap, I would have suggested that they be certified! In spite of all the problems of recent years, up until 1995 the number of excursions each year has been maintained — or surpassed.

How it all began. The triumphant return of steam to the main line after a three year total ban saw 6000 King George V *passing Magor en route for Tyseley on the 2nd October 1971 — the first day of its week long tour with the Bulmers Cider train.*
(Toni Ballantyne)

Steam did return to the main line in two ways in 1969. On 29th June, No 4472 *Flying Scotsman* hauled a special train sponsored by the North Eastern Locomotive Group from Newcastle to Keighley via York and Leeds, and then made the return journey to Carlisle by way of the West Coast main line and Shap. Rather less adventurous in nature, but no less welcome was British Rail's decision to allow LMS 'Black 5' No 5428, LMS 'Jubilee' No 5593 *Kolhapur* and GWR 'Castle' No 7029 *Clun Castle* to appear in steam at the "Open Day" at Cricklewood depot in July 1969. These locomotives were allowed to haul passengers up and down a specially selected length of track. Once No 4472 *Flying Scotsman* was taken off to the USA in 1969 by its then owner, Alan Pegler, "The Ban" became virtually complete — apart that is from the steam-hauled services which ran on BR's 1ft 11½in gauge Vale of Rheidol line.

Two years were to elapse before steam again appeared on the main line. The closest that enthusiasts got to seeing a steam locomotive back on British Rail tracks was when 'Jubilee' No 5596 *Bahamas* was towed in light steam by a diesel from Dinting Railway Centre to Glossop station where it appeared in the Festival of Vintage Transport on 18th April 1971.

Steam enthusiasts are nothing if not resilient and optimistic as the very nature of their hobby requires them to be. From the end of BR steam in 1968, the "Return to Steam"

committee of the Association of Railway Preservation Societies had been carefully and diplomatically negotiating with BR to effect the return of steam specials to the main line. The appointment of Richard Marsh as Chairman of the British Railways Board in 1971 coincided with a remarkable change in heart by the Board, and a trial tour was authorised for October 1971, to be worked by No 6000 *King George V*. This involved an eight-day tour, with stop-overs for exhibitions and the train was formed of five Bulmers Pullman cars and three BR Standard coaches. The train's route included London, Swindon, Newport and Birmingham and proved to be a resounding success. People flocked in huge numbers to see the passing of this pioneering special.

It was a beginning. No one then could possibly have foreseen what it would lead to in so short a space of time.

Of necessity, steam returned to the main line cautiously, British Rail having made it clear that a return to the free-for-all conditions of the last years of steam on the main line would not be tolerated. Uppermost in the authorities' minds were the need for safety, and for commercial viability.

No 6000 *King George V*'s outing of October 1971 was regarded as an experiment to identify the potential difficulties that might arise in the diesel age with the isolated operation of a steam locomotive on the main line. The apparent obstacles posed in ensuring satisfactory coal and water supplies were demonstrated as not unsurmountable — merely challenges for the organisers. The provision of steam crews again proved to be less of a problem than had been feared. Perhaps the biggest concern was whether the mechanical condition of the steam locomotives would ensure reliability. Failures on the main line might easily have led to a resumption of "The Ban".

For negotiations with British Rail and co-ordinating the involved planning required for the return of steam to the main line, a Steam Operating Consortium was formed jointly by the Association of Railway Preservation Societies and the main steam depots of the time — Tyseley, Didcot, Hereford and Carnforth. British Rail agreed to open up some 300 miles of track to steam traction and twenty-three locomotives were approved for use in the initial "Return to Steam" programme. Five steam routes were designated, these being Birmingham-Didcot, Newcastle-Carlisle, York-Scarborough, Newport-Shrewsbury, and Carnforth-Barrow.

It is worth looking at the list of approved locomotives in detail at a distance of 25 years — would that they all remained available for operation. Out of the 23 locomotives, only three are currently active on the main line. These are 35028 *Clan Line*, 60532 *Blue Peter* and 4498 *Sir Nigel Gresley* (currently running in BR livery as No 60007).The rest are now confined to steam centres or preserved railways, some in working order, others awaiting repair. They are 7029 *Clun Castle*, 5593 *Kolhapur*, 6000 *King George V*, 6998 *Burton Agnes Hall*, 44871, 44932, 45231, 5407, 5428 *Eric Treacy*, 7752, 7760, 6106, 6697, 1466, 5322, 92203 *Black Prince*, 75029 *The Green Knight*, 60019 *Bittern*, 5596 *Bahamas*. and 4079 *Pendennis Castle* (sadly no longer in this country). Although approved for operation, some of these locomotives were destined not to appear on the main line.

The first of the "Return to Steam" Railtours took place over the weekend of the 10th and 11th June 1972. No 7029 *Clun Castle* had the honour of hauling the first special from Tyseley to Didcot on the Saturday, and the reverse journey on the Sunday. The following Saturday — the 17th June — 4498 *Sir Nigel Gresley* returned to the main line hauling the

"Steam Safari" railtour between Newcastle and Carlisle. Further trips followed. 'A4' No 19 *Bittern* worked the 'Scarborough Flyer' of the 16th September, and 'Black 5s' Nos 44871 and 44932 each worked a train from Carnforth to Barrow and return on the 23rd September. No 6998 *Burton Agnes Hall* featured on a return trip from Didcot to Tyseley on the 1st October, and 5596 *Bahamas* and 6000 *King George V* each operated a leg of the Shrewsbury — Hereford return trip of the 14th October.

One significant working — a forerunner for many others — took place on the 11th November 1972 when 6000 *King George V* ran from Hereford to Newport at the head of the Bulmers Cider train. The object was to provide a film company with sufficient and suitable action material for a documentary entitled "The Golden Age of Steam". Since that first charter, several steam locomotives have featured in films, TV series, TV adverts and promotional videos. All have generated welcome finance for the preservation societies and locomotive owners concerned.

All in all, during 1972 twelve trips operated on the main line. In commenting on the programme the official BR statement noted that "No real difficulties were encountered, and the steam excursions made a small profit." This encouragement was no doubt gratifying to the dedicated people who in one way or another had striven to return steam to the main line.

By today's standards, 1972's twelve trips might seem miserly, but after three steam-starved years, it was nothing short of miraculous. Irksome restrictions were applied — such as light engines being towed by diesels from their depot to the starting point of the tour — but the climate for steam trips was generally favourable, and a solid foundation had been laid.

Apart from steam-hauled excursions on the main line, another significant development in 1972 was the purchase of 5690 *Leander* from Dai Woodham's scrapyard at Barry, the intention being to restore it to main-line running standards. Some locomotives had already left, and many more were to follow *Leander* from that South Wales Aladdin's Cave. Some were to be lovingly restored to run again on the main line, others to be carefully brought back to life to act as the main-stay of a preserved line, and a few to remain in rusting heaps at their new homes as if attempting to propagate Woodham's yard in various parts of the country.

It is interesting to speculate as to what would have happened to British railway preservation had all the locomotives in Dai Woodham's yard been reduced to scrap in the 1960s. In all, 213 locomotives were purchased from this most famous of all scrapyards, the last being Churchward 2-8-0 No 2873 which was bought by the Wales Railway Centre, Bute Street, Cardiff on 29th February 1988. That was nearly 20 years after the first of many — Midland '4F' No 43924 — had been sold to the Keighley and Worth Valley Railway.

Had that treasure trove not been to hand, the number of locomotives available for use on the main line and the preserved lines would have been restricted. Arguably the scale of operations on the main line which was to grow from the late 1970s could not have been considered, let alone effected. Without the benefit of hind-sight, in those uncertain days of 1972 it was a monumental act of faith in the future of steam preservation for Oliver, Taylor, Crossley and Company to have paid — as has been reported — in excess of £50,000 (1972 figures) for the return of *Leander* to main line standards.

'A4' Pacific No 4498 Sir Nigel Gresley *worked the second 1972 "Return to Steam" excursion with a return journey between Newcastle and Carlisle on the 17th June 1972, connecting at both ends of the run with diesel-hauled excursions to and from St. Pancras. In this shot the eastbound "Steam Safari" rounds the curve at Brampton Junction.* (John Cooper-Smith)

Consolidation was the keyword for 1973 and again in 1974. A further 460 route-miles of track were approved by BR in 1973 for use by steam-hauled excursions. Included in the list were Kyle of Lochalsh-Inverness, Dundee-Lady-bank-Dunfermline-Cowdenbeath-Thornton-Dundee, Filey-Hull, Carnforth-Leeds via Keighley, Barrow-Sellafield, Guide Bridge-Dore & Totley, Oxford-Worcester-Hereford, Tyseley-Stratford via the North Warwickshire line and Hatton/Lapworth-Stratford as an addition to the already approved Birmingham Moor Street-Didcot route. Hopes were raised that on occasions cross-country charters spanning two of the designated lines would be authorised, to facilitate the appearance of steam locomotives away from their 'home' areas. As yet the number of steam runs was restricted and confined to the months of April, May, June, September and October.

For 1973 as a whole, the number of steam runs was double the previous year's total. The year started with the York Department of Tourism staging a special Easter Festival of Steam, which included on the 21st April, a special run behind No 4498 *Sir Nigel Gresley* from York to Scarborough, and then after a visit to the North Yorkshire Moors Railway, a second main line steam working with A4 No 19 *Bittern* hauling the 600 passengers from Filey to Hull.

May 5th saw the first "Cumbrian Coast Express" excursion in preservation times when 'Black 5s' Nos 44871/45407 doubleheaded a train from Carnforth to Ravenglass and return. On May 19th the Wirral Railway Circle and the Oxford Publishing Company ran two trains titled the "Royal Giants", featuring 9F No 922203 *Black Prince* on the Oxford-Hereford and reverse leg and No 6000 *King George V* on the Hereford-Newport and return leg.

Steam returned to Scotland in 1973 in the shape of 60009 *Union of South Africa* on the 5th May working a return trip from Inverkeithing to Dundee. Following the success of this venture two further runs were made by the A4 over this route on the 30th June and 8th September.

No 60009 was only one of several new locomotives approved for running on the main line in 1973, the others being 5690 *Leander* — fresh from its extensive and expensive overhaul at BREL Derby — 7808 *Cookham Manor*, 4771 *Green Arrow*, and 1306 *Mayflower*.

Several novel runs were operated during 1973, notably by Tyseley's Pannier Tank No 7752 which on the 13th May worked a shuttle service between Birmingham Moor Street and Stratford-on-Avon, and on 15th July, Didcot's 2-6-2 tank No 6106 appeared with No 6998 *Burton Agnes Hall* on the Marlow branch as part of the centenary celebrations for the Marlow — Bourne End line.

June 10th saw the return of V2 No 4771 *Green Arrow* to the main line after a major overhaul when it worked a series of three return trains from Birmingham Moor Street to Stratford-upon-Avon. A week later the Bahamas Locomotive Society brought steam back to the Hope Valley line for the first time since 1968 when 'Jubilee' No.5596 *Bahamas* worked the "Scarborough Limited" from Guide Bridge to Sheffield. This trip, with a return fare of £4.95, included a run behind A4 No 19 *Bittern* from York to Scarborough and return to York. Instead of working a complimentary train, which was cancelled, from Sheffield to Guide Bridge and return to Sheffield, the 'Jubilee' sat in Grindleford sidings for seven hours waiting to work the first train on its return to revenue earning service from Scarborough back to Guide Bridge.

On 5th May 1973, two of Carnforth's 'Black 5s' Nos 44871 and 45407 ran double-headed from Carnforth to Ravenglass and return. The "Cumbrian Coast Express" originated at Euston and was promoted by the Ravenglass & Eskdale Railway Company. The train is seen leaving Ravenglass on the return journey. The locomotives were coupled tender to tender because of difficulties in turning them at Ravenglass.

(Tom Heavyside)

Two other trains rounded off a very successful programme of main line steam in the first six months of 1973. On June 24th the Great Western Society ran the "Great Western Returns" tour featuring No 6998 *Burton Agnes Hall* on the Didcot-Hereford-Didcot leg and No 6000 *King George V* running Hereford- Shrewsbury-Hereford. On the return trip to Didcot via Malvern, the 'Hall' failed at Worcester with a blown superheater tube and required assistance from 46.151 for the rest of the trip to Didcot. Finally No 4498 *Sir Nigel Gresley* and No 4771 *Green Arrow* were the motive power on two trains titled the "Gresley Commemorative Special" from Tyseley to Didcot and return on the 1st July.

Problems, however, began to surface. "The Phoenix" railtour planned for 28th May featured GWR 2-6-0 No 5322 and was advertised at £4.50 per head. Scheduled to run between Newport and Hereford the special had to be cancelled because of insufficient support. Two trips between Inverness and Kyle of Lochalsh advertised for haulage by 1306 and a 'Black 5' were also cancelled due to lack of support. A steam tour on Southern lines by 35028 *Clan Line* had been proposed for the 13th October but was cancelled by BR just six weeks before — a consequence of concern at trespassing by enthusiasts on electrified track during the Eastleigh Open Day of May 13th.

Lessons were there to be learned, by the Steam Operating Consortium, and not least by the enthusiasts. The first lesson was that the scheduling of a steam locomotive for a main line run was no automatic guarantee of financial success. The paying public was proving to be selective, and promoters of tours would have to pay attention to the selection of routes, locomotives and rolling stock. The second lesson — and one sadly that remains to be learned — was that enthusiasts must demonstrate their responsibility and not trespass on railway property. Otherwise they risked a total ban being placed on main line steam.

September 1st saw the return of 'Jubilee' No 5690 *Leander* to the main line when it worked two circular trains from Kings Cross and Manchester respectively from Guide Bridge to Sheffield and return. September also saw No 6998 *Burton Agnes Hall*, now restored to health, work "The William Shakespeare" from Didcot to Stratford-upon-Avon and back on the 29th, carrying the original nameboard from 1951.

As the big event of the year, and to the delight of all steam enthusiasts, 4472 *Flying Scotsman* returned from the USA in February 1973, to set the seal on the return of steam to British Rail metals. On the 22nd September, 4472 *Flying Scotsman* double-headed 6000 *King George V* from Newport to Shrewsbury on a 15-coach train titled the "Atlantic Venturers Express" in recognition that both locomotives had been to the USA — albeit at a 40-year interval.

The final steam workings of the year saw LNER Pacific No 4498 *Sir Nigel Gresley* haul the A4 Locomotive Society 12-coach "Hadrian" tour between Newcastle and Carlisle on 6th October. The train was then diesel-hauled to Carnforth where LNER V2 No 4771 *Green Arrow* took it on to Barrow. In the meantime the A4 returned from Carlisle to Newcastle with the "Tynesider" special run by the LNER Society from London Euston.

Steam had well and truly returned to the main line.

The second LCGB "Gresley Commemorative" special train to Didcot from Tyseley on 1st July 1973 was hauled by 'V2' 2-6-2 No 4771 Green Arrow seen here leaving Tyseley.
(Hugh Ballantyne)

It will soon be 30 years since Gresley 'A4' Pacific No 4498 Sir Nigel Gresley *made its first appearance on the main line as a preserved locomotive. Here is one of the "earlier" preserved guises of this famous A4 as it emerges from Harbury Tunnel on an LCGB "Gresley Commemorative" special from Tyseley to Didcot on 1st July 1973.* (John Cooper-Smith)

Right:
LMS 'Jubilee' No 5596 Bahamas *appeared on the main line for the second time since the return to steam in 1971 when it worked the "Scarborough Limited" railtour from Guide Bridge to Scarborough and return on the 17th June 1973. It is seen climbing the 1:87 gradient near Bamford between New Mills and Chinley on the outward run.*

(John Cooper-Smith)

Ebb and Flow — 1974–1977

The years between 1974 and 1977 were crucial for the "Return to Steam" lobby. It was one thing to get steam back on to the main line — but an entirely different matter not only to keep it there but also to extend operations. Public interest had to be sustained, and the organisational problems of co-ordinating the running of the steam trips needed to be overcome, these challenges demanding hard work by some very dedicated people. On the mechanical side, it was essential that the locomotives were maintained to the highest standards.

For 1974, some minor changes were made regarding the routes available for steam running. The lines between Kyle of Lochalsh and Inverness, and Newcastle and Carlisle were removed from the list but the route between Stockton and Darlington was added.

The approved list of locomotives available for main line duty remained the same as for 1973, although disappointments and inconvenience ensued when booked locomotives failed to appear and substitutes had to be provided, often at short notice. All in all 14 advertised steam charter trains ran in 1974, with a further three private charters — No 6000 *King George V* on a Didcot-Tyseley and return working for Swindon Corporation on 25th March, No 4079 *Pendennis Castle* from Hereford to Shrewsbury on 7th April and No 4472 *Flying Scotsman* from York to Scarborough on the 29th September with the "Northern Gas Newcastle Festival Special".

On April 6th GWR No 4079 *Pendennis Castle* shared with No 4472 *Flying Scotsman* the working of two steam specials from Newport to Shrewsbury, there swapping trains for the return journey. A week later, A4 No 60009 *Union of South Africa* ran from Edinburgh to Aberdeen and return with the "Bon Accord" and on the 11th May worked from Edinburgh to Arbroath and return with the "Red Lichtie". Not to be outdone, No 4498 *Sir Nigel Gresley* worked the "Tyne-Dee Coastal" from Edinburgh to Aberdeen and return on 22nd June.

The 20th April saw No 6000 *King George V* work a Shrewsbury-Newport-Shrewsbury train — the "Royal Dragon" — as part of the Silver Jubilee celebrations of the Locomotive Club of Great Britain. No 35028 *Clan Line* finally managed its return to the main line 27th April when it ran from Basingstoke to Westbury.

Steam once again appeared in the Hope Valley on 16th June when 5690 *Leander* worked two circular trains, the "White Rose" running clock-wise from Leeds and the "Red Rose" anti-clockwise from Manchester, between Sheffield and Guide Bridge. 4771 *Green Arrow* worked both trains over the Carnforth-Leeds section.

Two specials on 21st September, Flying Scotsman Enterprise's "White Rose" from Leicester and the LNER Society "Red Rose" from St. Pancras, included steam haulage between Leeds and Ravenglass via Carnforth. Motive power was No 4472 *Flying Scotsman* on the "White Rose" and No 4771 *Green Arrow* with the "Red Rose" on the outward runs. At Ravenglass the locomotives changed over trains for the return workings. 'Black Five' No 44932 found fame when it was lit up hurriedly at Carnforth to substitute for 4771 *Green Arrow* on the Carnforth-Leeds section of a return trip from Sellafield when the V2 had been failed with a badly clinkered fire. The train was by now running very late, but No 44932 actually bettered the scheduled time allowed for No 4771.

Two more excursions ran on the 5th October, "The Palatine" from Liverpool and the "Midlander" from London. No 5690 *Leander* worked the "Palatine" from Oxford to Hereford via Malvern, there handing over to No 6000 *King George V* for the Hereford-Shrewsbury run. The locomotives then worked the "Midlander" in the reverse direction.

Perhaps the most exciting trip made in the year was the appearance of 7808 *Cookham Manor* and 6998 *Burton Agnes Hall* at the head of the Great Western Society's "Vintage Train" which ran from Didcot to Stratford-on-Avon on the 19th October. The "Vintage Train" was formed of eight beautifully restored Great Western coaches, and was a splendid spectacle until it made its last main line run in January 1980

Tours from Euston and Paddington on October 26th organised by the Locomotive Club of Great Britain and the Merchant Navy Locomotive Preservation Society jointly involved return workings for Southern Pacific No 35028 *Clan Line* between Didcot and Stratford, and LNER A4 No 4498 *Sir Nigel Gresley* between Newport, Hereford and Shrewsbury. Anyone who was at Stratford that day will remember the great difficulty that *Clan Line* experienced on the return working to Didcot in starting the heavy train from the station

In 1974, serious and well-intentioned suggestions were made in an attempt to prevent a repetition of the cancellations experienced in 1973. Some suggested that the only way to ensure capacity patronage of main line steam specials was to restrict them to just one or two trips a month — working on the basis of scarcity value. Certainly when two trips were planned to run on the 13th April, one of them — that scheduled for No 5690 *Leander* between York and Scarborough at £2.50 a head — had to be cancelled for lack of support, while the other which featured No 60009 *Union of South Africa* between Edinburgh and Aberdeen with tickets

On four Sundays in September 1975, main line steam excursions operated between Sheffield and Newcastle on the East Coast Main Line north of York. The 21st September saw 'A3' No 4472 Flying Scotsman *come to the rescue when the rostered engine on "The North Eastern" — 'V2' No 4771* Green Arrow *failed between Sheffield and York. with a smoking tender rear axlebox. In this picture 'B1' No 1306* Mayflower *is seen piloting* Flying Scotsman *north of York as the train approaches Thirsk.* (John Cooper-Smith)

at £4.75 a head was a huge success. This trip represented exceptional value for money and offered haulage by an attractive locomotive over an interesting route, as well as involving 260 miles of steam haulage — the longest trip yet to be done behind steam in the "Return to Steam" programme. Many factors needed to be taken into account, not least of all co-ordination of effort which at this time remained fragmented.

The year closed with a significant event. This was the transfer on the 2nd December of LMS 'Black Five' No 5025 from the Keighley and Worth Valley Railway to the Kilmarnock works of Andrew Barclay for the engine's complete overhaul as preparation for its service on the Strathspey Railway, and eventual use on the Scottish main lines.

If 1974 was a relatively quiet year, then 1975 provided appropriate compensation when the 150th anniversary of the Stockton and Darlington Railway was celebrated at Shildon. The highlight of the celebrations was the never to be forgotten cavalcade of steam locomotives on August 31st. As impressive perhaps was the sight of all the cavalcade locomotives later that day as they gathered at the site of the former Darlington steam shed.

For 1975, 22 steam locomotives were approved for main-line running, and some 23 routes were made available for steam excursions, comprising 1,056 miles of "authorised track". It is instructive to glance at the list of available locomotives at a distance of 21 years. Missing from the 1973 and 1974 approved lists were 5593 *Kolhapur*, 5407, 7752, 7760, 45231, 6106, 6697, 1466, 5322, 75029 *The Green Knight* and 60019 *Bittern*. Additions to the list in 1975 were 4767 *George Stephenson*, 5110 *RAF, Biggin Hill*, 1306 *Mayflower* and 3442 *The Great Marquess*.

Not surprisingly, most of the emphasis was directed towards the North-East, though Shrewsbury-Chester was added to the list of designated routes. Approval was given for ten steam hauled trains to operate over authorised routes in April, May, June and the first week in October.

Gresley 'A4' Pacific No 60009 Union of South Africa *worked the Kirkcaldy and District Lions Club "Silver Jubilee Special" from Edinburgh to Perth and return on the 28th May 1977. The massive grandeur of the Forth Bridge is seen to good effect as the train crosses on its outward run.* (Brian Morrison)

15

Steam hauled trains were also to be allowed on some Saturdays in June, July, August and September on the Battersby-Whitby line. Highlight of the 1975 main-line excursions was operation on four Sundays in September of steam specials between Sheffield and Newcastle, each routed over the East Coast Main Line north of York.

April 5th saw the welcome return to the main line of B1 No 1306 *Mayflower*, which double-headed "The Furnessman" from Carnforth to Sellafield and return with V2 No 4771 *Green Arrow*. The two engines appeared on this route again on the 21st June, double-heading a Carnforth-Sellafield train. No 4472 *Flying Scotsman* worked a second train to Sellafield that day, the locomotives switching trains for the return runs.

In the run-up to the Shildon celebrations perhaps the most interesting trips on the main line took place away from the North-East. On the 20th April, 92203 *Black Prince* ran from Westbury to Eastleigh and return, while on 14th June 7808 *Cookham Manor* and 6998 *Burton Agnes Hall* reappeared with the "Vintage Train", this time running from Didcot to Hereford and return. Also in June, 'K1' 2-6-0 No 2005 made its main line debut hauling several trains between Battersby and Whitby.

The first "Return to Steam" specials over the Great Western route north of Shrewsbury ran on April 26th taking a 'King' as well as a 'Merchant Navy' into Chester for the first time ever. "The Mayflower", which ran from London Euston, was steam-hauled from Hereford to Chester by No 6000 *King George V* and from Chester to Hereford by 35028 *Clan Line*. The Merchant Navy Locomotive Preservation Society train from Paddington was worked by the two locomotives in the reverse direction.

On May 31st 9F No 92220 *Evening Star* regained BR metals when it worked a special between Leeds and Carnforth with return to Keighley.

In Scotland, No 60009 *Union of South Africa* worked from Edinburgh to Dundee over the Forth and Tay bridges on the 7th June, returning to Edinburgh via Perth and Gleneagles.

The September Sundays' Newcastle-Sheffield trips made use of 4472 *Flying Scotsman*, 4498 *Sir Nigel Gresley*, 4771 *Green Arrow* and 1306 *Mayflower*. One train, the "North Eastern" of the 21st September, was double-headed throughout on the return working between York and Newcastle by 4472 *Flying Scotsman* and 1306 *Mayflower*. This came about when 4771 *Green Arrow* on the Sheffield-York leg ran a hot-box. 4472 *Flying Scotsman* was the stand-by engine and replaced *Green Arrow* on this 15-coach train. Considerable disappointment was caused by the non-appearance of No 532 *Blue Peter* which was originally diagrammed for one of the trips.

The final two charter trains for 1975, "The Welsh Borderer" on a round trip from Manchester and "The Cathedrals Express" on a circular trip from Leeds ran on 4th October. The first train was steam-hauled from Chester to Hereford by 5690 *Leander* and from Didcot to Tyseley by 7029 *Clun Castle*, the routes being reversed for the second train.

Apart from the main line charters that ran, and the preparations for Shildon, several developments occurred in 1975 whose significance was not appreciated at that time. In the February, the ARPS "Return to Steam" Committee was wound up. The majority of the locomotive owners (or operators) providing power for the main line steam excursions then formed the Steam Locomotive Operators Association — or SLOA for short.

The Association was set up to promote the continued operation of steam locomotives on British Railways' lines by ensuring the maximum co-operation between the locomotive owners, operators and the British Railways Board. Membership was open to all owners and trustees whose locomotives were approved for main line running in 1975. Until then, the negotiations for individual main line excursions had been a matter for particular locomotive societies, preservation groups, or private individuals. Initially, although steam trips continued to be separately promoted, agreement as to their operation was reached with BR by means of SLOA. As time went by, SLOA took over more of the burden of administration and organisation, and became an effective champion for main line steam.

Only a little less significant was 1975's rescue of 46229 *Duchess of Hamilton* from Butlins Camp at Minehead. The locomotive was towed by 25.059 from Minehead to Taunton on March 13th, and on to Swindon works by D1010 *Western Campaigner* on March 17th. After extensive renovation and repainting, the engine was finally moved to the National Railway Museum at York during the weekend of 20/21 May 1976. Few could have foreseen that the 'Duchess' was destined to become a force on the main line.

In 1973, the decision had been taken to establish the National Railway Museum at York, and the official opening by HRH. the Duke of Edinburgh took place on the 27th September 1975. One of the NRM's hoped-for roles was to serve as a depot for steam-hauled excursions — a function which exceeded all expectations during the 1980s.

Not surprisingly 1975 ended with a note of satisfaction, given the undoubted advancement of the main line steam scene, and with considerable confidence in the future. The New Year had scarcely dawned when the British Railways Board dampened expectations. They announced that they had formulated a policy for the years 1976 — 1979 inclusive as follows:-

(1) Steam would be allowed to continue for a further four years on the main line, but steam operations were expected to reduce gradually. The situation would be reviewed in 1978, but significant steam operation over BR lines was not foreseen after the early 1980s.

(2) Compared with 1975, some 290 miles of previously approved steam routes were to be deleted, including Sheffield-York-Newcastle, Oxford-Worcester-Hereford, Basingstoke-Salisbury and Eastleigh-Salisbury-Westbury. Some 100 miles of new routes were to be added including York-Harrogate-Leeds and Manningtree-Ely. This left a total mileage of 918 miles of approved routes.

(3) Locomotives were to be confined to their designated 'home' areas and could not be transferred — even dead — to take part in open days or exhibitions elsewhere.

(4) Although the Settle — Carlisle line would celebrate its centenary in May 1976, no steam specials would be allowed over the route.

(5) Steam specials would be restricted to the periods between Mid-March and June, and from September to Mid-October on Saturdays and Sundays, and on Sundays only in July and August.

(6) All applications to run steam tours had to be made through SLOA who would approach British Rail with specific proposals.

The BRB's policy statement enjoyed a hostile reception, and shock waves travelled throughout the preservation movement. A list of 23 approved locomotives soon followed, each being placed in one of eight designated areas. Notable newcomers to the list included 'S15' 4-6-0 No 841 *Greene King*, 6115 *Scots Guardsman* and 6201 *Princess Elizabeth*. In due course there followed a list of 21 approved tours for 1976 .

GWR 'Castle' No 4079 Pendennis Castle *shared the working of two steam specials from Newport with A3 Pacific No 4472* Flying Scotsman *on the 6th April 1974, swapping trains at Shrewsbury for the return journey. The 'Castle' approaches Donnington on the southbound journey from Shrewsbury.*

(Hugh Ballantyne)

As often happens, matters were not as bad as they seemed at the time. The first indication of better fortune came when Steamtown Railway Museum Ltd and Flying Scotsman Enterprises announced that agreement had been reached with the National Railway Museum and with British Rail to exchange 4472 *Flying Scotsman* for the Midland Compound No 1000 and LNWR 2-4-0 No 790 *Hardwicke*. The change-over trips took place on the 24th April and the return workings were arranged for the 19th June. Between these two dates many strange combinations took to the main line — mostly as a result of No 1000's prompt failure on arrival at Carnforth, but also as a consequence of other defective locomotives.

One example occurred on the 1st May when various special trains operated over the Settle — Carlisle line in celebration of the line's centenary. The original plan was for No 1000 and 44932 to haul one of these trains from Carnforth to Hellifield, the steam locomotives then giving way to diesel power for the northbound run over the S & C. After being turned on the Shipley triangle, the 'Compound' and '5' would return to Hellifield to take over the south-bound special from Carlisle for the run to Carnforth. In the event, both locomotives were unavailable which prompted instead the unlikely pairing of 4472 *Flying Scotsman* and 790 *Hardwicke*, the latter as pilot.

On the 22nd May, 790 *Hardwicke* again piloted 4472 *Flying Scotsman* this time between Carnforth and Ulverston, there to be replaced by 1306 *Mayflower* for the remainder of the trip to Sellafield. One of the most delightful main line runs occurred on the 9th May when 790 *Hardwicke* made four return trips between Carnforth and Grange-over-Sands. The venture was such a success that it was repeated on the 23rd May. Similar excursions were arranged for July and August this time booked for No 1306 *Mayflower*, but were abandoned after the first day, having proved a financial failure. On the 19th June, two double-headed trains ran

from Carnforth to York, featuring another strange pairing in the shape of 790 *Hardwicke* piloting 92220 *Evening Star* on the LCGB's "Fells and Dales" railtour. The second train was hauled by No 1306 *Mayflower* and 'Black 5' No 5407.

Although Carnforth featured extensively in 1976's main line steam activities, there were excursions elsewhere on the BR network and they operated with varying degrees of success. No 841 *Greene King* made its main line debut on the 3rd April, and sadly expired with a "hot box" at March. The Birmingham Railway Museum organised a steam-hauled railtour for 17th April which saw No 7029 *Clun Castle* run from Birmingham New Street to Stratford-upon-Avon and Oxford returning via Banbury and Leamington Spa. Another engine which made its return to the main line was No 6201 *Princess Elizabeth*. On the 24th April No 6201 and No 35028 *Clan Line* were in action between Hereford and Chester with two railtours — "The Gwentman" and "The Intercity" organised by the Midland and Great Northern Railway Society and the Wirral Railway Circle respectively.

A third excursion by the Great Western Society's "Vintage Train" took place on the 15th May between Didcot and Tyseley, powered by 5900 *Hinderton Hall* and 6998 *Burton Agnes Hall*. Stanier Pacific No 6201 *Princess Elizabeth* worked the "Stanier Centenary" from Hereford to Chester on the 5th June to mark the centenary year of Sir William Stanier who was born on 27th May 1876. LMS '5' No 4767 *George Stephenson* appeared on the main line on the 4th July for the Newcastle-Stockton leg of the "Scarborough Flyer", the York-Scarborough leg being covered by No 92220 *Evening Star*. The 6000 Locomotive Association "Mercian Venturer"

Having left for its American tours on 19th September 1969, 'A3' Pacific No 4472 Flying Scotsman *returned to Liverpool on the deck of the container vessel "Californian Star" on the 14th February 1973 under different private ownership. After overhaul and re-painting in BRE workshops at Derby, it spent the summer season on loan to the Torbay Steam Railway, and the autumn touring the North of England with the "Cider Express" mobile exhibition. One of its early runs on the main line took place on 6th April 1974 when, complete with its second tender, it worked from Newport to Shrewsbury and back — here passing Dorrington on its return run.* (Hugh Ballantyne)

A special train of vintage rolling stock was jointly promoted by British Rail, the National Railway Museum and Steamtown Carnforth on the 1st May 1976 to celebrate the centenary of the Settle-Carlisle line. Initially it was advertised as being steam-hauled between Carnforth and Hellifield by Midland Compound 4-4-0 No 1000 and LMS Class 5 -6-0 No 44871. Both these locomotives proved to be unavailable, as did substitute 'Black 5' No 44932, leaving the unlikely combination of LNWR 'Precedent' 2-4-0 No 790 Hardwicke *piloting LNER Class A3 4-6-2 No 4472* Flying Scotsman. *The train is approaching Clapham station on a wild and windy day.*

and a complementary tour from Euston, the Merchant Navy LPS "Marches Merchantman", on the 2nd October involved three steam engines between Hereford, Shrewsbury and Chester — No 35028 *Clan Line*, No 6201 *Princess Elizabeth* and No 6000 *King George V*. The charter train had been organised in celebration of five years of main line steam specials.

In September of 1976, Sir Richard Marsh completed his five years stint as Chairman of the British Railways Board, to be replaced by Mr Peter Parker. What a five year spell it had been for the advocates of steam on British Rail! Steam had progressed from the first hesitant steps of 1971 to the well-established operations of 1976.

Not for the first time in this story, nor unfortunately the last, the weather managed to disrupt 1976's programme of steam specials — it was much too hot and dry! Those trains scheduled to run during August and September were suspended because of drought conditions, thereby preventing 6960 *Raveningham Hall* from making its scheduled main line debut on the 1st August. As compensation for the cancellation, the steam season was extended with the "Scarborough Belle", scheduled to run on the 11th September, appearing on the 30th October. This featured No 5690 *Leander* on the Guide Bridge-Sheffield and return leg and No 92220 *Evening Star* on the York-Scarborough-York leg.

A new locomotive to appear on the scene was No 5305 — a Stanier 4-6-0 'Black 5' owned by Mr A. Draper of Hull. The Humberside Locomotive Preservation Group had been responsible for its restoration, and the loco was handed over to Mr Draper in main line running condition at the group's headquarters at Hull Dairycoates on the 15th August — ready for the 1977 season.

Although 1976 proved to be better than any had dared hope, the same cannot be said for 1977 when various reverses affected the preservation scene in general, and steam on the main line in particular. The portents for 1977 were favourable — there was the Queen's Silver Jubilee to celebrate in October, and *King George V*'s Golden Jubilee in July — No 6000 that is! For many enthusiasts, the early part of the year was given over to chasing the last of the 'Western' diesel-hydraulics — perhaps it might have been termed the "Year of the Western Wakes" instead of Jubilee year. A list of 26 main line steam tours was published, all approved by British Rail in conjunction with SLOA. No 4498 *Sir Nigel Gresley* was due back on the main line after an extensive overhaul and retubing, and on 30th April No 5305 was down for its return to the main line.

The first blow fell in February when it was announced that 4079 *Pendennis Castle* had been sold to the Hammersley Iron Pty Ltd in Australia, and so would be leaving the country. The engine ran a farewell tour on 29th May from Saltley to Didcot, returning to Dorridge, and then made its way to Bristol docks from whence it was shipped to Australia to arrive in Sydney on the 11th July.

BR '9F' No 92203 Black Prince *had only a short main line life in preservation in the earliest years. The East Somerset Railway's special from Newport to the "Open Day" at Eastleigh on 20th April 1975 was steam hauled from Westbury and featured David Shepherd's engine — seen here at Upton Scudamore.* (Hugh Ballantyne)

Next came the news of the cancellation of no less than five "Return to Steam" tours planned to run during June, as a result of insufficient bookings. Surprisingly, some of the most popular main line engines had been advertised as haulage, including 5690 *Leander*, 35028 *Clan Line*, 4498 *Sir Nigel Gresley* and 7029 *Clun Castle*.

The third reverse of 1977 followed the announcement on July 16th that 5690 *Leander* was to be sold as a result of business problems affecting Oliver, Taylor, Crossley and Company. *Leander* had been mortgaged against a debt, and the engine was officially repossessed as an asset, to be sold to the highest bidder. A figure of £80,000 was mentioned — a not unreasonable sum given that the engine had run just 1000 miles since being rebuilt at Derby. There were natural fears that the 'Jubilee' might follow No 4079 overseas.

To cap it all, on the 15th October, No 841 *Greene King* failed again soon after the start of its journey between Manningtree and Ipswich. This time the culprit was a seized left-hand piston valve which caused damage to the motion on that side.

But 1977 was not all doom and gloom. April 3rd saw the start of the year's programme when Great Western 4-6-0 No 7029 *Clun Castle*, from Birmingham Railway Museum, Tyseley, made two return trips to Leamington Spa. The first train carried Warwick Castle headboard "The Kingmaker" and after the passengers had alighted at Warwick, the engine was turned on Hatton triangle and then worked from Leamington Spa to Tyseley and back with the Coventry Evening Telegraph/Wight Locomotive Society "Midland Wightsman". Finally it became New Cavendish Books "The Bookman" for the final leg conveying Warwick Castle visitors to Birmingham.

The 23rd April saw 6000 *King George V* and 6201 *Princess Elizabeth* back on the main line between Chester and Hereford hauling 11 restored Great Western coaches from the Severn Valley Railway. On its first passenger workings over BR metals since restoration on April 30th, LMS

'Black 5' No 5305 hauled a ten-coach train from Leeds to Scarborough via York and return. On the same day LNER Pacific No 4498 *Sir Nigel Gresley* ran from York to its new home at Carnforth via Leeds with an A4 Locomotive Society 13-coach special from Newcastle. The locomotive had spent the previous night in the National Railway Museum, where the A4 LS held a dinner on the 29th April to celebrate the centenary of Sir Nigel Gresley's birth.

Steam haulage of the "Western Cavalier" special on the 25th June included No 7029 *Clun Castle* from Didcot to Dorridge and No 35028 *Clan Line* on the Newport-Shrewsbury leg of the tour. On the 3rd July, 6000 *King George V* celebrated its Golden Jubilee with a run between Newport and Shrewsbury at the head of the Great Western Society's restored stock.

Three Steamtown-based locomotives were involved in the LNER Society special from Euston on the 17th September, "The North Eastern Jubilee". The engines concerned were 4472 *Flying Scotsman*, 4771 *Green Arrow* and 4498 *Sir Nigel Gresley* who each worked a section of the Carnforth-Leeds-York-Leeds-Carnforth route. *Green Arrow* was the first locomotive to be overhauled on the National Railway Museum premises, and its debut run on BR metals after restoration was the 17th September run. On the following week two pairs of LMS design 4-6-0s were out over BR metals working two complimentary railtours. 5305 and 5690 *Leander* worked the Guide Bridge-Sheffield and return leg, whilst 44871 and 45407 ran from Carnforth to Leeds and return.

Great Western 4-6-0 No 6000 King George V *celebrated its Golden Jubilee on the 3rd July 1977 by hauling the Severn Valley Railway's GWR train, strengthened by the "Clapham Buffet", from Newport to Shrewsbury and return. The "Great Western Venturer" was sponsored by "Steam in Hereford Limited" — the forerunner of the 6000 Locomotive Association. In this picture No 6000 is about to leave Hereford for Newport with the empty stock.* (Tom Heavyside)

On the 1st October, a mammoth extravaganza was staged between Newport and Chester to celebrate the Queen's Silver Jubilee. A locomotive from each of the Big Four companies hauled the train over a section of the route, commencing with 35028 *Clan Line* between Newport and Hereford, followed by 6201 *Princess Elizabeth*, 6000 *King George V* and finally 4498 *Sir Nigel Gresley* for the Chester-Shrewsbury leg of the journey. Two trains ran in opposite directions, and such was the interest that the whole affair was repeated on the following Saturday — the 8th October.

The final steam-hauled special of the year ran on 29th October with two complimentary trains. The steam section of "The Pennine Venturer" was between Carnforth and Leeds with 4498 *Sir Nigel Gresley* and Leeds to York with 92220 *Evening Star*. "The Pennine Ranger" worked in the reverse direction.

So 1977 drew to a close. Looming ever closer was 1980, with its threatened end of steam on the main line. No one could have supposed that the bottom of the trough had been reached, even though suggestions had been filtering through to the effect that British Rail itself was poised to sponsor a programme of steam-hauled excursions, and the Leeds — Scarborough route was mentioned. In spite of all 1977's disappointments, a spring had returned to the steam enthusiast's step — better times seemed to be on their way.

The Shrewsbury-Hereford section of the "Midland Jubilee" of the 1st October 1977 was hauled by LMS 'Princess Royal' Class No 6201 Princess Elizabeth, *seen here passing Wooferton. The other locomotives involved were GWR No 6000* King George V *and SR Bulleid Pacific No 35028* Clan Line. *So successful were the trains that the whole itinerary was repeated the following week.*

CHAPTER 3

The Turning of the Tide — 1978–1979

Two items of good news ushered in 1978. The first was the announcement rapturously received by all railway enthusiasts that No 4771 *Green Arrow* would inaugurate the season's main line steam operations on the 25th March with a northbound run over the Settle — Carlisle line, returning south two days later. Next came confirmation of the rumour that British Rail would be marketing steam-hauled trains on the main line for the first time since 1968 — perhaps the single most important step forward since steam returned to the main line in 1971.

SLOA's advertised programme of 19 steam worked excursions, half in the spring and early summer and the remainder scheduled for autumn and winter, had expanded by two trains by the end of the year. In addition, on the 6th June 4472 *Flying Scotsman* emerged from a six-month overhaul at Vickers works at Barrow-in-Furness including fitting of a replacement boiler, and promptly returned to main line operations on the 13th June hauling a Press Preview of the "Cumbrian Coast Express" between Carnforth and Sellafield, No 4498 *Sir Nigel Gresley* working the return leg. Two days later *Flying Scotsman* worked a train of vintage stock from Hellifield to Carlisle, returning the following day. Fresh engines promised for the year included 70000 *Britannia*, 6115 *Scots Guardsman*, and 6960 *Raveningham Hall*. No 841 *Greene King* was withdrawn from the main line steam list before the season started.

BR '9F' No 92220 Evening Star *became the second locomotive to run over the S. & C. line following its opening to preserved steam when it headed the 6000 Locomotive Association Railtours "Border Venturer" from Hellifield to Carlisle and return on 13th May 1978, shown here crossing the spectacular Dent Head viaduct. The train originated in Cardiff, leaving at 06.40 and was timed to return at 23.30! Some day out for a fare of £12.50.*

Bulleid Pacific No 35028 Clan Line *leaves York with a thirteen coach train forming the Merchant Navy Locomotive Preservation Society's "Citadel Express" for Carlisle on the 23rd September 1978. Whilst the weather was sunny at York, low cloud and mist prevented any photography on the S. & C. above Horton.*

The "Humber Venturer" of the Humberside Locomotive Preservation Group on 8th April was headed by 5305 from Leeds to Carnforth, whence it set out for Sellafield behind LNER B1 4-6-0 No 1306. On the same day No 6960 *Raveningham Hall* ran on the "Cathedrals Express" between Hereford and Chester, but failed at Chester with a 'hot box'. This was one of a couple of failures because 6000 *King George V* also succumbed to a 'hot box' on the 7th October. Two of Steamtown's Class 5 locomotives featured in the running of two specials on 29th April. Nos 45407 and 44932, the latter currently in green livery, hauled the first train from Carnforth to York, there handing it over to A4 No 4498 *Sir Nigel Gresley* for its onward trip to Guide Bridge. The second train was sponsored by the A4 Locomotive Society, and ran from Guide Bridge to York behind *Sir Nigel Gresley*, and then to Carnforth behind the two 'Black 5s'.

Following the successful runs with 4771 *Green Arrow* on "The Norfolkman" over the Settle & Carlisle line in March, No 92220 *Evening Star* headed the 6000 LA Railtours "Border Venturer" from Hellifield to Carlisle and return on the 13th May.

On 20th May, No 70000 *Britannia* was 'renamed' and rededicated by its designer, R.A.Riddles at Bridgnorth but, sadly, the Pacific was subsequently failed by a British Rail inspector because of a welded repair found on the inside of the outer firebox.

King George V and *Princess Elizabeth* were out between Hereford and Chester working two complimentary steam specials on the 20th May. In Scotland, No 60009 *Union of South Africa* reached Aberdeen on the 25th March with the "Northern Belle" from Edinburgh, and on the 27th May, for the second year running, hauled the Kirkcaldy & District Lions Club "Lions Steam Special" from Kirkcaldy to Perth and return via the Forth Bridge.

For SLOA, 1978 was to prove the most successful year yet for steam-hauled excursions, and all but two trains achieved a minimum 95% loading to justify the cautious optimism which had accompanied the announcement of the 1978 programme.

A third encouraging development for 1978 came with the news that Bill Ford and David Clarke, then both directors of the Main Line Steam Trust at Loughborough, had purchased No 5690 *Leander* for a sum reported to be around £65,000, and had probably saved the export of the locomotive in the way that had happened to 4079 *Pendennis Castle*. Later in the year the new owners announced that *Leander* would not be going to Loughborough as originally planned, but instead would be based at Steamtown, Carnforth and made available for main line operation on BR's "Cumbrian Coast Express".

British Rail's sponsored steam-hauled excursions were promoted under the banner "Full steam ahead — for all the family". The London Midland Region was responsible for the "Cumbrian Coast Express", a train originating at Blackpool and picking up passengers at Preston and Lancaster. Steam was to be attached at Carnforth for haulage of the "CCE" to Sellafield, a second engine running light to Sellafield, to return with the train to Carnforth. The two designated locomotives were No 4472 *Flying Scotsman* and No 4498 *Sir Nigel Gresley*. Trains ran on Tuesdays from 27th June to 29th August inclusive, and the full adult fare was just £4. The Eastern Region's train — the "Yorkshire Circular Steam Tour" — was scheduled to make two round trips every Sunday from 25th June to the 3rd September. The route was circular, leaving York at 09.55 and 13.45, and running via Leeds and Harrogate before returning to York. The scheduled locomotives were No 92220 *Evening Star*, No 4771 *Green Arrow* and No 5305. The cost for the full round trip? £2.25!

Right:
LMS 'Royal Scot' 4-6-0 No 6115 Scots Guardsman *had its second outing to York during its short-lived renaissance in 1978 on the 11th November. It is seen here bursting out of New Mills tunnel, crossing the River Goyt with 6000 LA Railtours "Yorkshire Venturer".*

Below:
A new excursion train entitled the "North Yorkshireman" was introduced by BR in 1979 to run on summer Wednesdays from Grange-over-Sands to Skipton. Perhaps "Chop-em off Charlie" was the driver on the 5th September 1979 when the "North Yorkshireman" was being hurried along behind LMS 'Jubilee' No 5690 Leander, *storming up the bank at Clapham on the Wennington line.*

Details of the performance of these excursions, and the patronage they attracted was eagerly, if nervously, awaited by main line steam enthusiasts. Obviously British Rail's experience with these trains would have consequences for the organisation's attitude to main line steam specials in the future. It soon became clear that there was no need for concern, because, of the 5,100 seats on offer on the "Cumbrian Coast Express", 46% were sold a week before the start of the trips, a figure that rose to 64% occupancy after the first week of running.

Because of the pressure of bookings for the 'CCE', British Rail increased the service by a further train which ran on Wednesdays from 12th July to 30th August. By the end of July all 9,230 seats on offer on the 19 trains in the "Cumbrian Coast Express" programme had been sold. On the Eastern Region business was just as good with 500 passengers being carried on each train. All in all, over 20,000 passengers travelled on 42 British Rail sponsored trains in the 1978 programme, and British Rail pronounced itself delighted, so much so that in mid-July it was announced that British Rail and SLOA had reached agreement in principle that the operation of main line steam excursions over British Rail lines would continue until 1985. Later in 1978 British Rail said it would continue with a further programme of sponsored trains.

One sad event affected the euphoria of the year, and that was the death at Appleby station on the 13th May of the Rt. Reverend Eric Treacy. He died whilst waiting to photograph 92220 *Evening Star*. If ever a man was a legend in his own time then that was true of Eric Treacy — an inspiration to anyone who has pointed a camera at a train. In a sincere tribute to a great and much loved man, two special trains were chartered on the 30th September to run over the Settle — Carlisle line to Appleby, in turn hauled by the three locomotives turned out on the day — 92220 *Evening Star*, 4472 *Flying Scotsman* and 35028 *Clan Line*. At the destination there was a moving and dignified commemorative service in the station yard. The two trains were titled the "Lord Bishop" and the "Bishop Treacy", and the occasion must be regarded as one of the most poignant and significant in the annals of railway preservation.

The second half of SLOA's main line steam programme started on 9th September when 35028 *Clan Line* moved north with the "White Rose" from Hereford to Sheffield. The journey was done in two parts, from Hereford to Chester hauling the special, then light engine from Chester to Guide Bridge, where it was re-attached to its train for the run through to Sheffield. The engine then proceeded light engine to York to await a taxing programme of runs. The 16th saw the engine work across to Carnforth with a Gainsborough Model Railway Society special to Sellafield, the second leg from Carnforth being worked by 4498 *Sir Nigel Gresley*. The following week the engine worked a thirteen-coach train, the "Citadels Express", from Leeds to Carlisle, and on the 30th was one of three engines rostered for the Eric Treacy memorial trains over the S & C.

6115 *Scots Guardsman* made an emotional return to the main line on the 21st September with a spirited run from Guide Bridge to York. The 'Royal Scot' was at York again on

the 14th October, heading the "Anniversary Express" which celebrated its fiftieth birthday and ten years of the Dinting Centre.

Two trains from London organised by 6000 LA Railtours on October 7th were to have been steam-hauled throughout from between Hereford and Chester and return, but 6000 *King George V* failed at Shrewsbury with a hot box and two class 25 diesels substituted. The other special, "The Fenman", ran from Hereford to Chester behind No 7029 *Clun Castle*. Sunday 15th saw GWR 4-6-0s Nos 5900 *Hinderton Hall* and 7808 *Cookham Manor* double-heading the Great Western Society vintage train between Didcot and Tyseley.

The NELPG ran "The Moorlander" on 22nd October with K1 No 2005 between Middlesbrough and Newcastle, and 4498 *Sir Nigel Gresley* from Carlisle to Leeds. Six days later, 'Jubilee' No 5690 *Leander* ran from Guide Bridge to York with "The Mancunian". The return working to Guide Bridge saw Midland Compound No 1000 piloting *Leander*, the 4-4-0 going on loan to Dinting Railway Centre from the National Railway Museum.

LMS 4-6-0 No 6115 *Scots Guardsman* was out on BR metals again on November 11th taking the 6000LA Railtours "Yorkshire Venturer" — which originated at Cardiff — from Guide Bridge to York. It then worked the M & GNJR Society "Yorkshire Ranger" back to Guide Bridge. This was the 'Royal Scot's' last main line run before falling victim to British Rail's new policy of a more careful scrutiny of locomotive superheater flue tubes. This understandable stiffening of standards was a consequence of an accident at Didcot Railway Centre on the 2nd April when 0-6-2T No 6697 suffered a collapse of a flue tube, and its driver and fireman were seriously injured when high-pressure steam enveloped them. Stringent checks were applied to all locomotives. In addition to No 6115's removal from the scene, all the 'Black 5s' at Carnforth were withdrawn from the main line list.

Offering presents for the children and seasonal refreshments, the 13-coach "Santa Steam Special" run from London Euston on December 30th was steam-hauled from Carnforth to Sellafield, and return by the two "resident CCE" locomotives, No 4472 *Flying Scotsman* and 4498 *Sir Nigel Gresley*. This innovative run, the first of many "Santa Specials" on the main line, crowned a year which had generally been recognised as a make or break year for the commercial viability of steam-hauled special trains.

For 1979, the portents were favourable. In January, SLOA announced its provisional programme of steam tours — 18 in all — to run in spring and early summer, autumn and winter. True No 92220 *Evening Star* had been withdrawn from the list of approved locomotives because British Rail had issued an edict that locomotives with flangeless driving wheels were no longer acceptable on the network because of changes in levels at which check-rails were now installed. After its brief main line foray, No 6115 *Scots Guardsman* was also removed from the main line list as it required an extensive boiler examination before it could be considered again for main line running.

More happily, Nos 46229 *Duchess of Hamilton*, 4468 *Mallard* and 925 *Cheltenham* — all based at the National Railway Museum — were being mentioned as candidates for main line running. Later in 1979, the Friends of the National Railway Museum launched an appeal to raise funds for the restoration of No 46229, the centre-piece for this appeal being the commissioning of an oil painting from Terence Cuneo of the Pacific climbing Beattock Bank. A limited edition of signed prints of this painting was sold as part of the appeal.

Opposite left:
LMS 'Jubilee' No 5690 Leander **and 'Midland Compound' No 1000 storm through Horsforth station on the 20th October 1979 with the "Leander Enterprise" sponsored by the** Leander **Locomotive Society.**

British Rail's plans for its sponsored trains were published in February under the heading of "We're raising steam again". A much more ambitious programme was offered by the London Midland Region. The "Cumbrian Coast Express" was to run on Tuesdays and Thursdays, starting on 29th May and then from 26th June to 6th September inclusive. In addition, there was a new train titled "The North Yorkshireman" which was to operate on Wednesdays from Grange-over-Sands to Skipton and return, starting on 30th May and then every Wednesday from 28th June to 5th September. The rostered engines for the LMR's trains were 4472 *Flying Scotsman*, 4498 *Sir Nigel Gresley*, 35028 *Clan Line* and 5690 *Leander*. The "York Circle" trips of the Eastern Region were to remain with the previous year's formula, but their season was also extended. The booked engines in this case were No 5305, and No 4771 *Green Arrow*. A ticket on the "Cumbrian Coast Express" was £5, the "North Yorkshireman" £4.50 and that on the "York Circle" £2.95.

The year started well with No 5690 *Leander* working the "Leander Envoy" from Guide Bridge to Carnforth via York, transferring its base to Steamtown in order to work on the CCEs.

Life is never straightforward. No sooner had the season commenced than disaster struck. On the 1st March, 6000 *King George V* was permitted to work out of Paddington on a special to Didcot as part of the station's 125th anniversary celebrations. On the outward journey a driving wheel axlebox ran hot and the engine limped to Didcot where it was removed from the train, and a diesel substituted for the return to Paddington. Then at 03.42 on the 17th March, 35 yards of the roof of Penmanshiel Tunnel, north of Berwick, collapsed and blocked the East Coast Main Line. Trains had to be diverted and one route was over the Settle & Carlisle line with the result that the early part of the season's steam-worked programme was disrupted, and several trains had to be cancelled or hurriedly re-arranged.

After these initial upsets, the steam programme soon got into its swing and another excellent and successful season was recorded. Because of the failure of *King George V* at Didcot two days earlier, No 5900 *Hinderton Hall* worked the Didcot-Hatton section of the 6000 LA Railtours "Shakespeare Venturer" on the 3rd March, No 7029 *Clun Castle* working from Hatton to Stratford and return.

The steam section of the SLOA "Northumbrian Limited" from Kings Cross on 7th April — which amalgamated the advertised trips of the 7th and 14th April over the S & C — instead of going to Carlisle, had to be revised because of the Penmanshiel Tunnel blockage, to feature a "mystery trip" based on York. This turned out to be a run to Sheffield and return with a York Circle included. The tour was worked by No 4771 *Green Arrow*. On the 14th April, 60009 *Union of South Africa* ran from Edinburgh to Aberdeen and back with the "Grampian", and on the same day 'Black 5' No 5305 took the "Humberside Envoy" from Hull to Dinting. The return working on the following week saw No 4771 *Green Arrow* work the "North Eastern" from York to Guide Bridge, with 5305 working the return train to Hull. *Green Arrow* and the

Midland Compound No 1000 returned from Guide Bridge with "The Curator" on the 26th May. The train was run as a tribute to the late John Scholes, former curator of Historical Relics at the Museum of British Transport, Clapham.

Having worked the Hereford-Chester section of a MNLPS/6000LA Railtours "Red Rose" special from Cardiff on April 28th, instead of rejoining the train at Guide Bridge for a Sheffield leg as originally planned, the "Merchant Navy" class 4-6-2 No 35028 *Clan Line* continued through to Guide Bridge via Altrincham, thus breaking new ground over a "non-steam route".

LMS Class 5 4-6-0 No 5000, belonging to the National Collection and on loan to the Severn Valley Railway, made its first run over BR metals since restoration on 2nd June with a Hereford-Newport-Hereford trip.

One unique event of 1979 foreshadowed the Rocket 150 celebrations planned for 1980. This was the appearance of the "Centenary Express" to mark 100 years of train catering. A nine-coach train including restored and historic dining cars was assembled by the National Railway Museum on behalf of Travellers-Fare and toured the main lines from 15th to 29th September, visiting most parts of the country. On three of the advertised excursions steam power, in the shape of 6000 *King George V* and 4771 *Green Arrow*, was used.

Ten steam-hauled excursions were advertised for September and October. Three of these were double-headed. "The Intercity" of the 22nd September saw the main line debut of 4930 *Hagley Hall*, double-heading the special with 'Black 5' No 5000 from Hereford to Chester and return. On the 6th October, No 7808 *Cookham Manor* and No 5900 *Hinderton Hall* worked the Great Western Society's "Capital Venturer", composed of its vintage train of ten GWR coaches, from Didcot to Dorridge. The second steam-hauled section for the train was from Shrewsbury to Newport behind 6000 *King George V*. Their reverse working that day was with 6000LA Railtours "Devonian Venturer". The third double-headed working on the 20th October saw No 5690 *Leander*, which had worked "The Leander Enterprise" by itself from Carnforth, being piloted round the "York Circle" by the 'Midland Compound' No 1000.

Two "Santa Steam Specials" were run on the 29th December, which provided a fitting climax to a successful year. Four locomotives were turned out to work the two SLOA specials from Euston and Hull to Sellafield. 'Jubilee' No 5690 *Leander* worked the 13-coach Euston train from Carnforth to Sellafield, with 4498 *Sir Nigel Gresley* on the return working. The Hull train was hauled throughout to Sellafield by 5305, with 4771 *Green Arrow* working the train back to Carnforth.

At the end of 1979 it was difficult to believe that just a couple of years earlier despondency and pessimism had reigned when talking of the future of steam on the main line. BR's threat to end steam running in 1980 had been withdrawn, and now the Board was sponsoring its own trains.

The tide had indeed turned.

Flood Tide — 1980–1981

The SLOA Marketing southbound "Cumbrian Mountain Express" of the 22nd March 1980 from Carlisle to Skipton produced one of those magical days that all photographers dream about, and all motorists hate. There had been a heavy fall of snow which made the drive from Appleby to Ais Gill summit hazardous. Once there the sun came out to enhance the beautiful Christmas card scene which was crowned with the appearance of LMS 'Black 5' No 5305.

As far as steam enthusiasts were concerned, 1980 started with a bang! Initially, the Steam Locomotive Operators Association advertised six "Cumbrian Mountain Express" trains for the months of January, February and March, running alternately north and south between Skipton and Carlisle. In the event, such was the demand for seats that a further six extra trains were organised, and over the first four months of the year over 5,000 passengers were carried on steam specials over the Settle & Carlisle route. Enthusiasm and support for steam on the main line was well and truly demonstrated.

The "Cumbrian Mountain Express" trains featured two locomotives, one on the Carnforth-Skipton leg and the second on the Skipton-Carlisle section. The first of these new style "CMEs" ran on the 19th January with 5305 on the bottom leg and 4498 *Sir Nigel Gresley* over the S & C.

The Spring programme of tours encompassed seven runs between April 19th and May 17th using 13 different locomotives, including '9F' No 92220 *Evening Star* whose ban had been temporarily lifted for the tour of the 17th May.

This was, of course, the year of Rocket 150, when the re-enactment of the Rainhill trials and the attendant locomotive cavalcade were scheduled for 24th-26th May inclusive.

The Welsh ponies flee as a southbound "Welsh Marches Express" heads away from Church Stretton bound for Hereford behind GWR 4-6-0 No 4930 Hagley Hall and LMS 'Black 5' No 5000 on the 11th April 1981.

Apart from the "Cumbrian Mountain Express", most of the steam charters in the first half of the year had the aim of working particular locomotives to the Manchester area in readiness for Rocket 150. The difficulties in achieving this were clearly shown when in April and May booked engines had to be replaced due to their unavailability. BR '4' 2-6-4T No 80079 had to substitute for Ivatt '4' 2-6-0 No 43106 on the "Black Countryman" excursion of 19th April, when it double-headed with No 5000 from Hereford to Manchester. Similarly LMS 5 No 4767 substituted for K1 No 2005 on the Middlesbrough to Newcastle let of the "Tyne-Tay" excursion on the same day, A4 No 6004 Union of South Africa working the Edinburgh-Dundee-Perth-Stirling ley. On the 3rd May, because 'Schools' No 925 Cheltenham had failed, No 4771 Green Arrow partnered the Midland Compound on "The Mancunian" from Leeds to Carnforth. LNER 4-6-2 No 4498 Sir Nigel Gresley worked the train back to Manchester via Gisburn and Clitheroe. The 'Schools' was destined never to haul a train on the main line.

The weather also decided to make its contribution and, because of the risk of lineside fires in the drought conditions, No 6201 Princess Elizabeth was required to be piloted by a diesel for its run between Chester and Manchester Victoria on the 17th May. On the same day No 46229 Duchess of Hamilton — though permitted by the Eastern Region to undertake a York circle — suffered a similar fate on its run from York to Carnforth when the Midland Region insisted on the provision of a diesel pilot over its territory.

The Carnforth-Sellafield leg of the "Cumbrian Coast Express" of the 1st September 1981 was hauled by LMS Class 5 4-6-0 No 5407. This doughty performer attacks Lindal Bank at Pennington.

A new main line performer in the shape of S & D 7F 2-8-0 No 13809, which is carrying a "Pines Express" headboard for its debut run on the 2nd May 1981, rushes through Grindleford en route from Guide Bridge to York.

Steam bans due to high fire risk are not a new phenomenon. In May 1980 many of the plans to move locomotives to the North West for the Rainhill cavalcade on special excursions were disrupted by the hot, dry weather. On 17th May 1980 two such trains required diesel pilots, but North British 0-6-0 No 673 Maude *showed the way by travelling down from Scotland to Manchester via the S. & C. line, here reaching Ais Gill summit.*

For the year, over 1000 miles of British Rail routes had been approved for the operation of steam specials, and several additional routes — such as Liverpool (Edge Hill) — Manchester Victoria and Guide Bridge — Manchester Victoria — had been specially cleared in connection with the Rocket 150 celebrations. 17 steam locomotives were currently approved for main line running with a further 19 provisionally listed. In addition, another 18 awaited temporary certification for inclusion in the Rainhill 150 cavalcade. The civil engineers ban on the operation of No 92220 *Evening Star* was withdrawn and several "new" locomotives made their debut on the main line.

In Scotland, North British 0-6-0 No 673 *Maude* made its return to the main line with a shuttle service over the Forth Bridge to Fife, and then became a star attraction on the 17th May when it travelled down from Scotland to Manchester over the Settle & Carlisle line, and via Hellifield and Blackburn. Amid unprecedented scenes of enthusiasm at the lineside and on stations, No 46229 *Duchess of Hamilton* returned to main line in glorious weather on the 10th May, running twice round the "York Circle" with "The Limited Edition".

British Rail announced its own plans for sponsored steam excursions under the marketing slogan "Full steam ahead — In Rocket 150 year", and later advertisements appeared which read (slightly paraphrased) — "now you've seen them at Rainhill, come and ride behind them". Because of the activity in the North-West, and the extra excursions which occurred as a result of Rocket 150, the Eastern Region did not promote any excursions in 1980. Although the York Circle trains had proved profitable in 1979, they were not as successful as in the previous year, and British Rail was casting around for an alternative route which might attract passengers. Negotiations were under way with Scarborough Borough Council with the aim of installing a turntable at the resort with a view to running steam excursions from either Leeds or York.

"The Mancunian" steam special from Leeds to Carnforth on the 3rd May 1980 was originally scheduled for 'Midland Compound' 4-4-0 No 1000 and SR 'Schools' class 4-4-0 No 30925 Cheltenham. **Sadly the 'Schools' failed and never appeared on the main line, LNER 'V2' 2-6-2 No 4771** Green Arrow **substituting. The unlikely pairing made a handsome couple, as can be seen as they work hard away from Hellifield.**

The London Midland Region promoted no less than three different routes. The tried and tested "Cumbrian Coast Express" once more ran on Tuesdays from July 1st to September 9th, but one or two changes had been made to the format of the trip. The train was now to start from Crewe instead of Blackpool, and the engine on the outward run was to continue to Carlisle via Maryport for use on the southbound "Cumbrian Mountain Express". Having worked the previous Thursday's northbound "CME", the locomotive for the southbound "CCE" arrived from Carlisle. On Thursdays from 3rd July until 11th September a "Cumbrian Mountain Express" would run in replacement of the previous year's "North Yorkshireman" which had loaded disappointingly. The third route to be used by BR-sponsored trains was that from Manchester Victoria to Liverpool Lime Street which would see trains on eight Sundays from 22nd June to 10th August inclusively. A variety of motive power was promised for this excursion but, as it turned out, LMS '5' No 5000 hauled the first train, No 6201 *Princess Elizabeth* the second, and the remaining six were in the hands of No 5690 *Leander*.

There were also other main line charters during 1980, other than those operated in connection with Rocket 150. No 5051 *Drysllwyn Castle* made its main line debut after restoration with excursions featuring the Great Western Society's "Vintage Train" on the 19th and 26th January, the second occasion being the last time that these GWR coaches appeared on BR metals. No 4472 *Flying Scotsman* hauled a special train from Liverpool to Manchester on the 12th March to commemorate the First Day of Issue of the Post Office's Rail 150 stamps. 'Jubilee' No 5690 *Leander* and 'Midland Compound' No 1000 teamed up again in a very pleasant pairing on the "Royal Wessex" from Carnforth to Sellafield on the 5th May, 4771 *Green Arrow* working the return train.

In Scotland, No 60009 *Union of South Africa* ran over the Highland main line from Perth to Aviemore on the 27th June and again on the 25th August.

No 35028 *Clan Line* made a farewell run from Liverpool to Hereford on the 21st June which featured a memorable performance. The Southern Pacific was then withdrawn for a major overhaul and boiler retubing. It would be 1984 before it returned to the main line.

In conjunction with the BBC's "Great Railway Journeys of the World" TV series, No 4472 *Flying Scotsman* ran throughout with a main line special over the 195 miles between Guide Bridge and Carnforth via York on the 15th June, and on the 11th November, 46229 *Duchess of Hamilton* made a memorable appearance over the Diggle route at the head of a special train from Liverpool to York in commemoration of the 150th Anniversary of Mail by Rail.

Several other interesting trains took to the main lines in 1980. Over the weekend of September 6th and 7th, Scotland enjoyed a feast of steam when on the first date No 60009 *Union of South Africa* crossed both Forth and Tay bridges with a charter from Edinburgh to Aberdeen and return, to be followed on the next day by D49 4-4-0 No 246 *Morayshire* hauling the "Taysider", traversing a circular route from Falkirk via Edinburgh, Dundee and Perth. The following Sunday, the 14th September, No 5051 *Drysllwyn Castle* appeared on the "John Mynors Memorial" train from Didcot

Huge crowds turned out for the inaugural runs round the 'York Circle' by newly restored LMS 'Princess Coronation' class 4-6-2 No 46229 Duchess of Hamilton *on the 10th May 1980. "The Limited Edition" — a reference to a painting produced by Terence Cuneo to raise funds for the restoration of the locomotive — left York with the first train in purposeful manner.*

to Saltley and return. Hull Locomotive Preservation Group's 'Black 5' No 5305 worked the "Humber Borderer" from Hull to Carlisle on the 20th September, while LMS Pacific No 6201 *Princess Elizabeth* returned from Carnforth to Hereford with the "Red Rose" on 27th September. Finally on the same day No 43106 — affectionately dubbed the "Flying Pig" — worked from Saltley to Didcot and back.

Life was seldom dull on the Settle & Carlisle with its steam workings although fortunes varied, often dramatically. One welcome newcomer to the line was SR 4-6-0 No 850 *Lord Nelson* which worked the southbound "CME" on the 31st July. No 6201 *Princess Elizabeth* made an impressive run with the southbound "Cumbrian Mountain Express" of the 4th September. No 5690 *Leander* was assured of immortality on the 21st August by rescuing failed diesel No 40.179 which was at the head of a freight train in front of the southbound "Cumbrian Mountain Express" between Kirkby Stephen and Garsdale. *Leander* left its train at Kirby Stephen station, ran wrong road past the stricken freight train, backed on to it to haul it into Garsdale station, where it was shunted by the 'Jubilee' into a siding. *Leander* then returned to Kirby Stephen to pick up its own train, by now running 1½ hours late. On its eagerly awaited inaugural trip over the Settle & Carlisle line on 1st November No 46229 *Duchess of Hamilton* blotted its copy-book when it stalled on the climb past Stainforth in adverse weather conditions and required rear-end assistance by 40.134 through to Blea Moor.

A "one-off" series of four return workings to mark the 200th anniversary of George Stephenson's birth featured namesake LMS 'Black 5' No 4767 George Stephenson, *seen here leaving Newcastle Central with the 13.15 for Hexham on the 6th June 1981. The locomotive had its BR certificate renewed especially for the occasion.*

The year ended with the further four "Cumbrian Mountain Express" trains booked for November and December being expanded to six, and four "Welsh Marches Expresses" from Shrewsbury to Newport along the North and West route. Throughout the year the popularity of the "Cumbrian Mountain Express" continued unabated. A total of 30 steam-hauled trains were run over the Settle & Carlisle line during the year, and that was before British Rail announced its intention of closing the line.

The grand finale for the year occurred on the 27th December with the running of two "Santa Specials". The first was organised by SLOA and departed from Euston, being most appropriately hauled to Carnforth by 86.240 *Eric Treacy*. There steam took over in the shape of No 850 *Lord Nelson* which worked the special to Sellafield. The second train was promoted by the Humberside Locomotive Preservation Group and began its day at Hull. It was hauled from Hull to Leeds by '5' No 5305 where a pilot was attached in the shape of No 4767 *George Stephenson*, the pair of '5s' working to Carnforth where No 5305 was detached. This engine was serviced at Steamtown while No 4767 *George Stephenson* continued with the train to Sellafield. At Sellafield another '5', No 5407, took over the Hull train for the return to Carnforth, where No 5305 was substituted and headed east. The return Euston train was hauled by No 4472 *Flying Scotsman* for the return run to Carnforth where electric traction took over for the run south. Over 1,000 passengers took full advantage of a marvellous day out.

By the early autumn of 1981, a decade of steam operation on the main line would have been completed. In the year more than 100 steam specials were to run on British Rail metals, an undreamt of number even three years earlier, let alone in 1971! The first half of the year was dominated by the SLOA excursions over two routes — the "Cumbrian Mountain Express" (north and southbound), and the "Welsh Marches Express". All the trains on both routes were exceptionally well supported.

In addition, 43106 returned to the main line with a return trip from Dorridge to Didcot on the 11th April, while SLOA triumphed with a most ambitious programme north of the border over the week-end of the 9th and 10th May, with its charter train titled the "North Briton". On the Saturday, hauled by No 60009 *Union of South Africa* the train ran from Mossend to Perth, Dundee and then back to Larbert. The next day, unhappily marred by thick fog for most of the time, the "North Briton" was double-headed by No 246 *Morayshire* and No 673 *Maude* from Larbert to Edinburgh and then to Mossend. Apart from the weather it had all proved a great success.

LNER class 'D49' 4-4-0 No 246 Morayshire **ran round the 'Fife Circle' on the 5th July 1981 with a private charter for Donald Monteith Travel Ltd. The train is on the last leg of its journey as it leaves Dalmeney for Larbert.**

32

In March 1981, in a bold initiative SLOA purchased eight former Metro-Cammell Pullman Cars, for use not only on steam charters, but also for Scenic Land Cruises worked by modern traction. As brake vehicles to complete the set two Mark 1 BCK's were also purchased, all vehicles being passed for 100mph running. The purchase was made in the face of the declining number of coaches in the BR fleet that were compatible with steam haulage. The move was particularly brave given that the cost of maintenance and 'plating' of the vehicles was in excess of their purchase price. Such charges had brought about the withdrawal of the GWS. "Vintage Train" and the Severn Valley Railway's set of GWR coaches used on the main line. Agreement was reached between SLOA and BR for the Pullman rake to be based and maintained at Carlisle Upperby Depot. The set made its main line debut with a special train over the Settle & Carlisle line on 2nd May with No 5407 as the motive power.

A newcomer to the main line was former Somerset & Dorset 2-8-0 No 13809 which ran from Guide Bridge to York and back on the 2nd May. Other new engines to main line work were No 5025 which appeared on the Perth-Aviemore line on the 6th July, and Bulleid Pacific No 34092 *City of Wells*, which worked the Carnforth-Hellifield leg of the northbound "Cumbrian Mountain Pullman" on 28th November. The next month, on the 12th December, in arctic conditions it worked a curtailed special from Carnforth to Skipton.

Of the year's total of over 100 trains, BR contributed 59. Its ambitious summer programme was promoted under the banner "Full Steam Ahead in 1981". The Eastern Region's contribution was an entirely new working, the "Scarborough Spa Express" which ran from York to Scarborough and back on Tuesdays and Wednesdays. This was the culmination of the negotiations between British Rail and Scarborough Borough Council which resulted in a 60ft diameter turntable from Gateshead depot being installed in an enlarged turntable pit west of the station. The local council contributed towards the cost of the installation. The first of the special trains ran on 23rd May, and was worked by No 46229 *Duchess of Hamilton*.

The London Midland Region planned to run no less than three different trains in its 1981 programme. The first was the "Cumbrian Coast Express" running on Tuesdays from 14th July to 1st September, but with slightly altered timings than before to allow passengers the opportunity to make a return trip on the Ravenglass and Eskdale Railway. Then there was the "Cumbrian Mountain Express" scheduled to run on Wednesdays from 15th July to 2nd September. The change over point between the top and bottom leg was altered this year to Hellifield from Skipton. The third train was a new format "North Yorkshireman", to run on the Bank Holiday Mondays 25th May and 31st August, and also on Tuesdays 23rd/30th June, 7th July and the 8th/15th September. Steam would come on the train at Carnforth, where the passengers had 50 minutes to visit Steamtown, and work through to Keighley where passengers had 3½ hours to

In 1981 one of the popular routes for steam excursions was Shrewsbury-Hereford-Newport-Hereford using two engines. The Hereford-Newport-Hereford leg of the SLOA Marketing "Welsh Marches Express" of the 14th February 1981 saw 4930 Hagley Hall heading south at Nant-Y-Derry.

explore the Keighley and Worth Valley Railway. The stock was stabled at Bradford whilst the locomotive was turned and watered at Shipley. Both regions were involved in a new service which was used for the transfer of main line steam engines between Carnforth and York the expense of doing so being offset by revenue from passengers. These were advertised as the "Red Rose" and the "White Rose", and ran on six Sundays between 26th July and 30th August.

In the Autumn, SLOA introduced a new route for steam excursions with the introduction of the "Trans-Pennine Pullman" which required the services of two engines. One leg was from Carnforth to Leeds, the other between Leeds and Northwich via the Diggle route, Stalybridge and Manchester. The trains were scheduled to run alternately south and northbound. The first southbound Pullman was on 26th September hauled by No 4498 *Sir Nigel Gresley* working the Carnforth — Leeds leg, with No 5305 continuing to Northwich. The following weekend, the first northbound run took place with No 5305 working the train from Northwich to Leeds.

Amongst several special trains which ran elsewhere in 1981, mention must be made of No 4767 *George Stephenson* which on the 6th July made four return trips between Newcastle and Hexham to celebrate the 200th anniversary of George Stephenson's birth. Then there was the mammoth excursion of 24th October to celebrate the 15th anniversary of the North Eastern Locomotive Preservation Group, when a train double-headed by K1 No 2005 and 'Class 5' No 4767

George Stephenson, ran from Middlesbrough to Newcastle, on to Carlisle where the engines were serviced, and continued over the Settle & Carlisle line to Hellifield, and back to the North-east.

Another entertaining main line operation took place on 20th September in connection with Old Oak Common depot's Open Day when No 92220 *Evening Star* and No 5051 *Drysllwyn Castle* "top and tailed" a series of shuttle workings between Paddington and Old Oak Common.

All seemed to be set fair for the continued success of steam on the main line. But one or two clouds were appearing on the horizon. The first sign of changed fortunes came with a disappointing response to SLOA's autumn programme. Eleven one-off trains had been included but two were cancelled because of insufficient bookings, two because of the non-availability of the booked motive power, and the original price quoted by BR for two of the trains could not be guaranteed as a result of poor bookings and had to be re-negotiated. The other five trains were successful though the non-availability of 'King Arthur' No 777 *Sir Lamiel* caused much additional administrative work. The "package" programme included four "Trans-Pennine Pullmans", three

The 12th December 1981 was one of the coldest days on record. In arctic conditions, newly restored SR Bulleid Light Pacific No 34092 City of Wells, *on its second outing on the main line, heads for Skipton at Kettlesbeck Bridge near Eldroth. The train was originally scheduled to run from Carnforth to Leeds and return, but was curtailed at Skipton so that passengers stood a chance of getting home the same day.*

"Cumbrian Mountain Pullmans" and three "Welsh Marches Pullmans". The "Trans-Pennine Pullmans" were a disappointment, with an average load of only 180 passengers. The "Welsh Marches Pullmans" loaded much better, but the level of bookings for the two trains programmed for October was distinctly discouraging.

These reverses were accompanied by a downturn in traffic growth on the preserved railways. The opinion was voiced more than once that from 1982 there would have to be a contraction in main line steam operations, and that steam workings would have to be concentrated on a limited number of depots where an adequate number of trained staff remained.

The most worrying set of conclusions came from the Railway Preservation Convention held in Manchester in 1980. It was noted that the nucleus of staff with steam experience was diminishing, that the costs of compliance with the ever

more stringent safety requirements were rapidly increasing, that internal boiler examinations would have to be made every six months, while the requirement for retubing was now reduced to five years, with a possible extension to a maximum of seven years.

George Hinchcliffe — then General Manager of Steamtown Railway Museum — calculated that at 1980 prices the cost of re-tubing an LMS 'Class 5' locomotive would be in the region of £12,000. When No 35028 *Clan Line* was withdrawn for overhaul in 1980, the estimated cost of re-tubing and other work was put at £30,000. As George Hinchcliffe pointed out, such sums of money could not be raised from ticket sales and private charters unless charges rose considerably. His quote was, "If you want your fun to continue, you must pay for it". Dan Cowan of BR's CM&EE Dept. at Derby added to the concern when he warned "We consider that the boiler of a steam locomotive has the greatest potential for disaster, and we will not make things easier for you in the future".

Such views underlined the problems facing main line steam at the end of 1981, and indeed are echoed in the situation 15 years later. After ten years of preserved steam on the main line, which had achieved far more than even the most optimistic enthusiast would have thought possible in 1971, the challenge was to face and overcome these problems.

High Water — 1982–1983

The outlook at the beginning of 1982 was slightly worrying, particularly for those locomotive owners faced with the major overhaul of their locomotives in the near future. Had the bubble of steam on the main line burst, and would their outlay on repairs be recouped — at least in part — by the revenue from main line charters?

The results of the first six months of 1982 gave the lie to those who thought that steam had peaked out on the main line. On 21 main line steam charters, SLOA carried 7,000 passengers — an overall load factor of 94%. Indeed 800 applications for seats had to be refused on fully-booked trains.

Because of the problems experienced during the autumn and winter programme in 1981, the annual steam excursion programme on the main line was now based on three different types of train. Firstly, there was the British Rail sponsored summer train. Secondly, there were the autumn/winter/spring repetitive package trains organised by SLOA. Finally occasional "one-off" individual trains, sponsored either by SLOA or the locomotive owner, were to be permitted. These were to be authorised only for special occasions such as anniversaries and celebrations, or for the specific purpose of transferring locomotives.

Between January and June, SLOA concentrated on three routes — the well-tried and trusted "Cumbrian Mountain Pullman" and "Welsh Marches Pullman", and the newer "Trans-Pennine Pullman". The last-named of these services proved to be a big disappointment — the bookings were poor. At the end of June it was decided that this route would be dropped.

Under the heading "Getting Steam Up in 1982", British Rail's summer programme included north and southbound "Cumbrian Mountain Expresses" on Tuesdays, "Cumbrian Coast Expresses" through to Maryport on alternate Wednesdays, and transfer trains between York and Carnforth on the other Wednesdays. The Eastern Region's "Scarborough Spa Express" now incorporated a York Circle on both the outward morning train and the evening train.

Initially there was a set-back to this programme when the threatened NUR strike caused the cancellation of the northbound "Cumbrian Mountain Express" on the 29th June. No sooner had this strike been settled than ASLEF came out on strike from the 4th to 19th July. All in all the London Midland Region lost five trains due to strike action and the Eastern Region three of its "Scarborough Spa Express" workings.

The first "Cumbrian Mountain Express" ran the day after the strike was settled — featuring 4472 *Flying Scotsman* with LMS '5' No 5407 on the Hellifield-Carnforth leg of the journey. The first "Scarborough Spa Express" ran on the 22nd July and again featured 4472 *Flying Scotsman* — the engine having arrived at York the previous evening with the "White Rose" originating at Carnforth. Motive power during that summer's season of BR sponsored trains included No 4472 *Flying Scotsman*, 4498 *Sir Nigel Gresley*, 46229 *Duchess of Hamilton*, 5690 *Leander*, LMS '5s' Nos 5305 and 5407, 777 *Sir Lamiel*, and 34092 *City of Wells*.

After an inauspicious start, the BR Specials ran with varying degrees of success. On the Midland Region, the "Cumbrian Mountain Express" trains were well patronised, but the "Cumbrian Coast Expresses" were disappointing, and patronage of the transfer trains — the "White Rose" and "Red Rose" — could only be described as "fair". On the Eastern Region, however, loadings were excellent with the high-point being a total of 670 passengers booked on one train leaving York for Scarborough after the morning York Circle.

Several "one-off" trains appeared during the year, and 5025 starred in several of the most exciting. On 29th May, the engine worked over the Inverness to Kyle of Lochalsh line with a train chartered by the Scottish Chamber Orchestra and members of the public attending a concert given at Dornish Castle by the orchestra. It was steam-hauled only as far as Dornish, where 5025 came off the train to return light-engine to Inverness. On the 12th June, No 5025 returned to the main line hauling the "Strathspey Express" between Perth and Aviemore, and on the 25th September hauled the "Ravens Rock Express" from Inverness to Kyle of Lochalsh. A busy season for the 'Black Five' was rounded off during the first week in October when on four successive days a train carrying journalists to a Toyota press event in Skye was hauled by 5025 from Inverness to Kyle of Lochalsh.

Further south, Ivatt '4' No 43106 and 7812 *Erlestoke Manor* ran from Hereford to Chester and then back to Shrewsbury on the 5th June after the cancellation of the "Yorkshire Pullman" previously due to be run on that day. The "Yorkshire Pullman" was finally run on the 18th September with 777 *Sir Lamiel* at the head of the train. This run was to test-market the route between York, Scarborough and Hull.

Between the two strikes, 4472 *Flying Scotsman* appeared at the head of two special school trips over the Settle — Carlisle line. The first, on the 1st July, ran from Langwathby to York and return, whilst the second, the following day, ran from Carlisle to York and return.

SLOA's autumn programme of steam-hauled Pullman trains proved outstandingly successful with a load factor of 98.9%. Indeed six out of the autumn and winter trains had to be strengthened, and more than 200 applications for seats were refused. SLOA had introduced a new train to its programme — the "Pennine Pullman" — running from Blackburn to Leeds and Carnforth via Manchester Victoria. The

A newcomer to the main line in 1982 was Urie 'Class N15' No 777 Sir Lamiel *which made its first main line trip on the "Cumbrian Mountain Express" of the 27th March 1982 double-heading with Stanier 'Black 5' No 5407. On the 21st July 1982, the 'King Arthur' was in charge of the "White Rose" — a transfer train between York and Carnforth — heading west at Bell Busk near Skipton.*

first train was hauled by 4498 *Sir Nigel Gresley* prior to its withdrawal for heavy repair and retubing — an exercise estimated to cost about £30,000.

In general terms, 1982 was a quietly successful year for steam on the main line. This was reflected during October with the announcement that British Rail had agreed to extend the period for main line steam running to 1990. But there was a sting in the tail with the announcement that beyond 1986, steam operations would be concentrated on three centres only — Carnforth, York and Hereford. The steady reduction in the availability of steam-heated coaches on British Rail meant that greater reliance would be placed on privately owned sets of rolling stock equipped with dual heating. It is interesting to note that between 11th April 1981 and 20th June 1982, the SLOA Pullman train covered no less than 21,800 miles.

The announcement of the extension of steam running to 1990 was particularly important not only for the owners of 4498 *Sir Nigel Gresley*, faced with a bill in excess of £30,000, but also for all other owners since it gave them the opportunity to re-coup some of the heavy costs of keeping a locomotive on the main line.

During the year, SLOA sounded a warning note which was largely ignored. It was pointed out that there was a yawning discrepancy between the true cost of a ticket on a steam special — particularly in the case of an inclusive ticket from a major centre — and its actual cost. They estimated that in 1982, each passenger journey was subsidised to the tune of £10.40. This figure was made up by the element of heavy repair charges (i.e. boiler overhauls) not covered by earnings of £3, 'free' volunteer labour — £3, 'free' help by British Rail staff — £1, cross-subsidisation from non-steam

services using the SLOA Pullman Set — £1, unrecovered administration costs — £1.50 and miscellaneous costs — 90p. In other words, without the voluntary contribution of a small number of dedicated people a ticket costing £15 would really cost £25. The significance of this statement only became apparent later when, perhaps in an effort to oust SLOA from its pre-eminent position in the marketing of steam charter trains on the main line, BR decided to abandon what the organisation saw as its own voluntary contribution to the fare charged for steam charters, and to force the fares up to what they regarded as realistic levels.

If 1982 was a success story for steam on the main line, then 1983 turned out to be an enigma. The year started favourably with a full programme of tours organised by SLOA, all of which were well supported. The highlight of this part of the year's programme was probably the run north over the Settle — Carlisle line in blizzard conditions by the Midland Compound No 1000 and No 5690 *Leander* on the 5th February.

One of the outstanding events in the first part of the year had promised to be the celebrations to mark the 60th Anniversary of 4472 *Flying Scotsman*. The Diamond Jubilee was celebrated on the 24th February in a ceremony staged at Steamtown, Carnforth which was followed by 4472 *Flying Scotsman* hauling a special train from Carnforth to Leeds. Because unsuitable coal was provided, the outward journey

was a lack-lustre affair, to put it mildly — although all credit was due to the footplate crew for getting the engine to steam at all! No 5407 returned the train to Carnforth in style.

Initially, a single celebration run on the East Coast Main Line was organised for the 27th February, with 4472 *Flying Scotsman* hauling the train from Peterborough to York. Not surprisingly the trip was an immediate sell-out. Two further trips were organised for the 6th and 13th March, and both were heavily over-subscribed. Indeed SLOA stated that the trips could have been sold "ten times over". The unacceptable face of rail enthusiasm was demonstrated at Newark when hundreds of people spilled over on to the tracks to get a better view of the engine and in the process not only risked injury to themselves, but delayed several scheduled Inter-City 125 services. Unsurprisingly British Rail was not amused.

Other interesting 'one-off' specials ran in the first six months of the year apart from the trips by 4472 *Flying Scotsman*. On the 11th June, No 6000 *King George V* hauled a private charter train from Bath to Bristol in celebration of the 150th anniversary of the appointment of Isambard Kingdom Brunel to the post of engineer to the Great Western Railway. On the evening of the same day, LMS '5' No 5000 hauled a train from Wapping Wharf to Bristol. The 1200 passengers from these two trains — all dressed in 1933 costume, that being the Brunel centenary year — then attended a Gala Evening and banquet in Temple Meads Train Shed which was then undergoing restoration. On the following day, 6000 *King George V* hauled the SLOA sponsored "Brunel Pullman" from Bristol to Hereford via Newport, and No 5000 then took over and hauled the train to Worcester via Ledbury. As Pullman coaches with inward

opening doors were being used, for this trip the ban was lifted on steam specials through Ledbury tunnel.

The following week — on the 18th June — 5690 *Leander* worked a one-off special to Sellafield on behalf of the "Leander Locomotive Society". During their stay at Carnforth the *Leander* support team and their families had become addicted to Cumberland sausage. Whenever *Leander* ran to or from Sellafield, a telephone order was placed with a butcher in Ravenglass for up to 55lbs of this delicacy, to be picked up as the train came through. Under the circumstances it was only right and proper that the special train of the 18th June should be titled "The Cumberland Sausage"!

On the 25th June, 5025 again appeared on the Highland Main Line hauling a steam special between Perth and Aviemore.

Perhaps the most significant series of trips organised for 1983 were the ones that ran on the 12th, 19th, and 26th June, which were titled "The Shakespeare Express". The trains worked from Paddington to Stratford-upon-Avon, steam-hauled from Didcot to Stratford, on two occasions by 5051 *Drysllwyn Castle* and once by 6000 *King George V*. Although the potential of these trips was enormous — given the opportunities for marketing them as an attraction for tourists rather than as trips for enthusiasts — support was at best lukewarm. Perhaps later developments with the opening up of Marylebone to steam were in part due to the initial limited success of these trains.

Having hauled a private charter from Inverness to Dornish in May 1982, LMS 'Black 5' No 5025 returned to the Highland Main Line on the 12th June with the "Speyside Express" from Perth to Aviemore and return. The locomotive heads south from Pitlochry on the return trip.

The summer season of steam specials clearly revealed the enigmatic nature of 1983. While the Eastern Region was pleased with a reported £30,000 profit on the 1982 season of "Scarborough Spa Express" trains, and was to run them again in 1983, London Midland Region was less happy with its experiences of 1982. With reduced availability of suitable BR-owned vacuum-braked stock, and falling demand from passengers particularly for the "Cumbrian Coast Express", the LMR invited SLOA to take over the running of the summer service using their Pullman stock.

SLOA duly acceded, but only after considerable thought. In the event, 14 trains were offered — a mixture of 8 "Cumbrian Mountain Pullmans", 3 "Cumbrian Coast Pullmans", and 3 "Welsh Marches Pullmans". With one exception the trains ran on Wednesdays between the 22nd June and 14th September. The weather attempted to take a hand, and two trains had to be piloted by diesels because of the fire-risk — the "Welsh Marches Pullman" of 13th July had 47.491 as pilot for 5051 *Drysllwyn Castle* and 6000 *King George V*" had 40.063 attached for the return trip of the "Welsh Marches Pullman" on the 10th August.

At the end of the programme, SLOA expressed themselves reasonably happy with an average of 80% capacity filled, though the "Cumbrian Coast Pullman" of 6th July ran with only 200 passengers. A potential body-blow occurred at the end of August when the SLOA Pullman set had to be withdrawn because of presence of asbestos insulation. The year's programme was completed using mixed sets of Mark 1 and Mark 2 stock provided by BR.

The final months of the year once more saw a full SLOA programme with two trips organised for 60009 *Union of South Africa* — one to Perth and the second to Aberdeen — and one trip run into Fife by NBR 0-6-0 No 673 *Maude*. New ground was broken when 4472 *Flying Scotsman* hauled a train between Annan and Ayr on the 22nd October as part of its move to the Ayr Rail Fair organised by BR on the 29th.and 30th October. Other locomotives to appear at the Rail Fair were 60009 *Union of South Africa* and 46229 *Duchess of Hamilton*. The return journey by 4472 *Flying Scotsman* took place on the 12th November.

Two notable "one-off" charters took place in September, the first being in connection with the Shildon Works Open Day on the 29th September, when K1 2-6-0 No 2005 hauled a series of trains between Middlesbrough and Shildon. Four days later Midland Compound No 1000 powered a private charter from York to Rochdale and Castleton.

The pairing of Severn Valley Railway engines — standard class 4 2-6-4T No 80079 and LMS class 4F No 43106 — looks right as the "Welsh Marches Pullman" of the 26th February 1983 heads north at Caerleon en route from Newport to Hereford.

No 850 *Lord Nelson* made a welcome return to the main line after repair. It's first duty was on the 7th September when working the Hellifield-Carlisle leg of the "Cumbrian Mountain Express". The year ended with the by now customary Santa Specials when No 5305 hauled two Santa Special trains over the Settle-Carlisle line — a northbound trip on the 28th December and a southbound run on the next day.

Several things happened in 1983 which provided an ominous portent for the future of main line steam. Early that year, SLOA issued a warning to those owners and societies restoring locomotives to main line standards, that these would not necessarily be allowed to run on the main line. It was emphasised that engines could only be placed on the list of those approved for main line running after stringent examination and with the agreement of SLOA.

Because of the economic climate, and the possibility of less main line work with correspondingly reduced fees for the owners of existing main-line approved locomotives, a new locomotive would not automatically gain admission to the approved list, especially if another example of the class was already approved.

The logic behind this announcement became clearer later in the year when, after spending six weeks working on the North Yorkshire Moors Railway — almost certainly in an attempt to maximise the locomotives income — 5690 *Leander* was transferred to the Midland Railway Trust at Butterley, in the first instance to work service trains on the railway, but also for minor repairs to be carried out during the winter months. Whilst there it was announced that 5690 *Leander* and unrestored sister engine *Galatea* had been sold to the Severn Valley Railway.

The main reason given for the sale was that the directors of Leander Locomotive Limited — Messrs Ford and Clark — had lost an estimated £50,000 keeping the engine on the main line. Two other reasons were also given for the sale, one being the virtual elimination of the profitable one-off charter specials, and the other being the advent of additional locomotives to share available main line work.

This sad event shows the economic pressures on locomotive owners and further fulfiled the prophecy of the 1980 Steam Preservation Convention held in Manchester which warned of hard economic times to come. With increasing charges being exacted by British Rail for locomotive inspections, the reduction in the numbers of enthusiasts charters run by SLOA in 1986, and BR's stated preference for large prestigious locomotives, the chances for owners of the medium sized locomotives to recoup some of their outgoings were dwindling fast.

The third event that caused major concern in steam preservation circles in 1983 was the announcement by BR that it wished to close the Settle & Carlisle line. All involved with steam on the main line reacted with dismay — after all, this was the line above all others which was the most popular and most lucrative route for steam hauled excursions. When the possibility of closure was first mooted in 1983, charter traffic on the line blossomed, and an extra train from York had to be run to Carlisle in the summer season. In addition, the ordinary service trains had to be strengthened — ten coach trains were the order of the day compared to the four coach trains planned when the Nottingham-Glasgow service first stopped running over the Settle-Carlisle line.

By the end of 1983, with the promise that steam specials would continue to run on the main line till 1990, the future looked promising and relatively secure. However storm clouds were gathering and the possibility of troubled waters lay ahead. In the next few years the railway preservation movement would have to meet and overcome a series of major problems and difficulties showing the same patience, flexibility and determination that had carried them through the first 12 years.

The "Cumbrian Mountain Express" trains in the first three months of 1982 were fully booked. On the 13th February, Bulleid Pacific No 34092 City of Wells made its debut on the southbound "Cumbrian Mountain Express", having travelled north the previous Saturday. The location is Howe & Co. sidings, Cumwhinton. Compared with 1981, the change-over point for the bottom leg train was altered from Skipton to Hellifield. During 1982, City of Wells worked 18 excursions on the main line.

The "Northumbrian Mountain Pullman" of the 22nd January 1983 from Stockton to Hellifield via Newcastle and Carlisle featured K1 No 2005, seen here rushing through Long Meg sidings at Little Salkeld between Carlisle and Appleby.

41

Above:
Another successful series of steam-hauled excursions in the early part of 1982 were the "Welsh Marches Express" trains. On the 17th April, newly restored GWR 4-6-0 No 7812 Erlestoke Manor, *making its main line debut, piloted GWR 'Hall' class No 4930* Hagley Hall *over Llanvihangel Bank on the Hereford-Newport section of the run.*

One of the most photogenic vantage points on the North and West route is Sutton Bridge Junction, Shrewsbury. GWR 'Castle' class No 5051 Drysllwyn Castle *heads south out of Shrewsbury en route for Hereford with the "Welsh Marches Pullman" of 9th April 1983.*

The northbound 'Cumbrian Mountain Pullman' of the 27th March 1982 was notable for the return to main line passenger working of SR 4-6-0 No 777 Sir Lamiel *after an absence of 20 years. The "King Arthur" piloted LMS Class 5 4-6-0 No 5407 on the Hellifield-Carlisle leg. On the bottom leg from Carnforth to Hellifield, S&DJR/LMS Class 7F 2-8-0 No 13809 is seen at Eldroth with Ingleton showing through the mist.*

On three Sundays in June 1983, steam returned to the Didcot-Birmingham line when the "William Shakespeare" excursion train ran from Paddington to Stratford-upon-Avon — the first regular through train to operate between the Capital and England's premiere tourist centre outside London for many years. Steam working between Didcot and Stratford featured GWR 'Castle' class 4-6-0 No 5051 Drysllwyn Castle *on the 12th and 26th June. On the 19th June, fresh from its overhaul at Swindon, GWR 'King' class 4-6-0 No 6000* King George V *rushes through Aynho on the outward journey. This was probably the first time that a 'King' had visited Stratford, for the line was prohibited to the class in ordinary steam days.*

A feast of steam was served up on the northbound Cumbrian Mountain Pullman on Bank Holiday Saturday — the 29th May 1982. The train was hauled from Carnforth to Hellifield by LNER A3 4-6-2 No 4472 Flying Scotsman, *then double-headed over the Long Drag by LMS Class 5 4-6-0 No 5407 and LMS 'Jubilee' 4-6-0 No 5690* Leander. *Amidst glorious scenery the two engines drift over Armathwaite viaduct on the last leg of their journey.*

Right:
SR 4-6-0 No 850 Lord Nelson *is really motoring between Langwathby and Culgaith on the southbound "Cumbrian Mountain Express" of the 3rd March 1984. The run took place in glorious early spring weather.*

Below:
Almost at a crawl after the taxing 1:45 and 1:50 gradients between Glenfinnan viaduct and Glenfinnan station, the newly restored North British 0-6-0 No 673 Maude *(formerly 'J36' No 65243) grapples with its four coach train on the foreshortened run to Arisaig on Monday, 28th May 1984. Because of the dry weather, several lineside fires were started, and the smoke from one of these can be seen in the background.*

Gresley 'A4' Pacific No 4498 Sir Nigel Gresley *made a welcome return to BR lines following a full boiler and mechanical overhaul at the head of a private charter from Clitheroe to York via Manchester on 9th June 1984. Later in the year — on the 27th October — the 'A4' approaches Ais Gill summit under Hangman's Bridge with a southbound "Cumbrian Mountain Express".*

"The Fenman" excursion from Manchester Victoria to Spalding via Sheffield and Nottingham on Saturday 10th November 1984 was conceived as a means of getting 'A3' No 4472 Flying Scotsman *to London for the Stratford (Low Level)-North Woolwich Royal Train carrying HRH The Queen Mother on Tuesday 20th November. With strong back lighting, the Gresley Pacific powers up to Cowburn tunnel.*

Right:
For a few short weeks in 1985, Stanier 'Black 5' No 5407 worked smokebox first out of Mallaig, giving undreamed of opportunities to explore new locations. On the 14th July 1985 the 18.00 hrs. train to Fort William leaves Mallaig station. The small boatyard in the foreground has now been replaced by Mallaig's new by-pass road.

Below:
On its second outing since returning to the main line following its extensive 4-year overhaul, an immaculate ex-SR 'Merchant Navy' class 4-6-2 No 35028 Clan Line *leaves Shrewsbury at Sutton Bridge Junction with the southbound Welsh Marches Express of the 20th October 1984.*

47

No 7029 Clun Castle *substituted for the non-available* City of Truro *twice in 1985 on the "Western Stalwart" trains with No 4930* Hagley Hall. *The two locomotives are seen passing Hereford at the end of the day on 6th July.*

Below:
In glorious autumn scenery, Stanier Pacific No 46229 Duchess of Hamilton *heads south at Baron Wood with the "Cumbrian Mountain Express" of the 26th October 1985. This was the locomotive's last run before coming out of traffic for overhaul on the expiry of its BR 7-year ticket.*

48

Troubled Waters — 1984–1985

1984 was a marvellous, if at times frustrating year. It started brimming with confidence in spite of the worrying trends previously mentioned. SLOA's winter and spring programme was well supported and new and exciting routes were introduced to complement the old tried and tested ones. Three engines returned to the main line after very extensive and expensive repairs. On the 4th February, 'Black 5' No 44767 *George Stephenson* marked its return to main line duty by hauling the bottom leg of the northbound "Cumbrian Mountain Express". No 4498 *Sir Nigel Gresley* returned on the 9th June with a private charter train from Clithero to York via Manchester and Leeds. Then on the 27th July, No 35028 "Clan Line" literally returned in a "blaze of glory" when while hauling empty stock on a running-in turn from Swindon to Bristol, it started more than 20 lineside fires. "Clan Line" had been out of service for some four years and the cost of restoring the locomotive to main line running condition was of the order of £48,000.

The two most eagerly awaited events in 1984 were the introduction of regular steam specials on the Fort William-Mallaig line using No 44767 *George Stephenson*, North British 0-6-0 No 673 *Maude*, and 'Black 5' No 5407, and the appearance of 60009 *Union of South Africa* south of the border for the first time since the return of steam to the main line in 1971.

The Fort William — Mallaig trains were a great success. The first runs took place over the Spring Bank Holiday weekend, with 5407 and 673 *Maude* sharing the work. Thereafter, steam services operated on Sundays from the 1st July to the 9th September, and on Wednesdays and Thursdays from 11th July to the 23rd August. It was soon obvious that 673 *Maude* could not cope with the severe gradients with anything like a full train. A new service was therefore introduced called the "Glenfinnan Flyer" which ran on some Fridays. *Maude* hauled two coaches to Glenfinnan and return — the passengers having time to visit the various historic spots at Glenfinnan. Over the season some 11,000 passenger journeys were made behind steam, representing a 20% boost to summer passenger travel over the line.

The appearance of 60009 *Union of South Africa* on the Settle-Carlisle line and on the "Scarborough Spa Express" resulted in huge crowds turning out, and was generally a great success though during a hot summer, lineside fires proved a problem. One particularly severe fire occurred at Baron Wood (between Carlisle and Appleby) on a southbound "Cumbrian Mountain Express", resulting in the 'A4' being taken off the northbound "Cumbrian Mountain Express" of the 28th April at Appleby, and D200 working to Carlisle.

Successes of 1984 included the appearance of the Dinting-based LNWR 'Coal Tank' No 1054 on twelve Wednesdays

that summer operating between Manchester Victoria station and Newton Heath in celebration of the 150th anniversary of Wilson's Brewery. Then there was the well-planned run carried out by 673 *Maude* with faultless timing on the 1st December between Glasgow and Edinburgh when it successfully dodged in and out of the paths of the fast-moving Glasgow-Edinburgh expresses, and the appearance of 4472 *Flying Scotsman* in the south-east during November. So that it could appear at the opening of the North Woolwich Museum by the Queen Mother, No 4472 *Flying Scotsman* ran from Manchester to Spalding with "The Fenman" on the 10th November. On the day of the opening — the 22nd November — 4472 hauled a short train from Stratford Low Level to North Woolwich, and two days later returned to Manchester from Spalding once more hauling "The Fenman", running via Nottingham, Chesterfield, Sheffield and the Hope Valley.

The year was not without its problems. The miners strike caused problems with coal supplies and resulted in the cancellation of SLOA's summer programme of Sunday "Cumbrian Mountain Express" trains, though the midweek trains still ran. The summer drought enforced cancellation of several trains in view of the fire risk, and all locomotives passed for main line running now had to be fitted with spark-arresting equipment. Only the "Scarborough Spa Express" trains seemed to escape any operational setbacks in the summer.

At a ceremony in York station on the 24th July 1984 whilst the engine was working a "Scarborough Spa Express", No 5305 was named *Alderman A.E. Draper* in memory of its late owner who rescued the engine from the scrap-yard.

Despite the bright start to the year, 1984 was disappointing. The "Scarborough Spa Express" trains recorded loadings of just over 60%, and SLOA only broke even on its summer "Cumbrian Mountain Express" excursions with loadings no more than 70% of capacity. Even with the return of 4498 *Sir Nigel Gresley* and 35028 *Clan Line* and the provision of a well-balanced programme, SLOA's autumn trips showed a down-turn in bookings.

One particularly sad event marred 1984, and that was the death on the 31st May at the early age of 54 of the photographer and writer on a wide range of railway subjects, Derek Cross. A prolific and exceptionally gifted photographer with a wide knowledge of railway matters, Derek Cross was also a talented writer. He will be missed not only for his expertise with the camera, and with words, but also as a good companion with a lively and endearing personality. I treasure his two books — done in conjunction with W.J.V. Anderson — on "Steam in Scotland".

All connected with the preservation movement forecast that 1985 was going to be the "make or break" year for

A volcano called Duchess of Hamilton *arrives at Helwith Bridge on the Hellifield to Carlisle leg of the northbound "Cumbrian Mountain Express" on a bitterly cold 4th February 1984.*

steam on the main line. The year had everything going for it — BR was set to sponsor no less than 180 steam-hauled excursions and SLOA a further 55. This was the year of the 150th Anniversary of the Great Western Railway, and a varied programme of celebrations had been lined up. Tragically the whole event was dogged by ill-luck, though some of the damage was undoubtedly self-inflicted.

The year started badly when on the 12th January 'Black 5' No 5305 worked "The Yorkshireman" rail tour through the Hope Valley from Sheffield to Manchester Victoria and then back to Leeds over the Diggle route. Due to poor bookings, some £1,500 was lost on the venture, and voices were raised in the railway press bemoaning the fact that so few people rode on the train, and so many were at the lineside photographing the train. Donations totalling £307 were received by the HLPG from lineside photographers as a result of the correspondence. The problem of providing an imaginative itinerary for steam charters which would incorporate run-pasts for the benefit of the passengers is one which has only really been seriously addressed in 1996 when it was finally realised that for steam to survive on the main line,the package must attract the customers.

SLOA's programme for the winter and spring included several interesting innovations, notably two runs from Newport to Swindon via Gloucester, which were effectively proving runs for the proposed Swindon-Gloucester trains due to be run in August as part of the GWR150 celebrations. On the 2nd February the first train was hauled by No 4930 *Hagley Hall*, and on the 2nd March, BR '4' No 75069 made

its debut on the main line on the second working. Both trains were mechanically and financially a success.

The most surprising development of the year was the introduction of steam excursions out of Marylebone despite persistent comment from BR previously that it was both impractical and likely to be uneconomic. Future developments proved these fears to be groundless.

The events leading up to the introduction of steam charter trains from Marylebone were fortuitous. On the 22nd January the Post Office issued a set of stamps featuring famous locomotives — including one featuring 4498 *Sir Nigel Gresley*. On the day of issue, 4930 *Hagley Hall* ran from Birmingham Moor Street station to Stratford-on-Avon with a mail train as a publicity exercise. With the same view in mind, 4498 *Sir Nigel Gresley* was brought down to London and appeared in steam at Marylebone on the 21st to preview the release. For some time BR had been considering the feasibility of introducing an up-market excursion train including full at-seat dining service. Stratford had not been considered as a destination, nor had there been thoughts of steam haulage.

Having got 4498 *Sir Nigel Gresley* down to Marylebone, it was too good an opportunity to miss. British Rail and SLOA

North British 0-6-0 No 673 Maude *spent an eventful 1984 summer on the West Highland line. Having failed to reach Mallaig on its inaugeral run on the 28th May,* Maude *finally made it piloting LMS Class 5 4-6-0 No 44767* George Stephenson *on the 1st September 1984 — seen here crossing the causeway at Loch Eilt. During the summer months,* Maude *worked the "Glenfinnan Flyer" — a much less demanding 2-coach train from Ford William to Glenfinnan. On the 20th July,* Maude *stands in Glenfinnan station as 37.188 approaches with the 12.20 service train from Mallaig. Alas the signals are now only a memory.*

got their heads together and, on the 26th January, SLOA ran a "Thames-Avon Express" from Marylebone to Stratford-on-Avon. This proved a tremendous success, so much so that BR decided to operate its own train — "The Sunday Luncheon Pullman" — on the 3rd February. Such was the popularity that this particular train was sold out even before it was advertised.

From then on the BR-sponsored trains really took off, and a rake of Mark 1 coaches and two buffet/kitchen cars were made available by Bounds Green Depot, and subsequently refurbished and turned out in InterCity livery. In 1985 the train was timed to leave Marylebone at 10.25, and after pre-lunch drinks, a three-course Roast Beef lunch was served prior to arrival in Stratford. On the return journey, afternoon tea was served. The cost in 1985 of the tour plus lunch was £32.50 with afternoon tea or high tea extra. The train was primarily aimed at the premium day-excursion market.

By the middle of July, about 2,500 passengers had been carried on ten BR-sponsored trains. An evening working out of Marylebone — a "Wine and Dine" train — was tried on the 30th April with 35028 *Clan Line* at its head on the outward trip to Banbury. D200 then hauled the train back to London. It was priced at £27.50, but was not a success. During August, September and October the "Shakespeare Lim-

ited" (as the train was now known) ran every Sunday with excellent loadings. During the autumn and winter, both SLOA and British Rail used this route for steam excursions, and its use continued throughout 1986 with excellent loadings. Dates were announced in December 1986 for the running of the train in the first four months of 1987. Locomotives used in 1985 on this route were 4498 *Sir Nigel Gresley*, 46229 *Duchess of Hamilton*, 35028 *Clan Line* and 34092 *City of Wells*. The one big disappointment was the non-appearance of 60009 *Union of South Africa* on these trains due to a spring failure which kept the engine at York.

GWR150 was the intended big attraction for 1985, and its triumphs and its tragedies are all too well known. Various events were organised, including an exhibition at Swindon Works from the 1st August to the 1st September, the running of a steam-hauled service between Swindon and Gloucester from the 6th August to the 1st September, and a series of special trains between Bristol and Plymouth, an exhibition train scheduled to run over most of the former Great Western territory, starting at Paddington on the 29th May and finishing at Swindon on the 22nd September which would be steam-hauled over some sections, and various special trains over selected routes hauled by selected Great Western engines.

By and large the whole programme was dogged by ill-luck and poor weather. The programme got off to a bad start on the 7th April when the inaugural Bristol-Plymouth train hauled by 6000 *King George V* and 7819 *Hinton Manor* ran into trouble even before reaching Taunton, where the 'King' was taken off the train with a hot box on a tender axle. With two class 37s attached to the rear of the train, No 7819 *Hinton Manor* struggled on to Exeter where it had to come off the train — again with a hot box. The train was then worked forward to Plymouth by the two class 37s. Thanks to some sterling work by the support crews and splendid organisation, the 'Manor' was ready for the return trip the next day and was joined by 4930 *Hagley Hall* which had travelled down overnight. A largely trouble-free trip back to Bristol was the reward for all the hard work.

Above:
GWR 4-6-0s Nos. 5051 Drysllwyn Castle *and 4930* Hagley Hall *emerge from one of the cliff tunnels at Horse Cove between Dawlish and Teignmouth on the 7th July 1985 with little sign of the problems to come at Dainton Bank.* (John Cooper-Smith)

Left:
After a photo stop, GWR 4-6-0 No 5051 Drysllwyn Castle *makes a rousing start out of Abergavenny on the bottom leg of the "Welsh Marches Express" of the 17th March 1984 from Hereford to Newport.*

At the end of May 1985 steam returned to Bristol's Portishead and Wapping Wharf branches alongside the River Avon, for the start of a summer season of special trains promoted by the Bristol Marketing Board, in celebration of GWR 150. Notwithstanding the unheralded appearance of Didcot's 2-6-2T No 5572 on the main line to Reading on Thursday 30th May 1985, Western Region decreed that there was no suitable small engine of GW origin available to work the inaugural "Bristol Harbour Special" on Friday 31st May. They accordingly conferred "special permission" for SVR's "Mickey Mouse" Mogul No 46443 to run the service. It was the engine's first taste of scheduled passenger service on BR lines as a preserved locomotive. On the 21st September it leaves Bristol Temple Meads for Wapping Wharf. (Brian Dobbs)

The next disaster to befall the celebrations was the unhappily timed announcement on the 13th June of the proposed closure of the Swindon Works which not only resulted in the cancellation of the Swindon exhibition but put at risk the Swindon — Gloucester steam excursions, though after a lot of re-planning the trains ran, and were successful — with some 17,600 passenger journeys made, a load factor of 77%.

Fingers were crossed and prayers said for the Bristol-Plymouth steam excursion of the 7th July, to no avail. A combination of poor coal, and a signal check at the foot of Dainton Bank led to 5051 *Drysllwyn Castle* and 4930 *Hagley Hall* stalling on Dainton Bank, and the train had to be assisted by a class 50 locomotive arriving in Totnes some 148 minutes late. The two steam locomotives came off the train at this point. As a result of their poor running, there were serious delays to 11 down West of England expresses — some running up to four hours late. The consequence of the disastrous run was that the return train on the 14th July was only steam-hauled between Newton Abbot and Bristol, and the trips of the 1st and 8th September were diesel hauled on the outward trips, and only steam-hauled on the return. The idea was that the engines should face the steep South Devon banks with clean fires, and fresh footplate crews.

Other problems associated with GWR150 included the non-availability of 3440 *City of Truro* until October. It was replaced on the "Western Stalwart" of the 6th July, the first steam-hauled excursion to reach Cardiff since the 1960s, by 7029 *Clun Castle* running double-headed with 4930 *Hagley Hall*. No 7029 *Clun Castle* again substituted for 3440 *City of*

Truro on the 6th September for the run between Plymouth and Truro. 3440 *City of Truro* did finally make it back on to the main line on the 20th October, working an excursion announced as a "mystery trip, somewhere in the West Country" at a cost of £45.00 per ticket. In fact, though no one was supposed to know of the route or the destination, photographers and onlookers greatly outnumbered the 95 passengers on the train for the run from Gloucester to Newport!

Other special trips which ran in connection with GWR150 included No 6960 *Raveningham Hall* running between Swansea and Carmarthen, and 7819 *Hinton Manor* and 46443 on the Bristol-Portishead line. Perhaps the most attractive spectacle was the appearance on the main line of No 2857 hauling a preserved freight train down to Newport to appear in the "Rail Freight Spectacular" held there on the 10th September.

West Country Pacific No 34092 City of Wells *leaves Bicester at Bucknell with a "William Shakespeare" excursion on 2nd November 1985.*

Elsewhere, steam specials ran with varying degrees of success. On the 9th March, No 92220 *Evening Star* worked four trips between Newcastle and Hexham to commemorate the 150th Anniversary of the opening of the first section of the Newcastle — Carlisle line. The next Saturday No 46229 *Duchess of Hamilton* broke new ground with its lengthy trip from Eaglescliffe via Sunderland and Newcastle to Carlisle and thence via the Settle-Carlisle line to Hellifield and Leeds. Both these excursions were well supported. Not so the private charter from Dundee to Edinburgh via Perth which ran behind No 60009 *Union of South Africa* on the 25th May which carried less than 50 passengers.

Steam returned to the West Highland Line on the 26th May over the Bank Holiday weekend. No 44767 *George Stephenson* managed to de-rail itself on the 28th May in Fort William goods yard, fortunately without causing any damage and 37.033 had to substitute on the "West Highlander" that day. The full five-days-a-week service started on June 17th., the trains running one round trip on Mondays to Thursdays with two round trips on Sundays, at the very reasonable price for an adult return ticket to Mallaig of £9.00. The loadings were again good with more than 13,000 passengers travelling behind steam — a 20% increase on the previous year when a profit of £20,000 was made.

The second engine to arrive at Fort William for the season was 'Black 5' No 5407. For $3\frac{1}{2}$ weeks it ran smokebox first out of Mallaig before it was turned, providing exciting new photographic opportunities. On Fridays throughout the summer the luxury sight-seeing train, the "Royal Scotsman" was steam-hauled over the line as part of a 30-passenger six-day tour of Scotland, at a cost in 1985 of £1650 per person, with a £610 supplement for a private bathroom!

Prior to arriving at Fort William, 5407 hauled two private charter trains for McKinlays the distillers. The first train ran on the 2nd July between Edinburgh and Perth with return to Glasgow, and the second ran on the following day from Glasgow to Perth. For these two excursions 5407 carried the name *Black Watch*.

The Birmingham Railway Museum put on an extravaganza on the 8th and 9th June which involved four return trips on each day between Tyseley and Stratford-upon-Avon. The locomotives featured were 7029 *Clun Castle*, back on the main line after repairs, and 5593 *Kolhapur* — also returning to the main line after many years of absence. The "hot box gremlin" struck again, 5593 *Kolhapur* retiring with a hot box on the leading driving wheel axle after its first trip on the 8th., leaving 7029 *Clun Castle* to work the rest of the weekend's trains. The coaching stock used on this run was Mark 1 stock painted chocolate and cream livery and used for some of the GWR150 specials. Over 3,000 passengers were carried on the two days. The event was so successful that it was repeated in 1986. 5593 *Kolhapur*, after repair, subsequently hauled ten empty coaches from Tyseley to Derby and return on a successful running-in turn on the 29th October, proving itself a certainty to return to the main line in 1986.

The "Scarborough Spa Expresses" run by Eastern Region, and the "Cumbrian Mountain Expresses" and "Cumbrian Coast Expresses" run by SLOA on the London Midland Region during the summer were rather overshadowed by GWR150. The loadings on these latter trains were satisfactory, but in spite of introducing two locomotives on each run, the locomotives being changed at the end of the morning "York Circle" run and before the evening "York Circle" run, the "Scarborough Spa Expresses" lost approximately £25,000 over the summer season and loadings were poor. No 4771 *Green Arrow* had to be withdrawn after one trip round the morning "York Circle" on the 25th August with a hot box on the left-hand trailing driving wheel.

Two other noteworthy "one-off" trips which took place during the year were the "White Rose" of the 15th June when 92220 *Evening Star* ran from York to Shrewsbury via Manchester and Chester, and the "Nithsdale Express" which ran on the 31st August, this being organised by the Scottish Railway Preservation Society to enable No 44767 *George Stephenson* to return south from its stint of duty on the West Highland line. The train ran first from Edinburgh to Glasgow and then on down to Ayr where all the passengers alighted to enjoy the Ayr BR "Open Day". 44767 *George Stephenson* then hauled a train from Ayr to Kilmarnock and return before leaving Ayr with its original passengers for the run down via Kilmarnock and Kirkconnel to Dumfries where it came off the train before proceeding light-engine to Carlisle. The charter train was hauled back north by a class 37 locomotive.

60009 *Union of South Africa* again came south, but this time with a less happy outcome than the previous year, a spring failure resulting in the locomotive being laid up at York for several weeks. The locomotive never reached Marylebone as had been planned, but finally managed to return north on the 30th November, travelling from York to Carlisle via Leeds and Settle.

Prior to this, the 7th November saw the successful return to the main line of 4771 *Green Arrow* on a Sheffield-Manchester Victoria-Leeds-York train. Two weeks earlier, on the 26th October, 46229 *Duchess of Hamilton* made its farewell run on the main line before its major overhaul, running from Carlisle to Leeds.

On the 3rd November Carnforth 'Black 5' No 44932 made its return to the main line hauling a series of "nostalgia" trips sponsored by the "Southport Advertiser" between Wigan and Southport. The trips were a great success all-round, and at the time regarded as an example of a steam operation with a low commitment in terms of time and money alike that might provide a blueprint for future main line activity.

A similar form of steam excursion was organised by the Scottish Railway Preservation Society on the 14th and 15th December, with equally good results. That weekend more than 2,000 people enjoyed travelling behind No 673 *Maude* hauling special trains round the Edinburgh Suburban Circle line from and to Waverley station.

The year ended with 'Black 5' No 5305 working a "Santa Special" train from Hull to Scarborough and return on the 28th December as thick snow lay on the ground, and 3440 *City of Truro* and 4930 *Hagley Hall* double-heading a "Santa Special" between Kidderminster and Hereford on the 30th December.

What a mixture the year had been — of triumphs and disasters. It ended, however, with yet another worrying sign when bookings for SLOA's autumn trains took a marked down-turn. Had the flood of steam excursions on the main line, and the accompanying flood of disasters, so coloured the outlook, particularly of British Rail, that the end of steam on the main line as we had known it since 1972 was on the brink of being submerged and changed out of all recognition? Were we becoming too conservative and hidebound in our outlook for the overall good of the railway preservation movement? In 1986 these questions would have to be faced up to and answered.

Storm Warning — 1986

Uncertainty was the name of the game late in 1985 and the early part of 1986. How much this uncertainty was due to the disasters of 1985, and how much was due to the unreasonable expectations of the supporters of main-line steam is difficult to gauge. There is no doubt that towards the end of 1985, demand for seats from SLOA for their autumn series of excursions had dropped quite dramatically. Fears were expressed that the market had been oversaturated, and when one thinks about the number of trains on offer in 1985, it is hard to deny that there is an element of truth in that argument. In addition costs were soaring — in 1985 there was a 20% increase in charges made by British Rail and insurance premiums rose dramatically. The cost of a day out on a traditional steam excursion continued to rise — for good market reasons — and there was evidence that the travelling public were being driven away from steam specials as a result of over-familiarity with certain routes being covered by the same locomotives.

In the light of the events which took place in 1986, I think it is worth while stating at this point a few elementary — and uncomfortable — truths, which enthusiasts (including SLOA) had perhaps forgotten in the euphoria of seeing steam-hauled excursions on the main line in such large numbers.

Firstly, it is the paying public — the passengers — who make steam specials a possibility, and their voice and expectations have to be of primary consideration. By themselves, railway enthusiasts cannot hope to sustain the level of steam specials on the main line. Indeed it was quite clear towards the end of 1985 that even the most dyed-in-the-wool enthusiast was getting bored by travelling over familiar routes hauled by the same locomotives — and they were beginning to vote with their feet. In 1986 a policy of continual innovation would be required to capture and hold potential passengers.

Secondly, and following on from that point, steam does not appear on the main line simply to satisfy the interest and enthusiasm of steam locomotive owners, nor simply because British Rail wish it to appear — though as Sir Peter Parker correctly put it, it warms British Rail's market by bringing folk to the railway who would not otherwise be there. It has to pay its way.

Finally, since SLOA had for years negotiated with British Rail on behalf of all locomotive owners and provided all the locomotives and support crews, without whom there would be no available locomotives, they were perhaps lulled into a false sense of security as to the strength of their bargaining position with British Rail. The thought that some owners might negotiate separately with British Rail appeared not to have crossed their minds until 1985.

I think that it is fair to say that the GWR150 celebrations in 1985 stretched to the limit not only the market, but also the support crews and locomotives. In addition, as a result of the non-availability of some locomotives on advertised trains — some through failures, but many more through the locomotive's restoration not being completed on time — and the failures of others whilst out on the main line, which in BR's eyes rose to unacceptable levels — BR's tolerance of steam operations on an ever increasingly modern railway system became stretched to the point where some rationalisation of steam excursions had to be made. Steam had been living for years on a credit of good-will stretching back to 1971.

Suddenly a lot of that goodwill evaporated, and the overdraft was called in by the bankers — BR. It was an unexpected shock at the time, but one which should have been foreseen. The "amateur" approach to steam excursions of the early 1970s when 10 trains ran in a year was something which could be tolerated by an amused, avuncular British Rail. In 1985 with 180 steam excursions on the main line, some of those causing considerable disruption to normal main-line traffic, BR obviously decided that "amateurism" — so beloved by the British in all of their activities — had to end. The credit was stopped, the overdraft called in, and the receiver — in the guise of Mr. David Ward of British Rail — took over to run steam on the main line in a much more professional way.

The first step in this policy of rationalisation was taken in November 1985 as a result of a detailed study carried out by British Rail into the costs involved in running steam excursions. This showed quite clearly that the steam-hauled excursions were failing to meet their direct costs by a substantial margin. As a result, for the 1986 season, British Rail no longer had one flat rate haulage charge, but applied a variable scale related to the cost of the actual operation requested. This meant increases of between 46% and 82% on the previous flat rate.

A further examination by SLOA and Pullman-Rail (the company which had taken over the marketing of the former SLOA Pullman set of coaches after renovation) identified substantial cost increases relating specifically to the maintenance and servicing of the locomotives and rolling stock. In doing this they highlighted SLOA's warning note of 1982, previously discussed, which pointed out that in 1982-cost terms, each ticket on a steam excursion was subsidised to the tune of £10.40.

SR 'King Arthur' 4-6-0 No 777 Sir Lamiel *briefly assumed its original late-1920s appearance, running through Washwood Heath without smoke deflectors during the 22nd March 1986 "South Yorkshireman" railtour which it hauled from Sheffield to Saltley. The 'King Arthurs' were the first British locomotives to carry smoke deflectors after enginemen complained to designer R.E.C. Maunsell about drifting smoke obscuring their vision. The experiment to remove the smoke deflectors by the Humberside Locomotive Preservation Group was not a success and they were refitted before the loco's next main line outing.*

As a result of these cost increases, British Rail and SLOA agreed on an outline programme for 1986 featuring three categories of train.

1. There would still be available the traditional family holiday season train such as the "West Highlander" and the "Scarborough Spa Express".

2. "Up-market" dining trains such as the existing Marylebone-Stratford Sunday Luncheon trains would increase in scope, and would be aimed at the tourist market. A new initiative in this category comprising 18 mid-week trains in the summer over the Settle-Carlisle line and run by Pullman-Rail was announced.

3. A strictly limited number of trains for the "enthusiast" — possibly between 20 and 30 during the year — operating on approved routes and using a wide variety of motive power. It was hoped that by limiting the number of such trains, a high loading factor would result.

Amongst other factors considered was the numbers of locomotives on the "approved" list. Suggestions were made to limit the numbers on this list in order to reduce inspection costs, concentrate earnings on a smaller fleet and ensure that locomotives were in top condition to appear on the main line. The list at the beginning of 1986 amounted to a total of 59 possible runners. It was thought distinctly possible that this number might have to be cut to about 30.

The non-availability of some locomotives, and the failures of others in 1985 rose to unacceptable levels in the eyes of BR — on twenty occasions during 1985 a booked locomotive had been either unavailable or had failed — and they were not prepared to countenance a continuation of this situation. As a direct result of this, SLOA were forced to agree to new charges by BR for a six-month's locomotive certificate.

For the traveller, this meant that the forecast fare for a train hauled by a single locomotive would be in the order of £32, and the fare for a double-header around £36. One result of the six-month certificate inevitably would be the intensive use of a small number of locomotives during the validity of the certificate. A balance would have to be struck between the locomotive owner's desire to use up the six-monthly charge and the need to provide an attractive and varied main-line programme.

The second step took place late in 1985. When SLOA presented its proposed programme for the first half of 1986, BR rejected it as "unrealistic and too costly, involving some unnecessary light-engine movements". As a result, SLOA had to reconsider its whole programme and no SLOA-sponsored train appeared on the main line in the first 11 weeks of 1986. During that period steam-hauled workings were restricted to four BR-sponsored "Shakespeare Limited" trains out of Marylebone, two private charters over the same route — 4472 *Flying Scotsman* and 4498 *Sir Nigel Gresley* sharing the duties — and two other private charters which ran in the North of England.

The first of these, run on 3rd February, was perhaps the shortest charter in the history of steam on the main line. 4771 *Green Arrow* was chartered by Keith Johnson Photographic to pull a train the 20 miles from York to Harrogate where a photographic convention was being held. The second charter was one by the West Yorkshire Metropolitan Council involving 'Black 5' No 5305 hauling a train from Leeds to Carlisle on the 8th March. This train was basically run to publicise the case for the development of the Settle-Carlisle line, which BR was still actively trying to close. The charter train also marked the publication of a hard-hitting book about BR's proposals to close the line entitled "To kill a Railway". It is interesting to note that even with the shadow of closure hanging over the Settle-Carlisle line, once SLOA's programme for the first six months of 1986 was

approved by BR — involving the use of 11 locomotives on eight trains over some interesting routes — it included just one excursion booked to work over its most lucrative route, the S & C.

The third step came on the 14th February when BR announced that it was not going to continue with the York-based "Scarborough Spa Express" as it was felt that the popularity of the promotion had passed its peak. Losses in 1985 had been of the order of £25,000 to £30,000 in spite of efforts to attract more support by providing two locomotives for each trip. The other factor was the shortage of "prestigious" motive power. Apart from this being a blow to enthusiasts, it was also a blow to Scarborough Borough Council who in 1981 paid out a reported £56,000 towards the cost of installing a turntable at Scarborough, albeit on the basis of a three-year running agreement with British Rail, and contributed £1,000 a year to help offset the costs of running the service. The other body not happy with the situation was the Humberside Locomotive Preservation Group whose two engines — 'Black 5' No 5305 *Alderman A.E. Draper* and 'King Arthur' No 777 *Sir Lamiel* — relied heavily on the "Scarborough Spa Express" to pay for their upkeep.

A third season of steam running on Scotrail's West Highland extension began on 5th April 1986 with Stanier 'Black 5' No 44767 George Stephenson *working a private charter train for South Tynedale Travel from Fort William to Mallaig and return. With safety valves lifting, the 'Class 5' proceeds towards Banavie, with the snow-covered bulk of Ben Nevis (4,406ft) looming in the background.*

Happily, York Area Manager, Philip Benham, and Inter-City Manager, Simon Fraser, re-opened discussions with Scarborough Borough Council, and the "Scarborough Spa Express" was re-instated, though in a much more modest form, the morning and evening York Circle tours being withdrawn. The inaugural trip on the 9th July was something of a one-off, with 4468 *Mallard* making its debut on the main line after restoration, gracing a train set mostly comprising the 10 Western Region chocolate and cream liveried Mark 1 coaches that were repainted for GWR150. The train ran from York to Scarborough, and then after servicing, continued on to Hull, to regain York via Selby and Church Fenton.

The "Scarborough Spa Express" started in earnest on the 20th July with No 5305 used for two return trips. Further trains ran on Sundays 27th July and 3rd, 10th., and 17th August with the final train running on Bank Holiday Monday 25th August. The undoubted successes of the short series of trains were 3440 *City of Truro* on the 10th August and 4468 *Mallard* on the 25th August. This latter train had to be strengthened to 13 coaches, such was the demand for tickets, and there were reputed to have been 800 passengers aboard the final Scarborough-York train of that day. Overall a guarded verdict of "A qualified success" was given, though one or two of the earlier trains did record disappointing loadings — the trains hauled by 5305 being only a third and a half full on the 20th July.

After the initial shocks and set-backs in the first 11 weeks of 1986, things began to sort themselves out. Nine "Shakespeare Limited" trains ran up to the end of May, the cost of an all-inclusive ticket being £35.

The belated SLOA programme got under way on the 22nd March with 777 *Sir Lamiel* running in its original 1920s condition — without smoke deflectors — from York to Saltley, where 75069 took over for the second half of the trip to Marylebone via Banbury. On the 29th March there were two 'Jubilees' on the main line when No 5690 *Leander* ran from Hereford to Shrewsbury and return, with 5593 *Kolhapur* taking over for the run to Gloucester via Newport. This marked the return of 5593 *Kolhapur* to the main line after its failure during the first day of the "Shakespeare Express" on the 8th June 1985.

75069 returned from Marylebone to Stratford on the 12th April, handing the train over at Stratford to 777 *Sir Lamiel* for the return journey, the smoke deflectors having been replaced for this trip at the request of the train crew. No 777 *Sir Lamiel* thus reached London for a spell of duty on the "Shakespeare Limited". The "West Riding" — a York-Manchester-Leeds-York circle on the 26th April. — was advertised with No 92220 *Evening Star* as the train engine. However with the '9F' marooned on the North Yorkshire Moors Railway as a result of a landslip at Beckhole, No 4771 *Green Arrow* substituted.

Above:
The Great Western Society engine No 6998 Burton Agnes Hall, *an 11th hour substitute for 'King Arthur' No 777* Sir Lamiel *which had been undergoing repairs to a cracked frame at London's Stratford works, accelerates hard upgrade from Tisbury with the 10.03 ex Salisbury for Yeovil "Blackmore Vale Express" of the 19th October 1986.*

Right:
Webb 0-6-2 "Coal Tank" No 1054 *rushes through Haughton on 18th October 1986 with the "SLS Special" in honour of Bill Camwell's 80th birthday. This was the locomotive's last main line appearance.*

Opposite:
On Saturday, 24th May 1986, former Great Western locomotives double-headed on the main line for the first time since the GW150 events of 1985. **'City' 4-4-0 No 3440** City of Truro *leads* **'King' No 6000** King George V *near Dorrington on the return working from Shrewsbury to Hereford. Although officially entitled the "Welsh Marches Express", the train ran with neither headboard nor the frequently-used GWR reporting numbers.* **'Castle' 4-6-0 No 7029** Clun Castle *took over the train at Hereford for the onward journey to Newport and Gloucester.*

Originally 92220 *Evening Star* went to the North Yorkshire Moors Railway on the 8th April for a two weeks stay, the purpose being to celebrate the 150th anniversary of the Whitby and Pickering Railway on the 23rd April. It had been hoped to run a train from Whitby to Pickering, but this idea was abandoned when BR's charges were found to be prohibitive. On the 22nd April, two areas of subsidence were discovered 150 yards apart on the 1 in 49 section at Beckhole shortly after 80135 had passed with a routine service train. The track had in fact dropped by four inches and moved sideways by $1\frac{1}{2}$ inches towards the edge of the embankment which falls sharply down to the River Esk. 92220 *Evening Star* rode light-engine over the area heading south and reported the track to be "spongy". As a result the engine was trapped on the North Yorkshire Moors Railway, and though repairs were effected, and the trains started running again between Grosmont and Goathland by the 22nd June, the engine remained on the railway till mid-August — returning to the National Railway Museum at York on the 3rd September.

On the 10th May 'Black 5' No 5305, deputising for No 4771 *Green Arrow*, ran from Carlisle to York with the "Thames-Eden Express". There was only a 60% loading for this trip, but those on board enjoyed a storming run up to Ais Gill in glorious sunshine.

Another attractive train was the 24th May "Welsh Marches Express" which involved the use of 3440 *City of Truro*, 6000 *King George V* and 7029 *Clun Castle*. *City of Truro*, and King *George V* ran from Hereford to Shrewsbury and return, with *Clun Castle* used for the run to Gloucester via Newport.

The final two trips of the first half of the year involved two transfer trains running between Swindon and Hereford, titled the "Red Dragon". They were run in connection with the Great Western Society's 25th Anniversary which was being celebrated at Didcot Railway Centre from the 24th May to the 1st June. On the 31st May No 5051 *Drysllwyn Castle* and No 6998 *Burton Agnes Hall* (celebrating its return to the main line) ran from Swindon to Hereford via Gloucester and Newport, with No 5690 *Leander* and No 75069 covering the reverse journey to Swindon from Hereford. The same engines ran in the reverse direction, on the 28th June.

Of these eight trains, three ran with very poor loadings. 5305's trip on the 10th May has already been mentioned, but the "William Shakespeare" trips involving 75069 and 777 *Sir Lamiel* which ran on the 12th April only had 65% loadings with 160 passengers, and the 31st May trip involving four engines carried only 196 passengers.

Several successful private charter and one-off excursions were run in the first six months of 1986. On the 22nd March No 44767 *George Stephenson* worked the "Nith Valley Express" from Carlisle to Kilmarnock, en route for Fort William, the train being hauled from Carlisle to Annan and from Kilmarnock back to Carlisle by D200. Over the same weekend — the 22nd and 23rd March — 4930 *Hagley Hall* appeared on the main line for the "Andover Rail Event, 1986", hauling five trains on each day on the truncated Andover to Ludgershall section of the former Midland and South Western Junction Railway. Also on the 23rd March, former LNER J36 0-6-0 No 65243, now more popularly known as North British No 673 *Maude*, returned to the once familiar metals of the Edinburgh-Bathgate line, running a series of 14 passenger shuttles from Bathgate to Livingstone on the day of the re-opening of a passenger service on this 11-mile branch line. Happily every train was loaded to capacity.

Scotland continued to provide some interesting private charter work in the second quarter of the year. Steam returned to the Fort William-Mallaig line on the 5th April when the "Tynedale Travel" club chartered the "West Highlander". Two days later, 4771 *Green Arrow* and 92220 *Evening Star* double-headed a private charter train, the "EMI Music Express", from Edinburgh to Gleneagles in spectacular fashion, the empty stock going on to Perth. This was the first visit to Scotland by 92220 *Evening Star*, the two locomotives giving a sparkling performance hauling a ten-coach train.

Then on the 5th June, 673 *Maude* ran with three maroon coaches from Falkirk to Edinburgh Waverley, having been hired by the Scottish and Newcastle Breweries to promote the McEwan International Jazz Festival 1986. Two circuits of the Edinburgh Suburban Circle followed, with the press being entertained on the first circuit, and friends of the Scottish and Newcastle Breweries on the second. On each trip a jazz band was located in the guard's van. A third circuit of the suburban circle was performed to return the empty stock to Falkirk.

On the 7th and 8th June, Birmingham Railway Museum repeated its two day "Shakespeare Express" programme to and from Stratford-upon-Avon with four return trips each day using 7029 *Clun Castle* and 5593 *Kolhapur*. Whilst loadings on the Saturday were described as "disappointing", the loadings on the Sunday were good.

There was a wealth of steam on the main line during the summer. On the 5th July, 60009 *Union of South Africa* appeared on the "Bon Accord" — a Perth-Edinburgh-Perth-Dundee special in connection with the Commonwealth Games.

The BR-sponsored "Shakespeare Limited" continued to prosper and ran every Sunday in June, July and August except for the 29th June. Motive power included 4472 *Flying Scotsman*, 4498 *Sir Nigel Gresley*, 777 *Sir Lamiel* and 35028 *Clan Line*, the last making a welcome return to the main line after an extensive overhaul.

Apart from *Clan Line*, all the other three engines encountered mechanical problems at one time or another. 777 *Sir Lamiel* was failed at Banbury on the 8th June when a little end ran hot — the result of a bent coupling rod sustained at Ashford (Kent) the previous day when it appeared at the Chart Leacon Open Day. 4498 *Sir Nigel Gresley* was taken out of service from the 24th June to have its inside big end re-metalled, and for attention to its coupling rod bushes. No 4472 *Flying Scotsman*, however, was the engine that suffered the most trouble, with recurrent failures involving its motion and bearings. This was disappointing in that the engine had only just arrived at Marylebone after a year-long overhaul at Carnforth where major work had been carried out on the boiler, front end and all axle boxes, with complete re-painting. Problems on the return working to Marylebone on the 5th May when the engine started to run on only two cylinders at High Wycombe resulted in the withdrawal of the engine for further remedial work, and it was only after a test run to Banbury on the 14th September proved successful that *Flying Scotsman* was allowed to return to the main line on the "Shakespeare Limited" apparently back to its old form. Certainly the engine gave two storming performances on its runs on the 26th October and the 2nd November.

Perhaps these problems with 4472 *Flying Scotsman* were in part responsible for Bill McAlpine's decision to lease Southall Diesel Depot's two-road repair shop to provide an operational base for main-line locomotives working public and private charters in the London area. The workshop —

Back on the main line after four years overhaul at Bulmers Railway Centre, Hereford, and celebrating the Golden Jubilee of its record-breaking non-stop run between London Euston and Glasgow, LMS 'Princess Royal' class 4-6-2 No 6201 Princess Elizabeth **powers through Bell Busk on the Leeds-Carnforth section of the "Princess Elizabeth Golden Jubilee" excursion of the 15th November 1986.**

which can stable up to eight main-line engines — boasts many useful facilities including illuminated inspection pits, interior heating, a wheel-drop and a white-metalling hearth. Initial approaches were made in September 1986, and by early December negotiations for the short-term lease (of between one and three years) of the depot by Flying Scotsman Enterprises was well under way. The depot's value had clearly been demonstrated earlier in the year when 35028 *Clan Line* underwent an extensive overhaul there.

Two new steam workings were proposed for 1986 — both to be promoted by Pullman-Rail. The first was planned to operate fortnightly from the 29th June, from Derby to Matlock with the opportunity to visit Chatsworth House, using 4472 *Flying Scotsman* and ex-S&DR 2-8-0 No 53809 as motive power, but it never got off the ground. The second was titled the "Pennine Limited", a dining train that was originally scheduled to run on every Tuesday from 3rd June to the 30th September, operating from King's Cross to Appleby, with steam-haulage one way between Leeds and Appleby. The fare of £45 included morning coffee with biscuits or

a Danish pastry, a light lunch of salad, gateau and coffee, and a three course dinner on the return journey. It had been hoped to attract American tourists but threats of international terrorism saw them stay at home and the programme was truncated.

The first train ran on the 3rd June, then the "Pennine Limited" operated at fortnightly intervals from the 15th July to the 23rd September. All the early trains were worked by No 34092 *City of Wells*, much interest being shown in the locomotive's performance following the fitting of a Giesl Ejector in May 1986. This was done to improve forward vision, improve steaming and to reduce spark emission, and certainly the results seemed to justify the efforts made. Unfortunately the Pacific slipped in Birkett Tunnel with the return "Pennine Limited" of 9th September and suffered two badly buckled coupling rods, and a slightly bent connecting rod.

A private charter train on the 13th September from Leeds to Carnforth and return for the tea and coffee merchants, Taylor Bros of Harrogate, which was to have been hauled by 34092 *City of Wells*, had 5305 *Alderman A.E. Draper* at its head instead. This mishap to 34092 *City of Wells* also caused the cancellation of SLOA's "Yorkshireman" on the 27th September. 5305 *Alderman A.E. Draper* worked the final northbound "Pennine Limited" from Leeds to Appleby, and thereafter worked on up to Fort William where it took over from 44932, working the remaining "Royal Scotsman" trains each Wednesday up to and including the 22nd October, and also Pullman-Rail's "West Highlander" of the 19th October.

The "Pennine Limited" trains were an undoubted success — all but one having loadings in excess of 200 (there being a maximum of 252 seats available.) As a result it was proposed to run a series of 16 similar trains in 1987 at an unchanged price of £45 — with a reduced fare of £35 for passengers being picked up at Sheffield. Eight of these trains were scheduled to run on Saturdays, 6201 *Princess Elizabeth* being rostered to haul the first north-bound train on the 7th February

The "Royal Scotsman" and "West Highlander" trains on the Fort William-Mallaig line in Scotland were also hugely successful. The "Royal Scotsman" enjoyed an extended season compared with 1985 with loadings of the order of 90%, appearing on the Mallaig extension on Wednesdays from 16th April to the 22nd October.

It was the "West Highlander" trains, however, that really prospered. 53 trains were planned for 1986 compared with 72 in 1985, running from the 22nd May through to the 25th September — an adult return fare being £9 (including the steam supplement). One train was cancelled — that of 1st July after 44932 had started two lineside fires on the previous day. Some 15,812 passengers were carried — an average loading of 84.7% and an absolute increase of 2,250 passengers over the 1985 figures. Demand towards the end of the season was very heavy — the last train on the 25th September leaving with all its 359 seats full. The service was worked by the two 'Black 5's' — 44932 and 44767 *George Stephenson*. Both suffered from considerable tyre wear due to the tight curves on the line. As a result of 44932 having trouble with its tyres, 5305 *Alderman A.E. Draper* was dispatched to Fort William after its northbound run on the "Pennine Limited" of the 25th September to finish the 1986 season. As a result of the success of the year's programme, plans were made to increase the 1987 programme, with a new Saturday "West Highlander" from Fort William during July and August. 'Black 5' 5305 *Alderman A.E. Draper* and K1 2-6-0 No 2005 were the locomotives provisionally rostered for 1987, and a new rake of Mk.1 stock was promised.

The summer programme of SLOA charter trains proved to be a big disappointment with only three out of the six trains running, and one of these with just 186 passengers. The first train, the "City to City Limited" featuring 3440 *City of Truro*, was scheduled to run on the 12th July between Birmingham and York, but was cancelled because repairs to the locomotive could not be carried out in time. As a consequence, 3440's turn of duty on the "Scarborough Spa Express" of the 27th July was taken by 4771 *Green Arrow*. The engine did, however, finally reach York on the 1st August, and after further work was carried out on it at the National Railway museum, it managed to reach Scarborough on the 6th August with a test train of empty coaching stock. It made its inaugural run on the "Scarborough Spa Express" on the 10th August when it hauled 397 passengers in a ten-coach train.

SLOA's second train — scheduled for the 26th July — was "The North-Eastern". The original plan was for 4771 *Green Arrow* to haul the train from Leeds to Appleby, and then from Carlisle via Newcastle to Eaglescliffe. In the event, 2005 and 5305 *Alderman A.E. Draper* were the substitute locomotives which ran throughout from Leeds to Newcastle via Carlisle. Surprisingly, this was only the second SLOA train over the Settle-Carlisle line in 1986 — previously SLOA's premier route. 2005 was the pilot engine from Leeds to Carlisle, but 5305 *Alderman A.E. Draper* took over this duty on the Carlisle-Newcastle leg so that it could arrive first in Newcastle — where it had been built 49 years

ago. A healthy 90% loading — 374 seats — was achieved on this train, at £32 a head.

The third train, which ran on the 16th August, was originally titled "The Lincolnshire Poacher". It was scheduled to be hauled by 53809 from Nottingham to Lincoln and thence to Gainsborough and Sheffield. It suffered several route alterations — first of all to a Sheffield-Leeds-Keighley and return route and finally to a Sheffield-Leeds-Carnforth-Leeds itinerary. Undoubtedly all these changes of routing affected the bookings — only 186 seats being sold. Poor time-keeping resulted in a fairly late arrival of this train back in Leeds.

The fourth train — the "Lancashire Coast Express" — ran on the 25th August in very poor weather. It was run in order to transfer 5593 *Kolhapur* from Tyseley to Southport. Again the route was changed, the steam section beginning at Derby instead of at Birmingham. The route taken was Derby-Sheffield-Manchester Victoria-Southport.

The fifth and sixth trains, involving 4498 *Sir Nigel Gresley* on a Marylebone-Tyseley train — "The Tyseley Connection", and 5593 *Kolhapur* on a Cumbrian Mountain Express scheduled for the 6th September, were cancelled. The reason given for the cancellation of this latter train was that because of the introduction of the new Skipton-Carlisle DMU service, there was no path available for the train.

The disappointment of SLOA's summer programme was offset by some excellent private charters and one-off trips including a return special from Newcastle to Carlisle on the 20th July with "The Citadel", the return train being titled "The Tynesider", with No 4771 *Green Arrow* which was run to coincide with Carlisle Upperby Open Day. Three SRPS special charter trains on the 2nd, 16th, and 30th August, had steam-haulage from Fort William to Mallaig and back.

One of the most unusual workings took place on the 31st August, when 44767 *George Stephenson* hauled a special from Inverness to Helmsdale in order to test the radio signalling equipment planned for introduction in 1987 on steam locomotives working between Fort William and Mallaig. For a £10 fare, some 200 passengers travelled on this train which worked over the Far North route otherwise not approved for steam running. Having performed its duty, 44767 *George Stephenson* returned to Carlisle in time to work an SRPS special from Carlisle to Keighley on the 6th September, and then remained on the Keighley and Worth Valley Railway till the end of October.

Another less usual operation was staged as part of the celebrations marking the 125th anniversary of the Stockton and Darlington Railway Extension, when K1 No 2005 ran two return trips on the 17th July from Newcastle to Saltburn on the "Saltburn 125" — the event being sponsored jointly by Langburgh Council and the North Eastern Locomotive Preservation Group. On the 16th September, 5593 *Kolhapur* was used for "The Southport Visitor" workings with four Manchester trains and two Wigan trains, the event being jointly sponsored by the "Southport Visitor" newspaper, Sefton Council and a local hotel.

The return of *Mallard* to the main line after a £35,000 overhaul at the National Railway Museum was probably the outstanding event of 1986. The cost of this work was largely funded by Scarborough Council from its tourism budget, on the understanding that each year the engine would make at least one appearance at the resort with a passenger train. As overhauled, the engine was restricted to a maximum of 26 main-line appearances over a five year period. This was to avoid competition with the other A4s currently approved for main line running, and to reduce restoration costs as oth-

'V2' 2-6-2 No 4771 Green Arrow *and BR Standard '9F' No 92220* Evening Star *rush through Blackford with the "EMI Music Express" private charter train from Kings Cross to Glen-eagles on 7th April 1986. The 10 "raspberry ripple" coaches were no real test for such a powerful combination, which took over the train at Edinburgh. After dropping its passengers at Gleneagles, the empty stock worked through to Perth.*

erwise a number of fire-box stays would have had to have been replaced before expiry of the normal five to seven years between internal examinations. By restricting the number of runs to 26, renewal would not be required till the end of the five year period.

After a steam test on the 16th March, 4468 *Mallard* made a test run with one coach from York to Scarborough and then on to Doncaster via Bridlington and Hull on the 25th March where it appeared at Doncaster Works Rail Weekend on the 3rd May, repainted, but unlettered and unnumbered. Its first revenue earning run on British Rail took place on the 9th July when the train had to be strength-ened to 12 coaches. It ran from York to Scarborough, and then via Bridlington, Hull and Selby back to York. Its next outing on the main line was on the "Scarborough Spa Express" of the 25th August. Again the train was a sell-out, being strengthened this time to thirteen coaches, with about 800 passengers on the final run back from Scarborough to

In glorious weather Stanier 'Black 5' No 5305, now named Alderman A.E. Draper, *crosses Ais Gill viaduct on the 10th May 1986 with a southbound "Cumbrian Mountain Express" from Carlisle which ran through to York.*

York. A proposal that *Mallard* should travel to the SNCF National Museum at Mulhouse, France over the weekend of 27th and 28th September did not materialise,and after working a charter train to Scarborough and back on the 4th September the engine took the "South Yorkshire Pullman" from York via Sheffield, Derby, Birmingham and Banbury to Marylebone on the 4th October.This train offered a full dining service with English Breakfast, lunch and afternoon tea at an all-inclusive fare of £50.

Having arrived in London, 4468 *Mallard* worked three extra BR-sponsored "Shakespeare Limited" Sunday luncheon trains — with fares being increased from £35 to £40 — which doubled up with the scheduled trains, leaving Marylebone an hour apart. The first runs were made on the 12th October, with 4498 *Sir Nigel Gresley* sharing the duties

with 4468 *Mallard*. On the two other Sundays — the 26th October and the 2nd November — 4472 *Flying Scotsman* hauled the second train. 4468 *Mallard* returned to York on the 8th November at the head of a special Pullman train which ran in honour of Sir Peter Allen, President of the Transport Trust, and sponsored by British Coal. This train again offered full catering facilities on both the outward and return journey, the return fare being £55. Hauling a 12-coach train, 4468 *Mallard* performed impeccably, although there were a few anxious moments towards the end of the trip when coal supplies ran low. With this run, 4468 *Mallard* ended its first season back on the main line. The expectations were that the engine would not re-appear until 1988. Provisional plans had been made for the locomotive to make several commemorative runs to mark the Golden Jubilee of its record-breaking run down Stoke Bank.

If the outstanding event of 1986 was the return of 4468 *Mallard* to the main line, probably a close second was the operation of steam specials between Salisbury and Yeovil during October. The decision to run a total of 12 trains was announced by BR on July 16th The train — titled the

"Blackmore Vale Express" — was scheduled to operate twice daily on Saturdays and Sundays, 4/5th October, 11/12th October, and 18/19th October, with No 35028 *Clan Line* and 777 *Sir Lamiel* as the chosen motive power. The idea was initiated by Salisbury Area Manager, Gerald Daniels, as a result of the success of the Andover-Ludgershall trains earlier in the year. The cost for a round trip was £16 — or £26 from London Waterloo.

In the event, 15 trains ran, three extra workings being added in response to demand, two on the 25th October and one on the 26th October. One major disappointment was the non-appearance of 777 *Sir Lamiel*, which spent all of October at London's Stratford depot where repairs were effected to the engine's cracked main frames. The initial "Blackmore Vale Expresses" were hauled by 35028 *Clan Line* and 6998 *Burton Agnes Hall*, with No 4498 *Sir Nigel Gresley* taking over for the last two weekends in place of the 'Merchant Navy'. In all, a total of 4,100 passengers were carried, representing a loading factor of 93%. Revenue from all sources for BR was estimated to be in the region of £70,000. As a result, provisional plans were made to repeat these trips in 1987 though there was speculation that following this success, something more ambitious could be tried — Salisbury-Yeovil-Exeter was rumoured.

The luxury "Royal Scotsman" tour train had a much earlier start from Fort William to Mallaig than did the "West Highlander", thus creating opportunities for different photographic locations. One such location where the sun was right only for an early morning shot was Beasdale Bank high up above Loch Nan Uamh, famous as the place where Bonnie Prince Charlie left Scotland after the failed '45 rebellion. Stanier 'Black 5' No 44767 George Stephenson **works hard up the gradient heading for Arisaig and Mallaig on the 4th June 1986.**

The "Peter Allen Pullman" of the 8th November 1986 from Marylebone to York was staged in honour of Sir Peter Allen, President of the Transport Trust, and was sponsored by British Coal. The train, hauled by A4 Pacific No 4468 Mallard, is passing Aynho Mill, precisely at the spot where the M40 now crosses the railway.

For SLOA, however, the autumn and winter was far from successful. The "Red Dragon" — featuring 6000 *King George V* — was originally scheduled to run on the 27th September from Hereford to Swindon and then back to Gloucester. Following a change of date to the 25th October — and a change of route to the familiar one of Newport-Hereford-Shrewsbury-Hereford, the tour was finally cancelled after bookings had reached no more than 150. The tour which was scheduled to take its place on the 27th September — the "Yorkshireman" — had to be cancelled owing to the non-availability of its rostered locomotive — 34092 *City of Wells* — as a result of its mechanical problems, and the "Cumbrian Mountain Express" of the 1st November was also cancelled because again the rostered engine — 44932 — was unavailable, having returned early from Fort William to Butterley with excessively worn tyres, with no other locomotive immediately available.

One star to return to the main line was No 6201 *Princess Elizabeth* which had last run on the 20th March 1982 with a "Welsh Marches Pullman", then being withdrawn for re-tubing and a complete mechanical overhaul. On the 28th June 1986, the Stanier Pacific returned to BR metals, hauling its support coach from Hereford to Newport, and then appearing at the BR Newport Open Day. A nine-coach test train was worked on 30th October between Hereford and Newport as a prelude to the planned first public trip of 15th November — the "Golden Jubilee Express" commemorating the record run by 6201 *Princess Elizabeth* on the West Coast Main Line in 1936. Considerable delays in obtaining route clearance — the route being changed on three occasions — meant that SLOA had to advertise a train without a route! Eventually, the itinerary for the steam section was agreed just one month before the scheduled date of the special as Stockport-Stalybridge-Leeds-Carnforth. Despite all these problems, the train was a sell-out, and a total of 456 passengers enjoyed a faultless performance from *Princess Elizabeth*.

It had been a year of escalating problems and setbacks for SLOA, and it came as no surprise when, after a meeting on the 11th October, SLOA Marketing Ltd announced that it was going to suspend its operations till late 1987 when the situation would be reviewed. They had struggled to run less than half of the proposed 30 steam specials in the year, and these operations had resulted in an overall financial loss in 1986. They felt they could not continue to market what was obviously a non-viable steam programme. SLOA itself would remain as a co-ordinating and advisory organisation. And so steam charter operations reverted to the position pertaining before the formation of SLOA Marketing.

Elsewhere, the story of autumn and winter steam-hauled charter trains was one of continuing success. On the 20th September, 673 *Maude* hauled a train from Falkirk via the Forth Bridge to Ladybank and Perth, with the return journey being routed through Gleneagles and Stirling, to celebrate the SRPS Silver Jubilee. *Maude* disgraced herself by failing on the the Forth Bridge — suffering from shortage of steam — having to be assisted into Inverkeithing by 47.562 on a following Edinburgh-Dundee train. After a spell in Inverkeithing sidings trying to raise steam, 673 *Maude* and its train were hauled to Ladybank by 26.036. The diesel came off here, and the stricken train struggled on to Perth arriving over two hours late. At Perth the fault was found — the blower pipe ring having come away from the blast-pipe. It only took a few minutes to rectify the fault, and steaming was transformed thereafter. Leaving Perth only about 15 minutes down, 673 *Maude* made a spirited run to Stirling.

On the 18th October, Bill Camwell — the man who pioneered the "SLS Special" steam rail tours of the late 1950s and 1960s — found himself the celebrity of his own rail tour marking his 80th birthday. Stephenson Locomotive Society members took advantage of the return working by LNWR 'Coal Tank' No 1054 from the Severn Valley Railway — where it had been a guest since its arrival from the Keighley and Worth Valley Railway early in August (travelling via Standedge under its own power on Friday 1st August) — to Dinting, to arrange a surprise SLS Special, steam-hauled by 1054 from Shrewsbury to Stockport. Some 150 members travelled on this unique train. On the following day, 35028 *Clan Line* ran from Marylebone to Banbury and then back to Marylebone from Stratford to celebrate the 60th Anniversary of the "Golden Arrow". Finally, 5305 *Alderman A.E. Draper* returning from its stint of duty on the West Highland line hauled a private charter from Perth to Edinburgh on the 8th November, and then with one support coach continued down the East Coast Main Line overnight to York .

To end the year, there was a very full programme of "Santa Special" trains. BR sponsored a series of trains from Marylebone to High Wycombe on the 13/14th December and the 20/21st December. Two return trips were advertised to run each day — the price of a return ticket being a modest £8 — but as all 3,200 seats were booked within three weeks of the trains being announced, four extra trains were put on for the first weekend in January 1987, and these too were all sold out well before Christmas. Motive power was 777 *Sir Lamiel*, 35028 *Clan Line* and 4472 *Flying Scotsman*. 4498 *Sir Nigel Gresley* was originally supposed to be in the pool of locomotives, but had to be withdrawn when ultrasonic tests showed that one of its tender axles might be flawed.

673 *Maude* met with similar success with Santa trains in Scotland when it ran six trips on each day round the Edinburgh Suburban Circle out of Waverley station on the 13/14th December. Again all the seats were sold out shortly after they were advertised, and further trips were arranged for the following weekend. All in all, 673 *Maude* made 24 circuits of the Edinburgh Suburban Circle, carrying in excess of 5,000 passengers.

Not to be left out of the pre-Christmas festivities, Eastern Region ran two trips from York to Scarborough on the 20th December, using the GWR150 set of coaches hauled by 3440 *City of Truro*. Santa, of course, rode on each train. The trains stopped at Malton where a Charles Dickens Festival was being held, hence the trains being titled the "Dickens Festival Express". An adult return ticket, including the steam supplement, was £9.90 with children being charged only £2.50. Finally, SLOA ran a "Scarborough Spa Santa Express" hauled by 3440 *City of Truro* on the 29th December.

The "Shakespeare Limited" finished the year on a high note, running two trains on the 28th December. The first, hauled by 4472 *Flying Scotsman*, had *Ethel 3* (a converted Class 25 diesel — 97.252) included in the train to provide electric heating. The ETHEL's were previously used on the West Highland Line sleeper trains before the advent of the 37.4s. Their use on the "Shakespeare Limited" had become necessary because of increased difficulty in maintaining steam heating equipment on rolling stock booked for steam haulage, and in particular difficulty in testing steam circuits. The second train was hauled by 35028 *Clan Line*. Overall the "Shakespeare Limited" trains were a great success in 1986, carrying over 12,000 passengers. As a result a full programme for 1987 was planned.

1986 was always going to be a difficult year. Overall some 160 steam specials were run — 87% of them sponsored by BR, 8% by SLOA and 5% by Pullman-Rail. On the positive side, the Inter-City sponsored "Shakespeare Limited" trains prospered, as did the BR sector promotions both in Scotland with the "West Highlander" and in the South West with the "Blackmore Vale Express". Less startlingly successful, though still returning a profit, were Eastern Region's "Scarborough Spa Express" trains, though without doubt the appearance of *Mallard* and to a lesser extent *City of Truro* on the runs made a significant difference. On the negative side was the failure by SLOA to market a successful programme of steam-hauled enthusiast trains, ending with the announcement of the withdrawal of SLOA Marketing from the scene during 1987.

The storms of 1986 had been weathered. The problem for 1987 was would the tide and current still be running with the steam preservation movement?

GWR 4-4-0 No 3440 City of Truro *passes Haxby with a full 10-coach load on the 20th December 1986. Passengers were given hot drinks and mince pies, children receiving gifts and a visit from Santa.*

Though never a Fort William engine during its 18 years in BR traffic, 'K1' No 2005 looks at home as it climbs away from Glenfinnan station with the "West Highlander" for Mallaig on the 29th June 1987.

Below:
Steam returned to the Cambrian Coast in May 1987 after an absence of almost 22 years. The first runs between Machynlleth and Barmouth took place in late May. On the 27th May GWR 4-6-0 No 7819 Hinton Manor *approaches Aberdovey at Trefri with the 13.40 ex Machynlleth for Barmouth.*

CHAPTER 8

High Pressure — 1987

Nobody likes change; it begets nervousness. SLOA Marketing had for so long been a part of the steam scene that the prospect of a year without their involvement led to a feeling of unease and uncertainty at the beginning of 1987. It soon became clear that we need not have been worried — indeed when the provisional main line steam programme for 1987 was announced it contained the staggering total of over 300 steam charters, with as many as two or three trains running in the spring programme on each weekend with most of the seats full!

BR now adopted a new policy of "franchising" steam hauled tours. Firstly BR local and area managers were encouraged to promote steam excursions where it could be shown that BR would generate worthwhile revenue. The concept was extended to include external bodies such as Pullman-Rail, Hertfordshire Rail Tours, British Nuclear Fuels and Traintours Ltd all of whom were invited to submit plans for approval by BR. In addition, a limited number of tours were to be allowed which were sponsored by individual members of SLOA.

The year started with BR's Marylebone-High Wycombe "Santa Specials" of the 3rd/4th January, which were completely sold out. January 18th saw the start of Intercity's popular and successful "Shakespeare Limited" trains, with further trains in the first half of the year planned for February 15th., March 8th and 22nd, April 12th and 19th., May 10th, 24th and 31st, and June 21st and 28th., though in a change to the previous format, steam haulage gave way to diesel at Banbury station to facilitate locomotive turn-round. The fare had risen from £35.00 to £38.00 with an add-on fare of £2.50 which covered travel from any station in the Network South-East to London.

LMS 5XP 'Jubilee' No 5593 Kolhapur *returned to the Settle and Carlisle line on the 21st March 1987 with a northbound "Cumbrian Mountain Express" almost 20 years after its last BR trip over the line on the 26th August 1967. Four weeks later it hauled its first southbound train — "The Mancunian" — from Carlisle to Leeds, here approaching Appleby at Keld.*

A highlight of the North Yorkshire Moors Railway Gala Weekend on 10th/11th October was the running, on the Sunday, of four special steam trains over the British Railways line between Whitby and Grosmont after an absence of 12 years, powered by Standard class '9F' 2-10-0 No 92220 *Evening Star*. *The last steam departure from Whitby was in 1975, when 'K1' No 2005 ran a series of specials from Battersby. In this shot, the '9F' leaves Whitby with the 11.25 for Grosmont and Goathland.*

Left:
Four special trains were run to celebrate the 50th birthday of 'A4' Pacific No 4498 Sir Nigel Gresley, and its 21st year in the ownership of the A4 Locomotive Society. On the 2nd May 1987 the locomotive worked from York to Scarborough via Leeds and Bridlington, with return to York by the direct route via Malton. On the outward leg, 4498 powers through the splendid display of semaphore signals at Gilberdyke.

The February 15th train had to be diesel-hauled when the rostered engine, No 4472 *Flying Scotsman*, was lit up overnight but failed with a fractured lubricator pipe to the middle cylinder. The stand-by engine, No 777 *Sir Lamiel*, was lit up and actually backed on to the train before being failed with its sight-feed lubricator not working.

The number of larger main line locomotives was perilously reduced with the premature withdrawal of No 4498 *Sir Nigel Gresley* in December 1986 after ultrasonic confirmation that one of its tender axles was flawed and would have to be scrapped. This put in jeopardy the four main line excursions due to be run by *Sir Nigel Gresley* commencing with a Manchester-Blackburn-Carlisle trip on the 28th March. in celebration of the engine's 50th anniversary and 21 years on the main line. The locomotive ran light engine to Doncaster works on December 15th where replacement axles were obtained from withdrawn BR class 08 diesel shunters. BR engineers machined three of these and pressed the A4's tender wheels on to them. The fourth axle was similarly treated at Steamtown, Carnforth in time for the "Thames-Eden Express" of the 28th March.

This train was dogged with bad luck. Because of high winds some of the power lines were down at London Euston resulting in the train being 2 hours 17 minutes late leaving. This resulted in the train being diverted at Hellifield to Carnforth instead of reaching its planned destination of Carlisle. The three remaining "Golden Jubilee" runs — "The Pennine Limited" southbound from Appleby to Leeds on 25th April, "The Scarborough Flyer" on 2nd May from York to Scarborough via Leeds and Selby, and "The Golden Jubilee" on 9th May from York to Marylebone — were successfully completed.

This left only 4472 *Flying Scotsman*, 35028 *Clan Line* and 777 *Sir Lamiel* to work the "Shakespeare Ltd." trains. Plans were made to bring 4771 *Green Arrow* down to London on the 21st March with a "South Yorkshireman" so that it could work the "Shakespeare Ltd" trains on 2nd March, 12th April and 10th May and an extra train on 17th May, returning to York on the 23rd May with a "South Yorkshireman". Unfortunately the National Railway Museum could not spare the manpower to prepare the engine for the 21st March "South Yorkshireman", so Hertfordshire Railtours filled the slot using 4472 *Flying Scotsman* on a Marylebone-Sheffield and return trip. Two weeks later Hertfordshire Rail Tours again promoted 4472 *Flying Scotsman*, this time on the 293 mile "Morecambe Bay Express" — from Marylebone to Carnforth. The train was an instant sell-out, and successfully completed the journey — albeit some two hours late due to the non-availability of watering facilities at Leeds station.

4771 *Green Arrow* finally made it to London with the "Green Arrow Limited" of the 18th July. After working three return trips to Stratford-upon-Avon, 4771 returned to York on the 29th August.

During 1987 Pullman Rail continued to offer its "Pennine Limited" diner trains at £45 per head from St. Pancras or £35 per head from Sheffield. Initially 16 trains were planned to run in the year, half on Saturdays and half on Wednesdays, from February 7th to October 7th. Two further trains scheduled to be hauled by 34092 *City of Wells* were subsequently added on October 24th and November 14th.. This latter train was eventually cancelled due to lack of support.

The train was steam-hauled from Leeds to Appleby or reverse, with 6201 *Princess Elizabeth* working the 7th February and 14th March trains, and 34092 *City of Wells* haul-

ing the train on 25th April . Both of the first two trips ran in poor weather, with the added disappointment that the first train — though 13 coaches strong — only carried 190 passengers. On the Appleby-Leeds train of the 14th March 6201 *Princess Elizabeth* stalled on the ascent to Ais Gill summit, due to the combination of a 20 mph slack, bad rail conditions and running out of sand. Driver Ted Doubtfire received a standing ovation from the onlookers when he managed to restart the 540 ton train in wet conditions on a 1:100 gradient — a tremendous and skillful demonstration of driving.

Much to the photographers disgust, a second Ethel had been commissioned and was based at Carlisle for use over the S. & C. line. This was *Ethel 2* — formerly 25.310 — and was used for the first time behind *Princess Elizabeth* on the February 7th train.

Steam once again returned to the Cumbrian Coast in the form of the "Sellafield Sightseer", which constituted a programme of five trains from various originating points, sponsored by British Nuclear Fuels Ltd as a PR exercise to attempt to persuade the public that nuclear power was safe. *Flying Scotsman* was BNFL's choice to haul all the excursions, the first train on April 25th being a sell-out. The run was eventful as two anti-nuclear protesters hand-cuffed themselves to No 4472's boiler handrail during a photo stop at Grange-over-Sands, causing some considerable delay to the train until they were removed. The offenders were in due course fined £275 each for their protest.

The intention had been that 4472 would be turned at Vickers' Eskmeals gun range, but the curves were found to be too tight, and so No 34092 *City of Wells* was provided for the return trips of the first two trains. The last three excursions — on May 25th, 30th and June 27th — were hauled both ways by 4472 following the commissioning of BNFL's own triangle at Sellafield.

4472 *Flying Scotsman* appeared once more on the Carnforth-Sellafield line with a private charter on October 17th When it arrived back at Carnforth, damaged white metal axle box bearings were noted on two of the axles. This was thought to be due to irregular tyre depths, so the locomotive was withdrawn from its rostered main-line duties till new tyres could be fitted.

In the early part of the year, various societies ran a number of interesting trains.

Birmingham Railway Museum kicked off with the first "owner-promoted" rail tour since the demise of SLOA Marketing when No 5593 *Kolhapur* hauled a Birmingham-Derby-Sheffield-York train on the 21st February. Four weeks later 5593 was again out on the main line with a Leeds-Carlisle "Cumbrian Mountain Express". This was an emotional trip since *Kolhapur* had last been seen on the S & C on August 26th 1967 at the head of an afternoon "Thames-Clyde Express" relief. The return trip was scheduled for the 18th April as "The Mancunian", but BR re-routed the train to Leeds. On the run back to Tyseley, *Kolhapur* ran a hot box at Derby. After repairs 5593 was out on the main line again on the 25th April with the. eagerly awaited "Buxton Spa Express" which was a sell-out. Sadly the "Hot Box gremlin" struck again, this time with the right side trailing axle on the light engine trip from Tyseley to Derby. Though the loco completed its booked turn, it failed again on a test run from Tyseley to Stratford-on-Avon on August 11th, in spite of having further attention to its axlebox bearings in preparation for its booked run on the "Derwent Explorer" on the 18th August. As a consequence, the Birmingham Railway Museum withdrew the engine from main line traffic until the end

'West Country' Pacific No 34092 *City of Wells* **accelerates the first of 1987's five "Scarborough Spa Express" BR specials past Strensall Common on Easter Monday 20th April 1987. It was quite remarkable that the engine was actually turned out after an accident in the days leading up to the run. The Bulleid engine miraculously survived a "York Circle" test run on Wednesday 15th April during which two fusible plugs were melted. A subsequent hydraulic boiler test showed that the firebox, which could have been wrecked, had escaped damage.**

of the year, abandoning the leaded bronze bearings fitted during its 1985 major overhaul in favour of plain white metal bearings.

On the 7th March, the Great Western Society ran "The William Shakespeare" rail-tour from Didcot to Tyseley via Stratford-on-Avon. The tour was undertaken for two reasons; as a farewell trip for 5051 *Drysllwyn Castle* prior to the expiry of its BR seven-year boiler certificate, and as a money-raising venture to buy *Drysllwyn Castle* at a fixed price from the family of the late owner, John Mynors, at the end of September 1987. The train was originally booked to run into Moor Street station, Birmingham, but this was changed to Tyseley when the train had to be strengthened from nine coaches to thirteen because of the demand for seats. After a series of traumatic delays during the trip caused by atrocious weather — there were blizzard conditions at Stratford and Tyseley — some passengers did not arrive back in London till 1 am the following morning.

Most of the anxieties which had been present at the start of the New Year disappeared during the hectic activity of the first few months of 1987. Indeed, BR's idea of "franchising" with area managers sponsoring their own trains produced some mouth watering — and in the end very exciting — new steam trips.

Perhaps the most eagerly awaited event was the return of steam to the Cambrian Coast line with "The Cardigan Bay Express" which comprised a total of 58 trains scheduled to run during Whit week (25th to 29th May inclusive) and from July 20th to September 2nd.

Most of these operated from Machynlleth to Barmouth and return — a round trip of 51 miles, initially priced at £6 but then increased to £7.50. But on three Sundays in July and August, there was a variation with a 115 mile Machynlleth to Pwllheli round trip, and on August 2nd, 16th and 30th an 85 mile Machynlleth-Aberystwyth-Barmouth round trip. This latter train was a complete sell-out, having to be strengthened from six coaches to ten. Motive power initially comprised 7819 *Hinton Manor* and 75069 from the Severn Valley Railway, but when the latter engine developed firebox leaks, 46443 was drafted in as a replacement and became the most regularly used engine of the three.

Apart from expressing their satisfaction with the exercise, BR did not release any figures of profitability except to report that revenue did not match expectations but that there had been an increase of £30,000 in the revenue from the line's sprinter trains. Certainly the service attracted large crowds, and a great deal of emotion. This was perhaps best summed up by the locomotive headboard which 7819 carried when it first headed for Machynlleth. It read "Rydw in mynd adref" — which translated says "I am going home".

Perhaps because of the good impression made by 46443 on these trips, the engine was selected for further main line duties on the 25th September when four steam-hauled round trips were made between Birmingham Moor Street and Dorridge to mark the closure of Moor Street Station. Some 2,000 passengers were carried on the "Dorridge Shuttle" — the last train being hauled by 7029 *Clun Castle*.

Following the success of the "Blackmore Vale Express" trains in 1986, which netted some £70,000 revenue when 4,100 passengers were carried on 15 trains (a 93% loading factor) further Salisbury — Yeovil trips were planned with two trips per day on June 6th, 13th and 20th. Fares were increased by £2 to £18 and the rostered locos initially were 34092 *City of Wells* and 777 *Sir Lamiel*. In the event, 35028 *Clan Line* took the place of 34092 *City of Wells* because of the latter's main-line commitments in the north, and when 777 had to drop out because of firebox stay leaks and worn wheel flanges the 'King Arthur' was replaced by 4472 *Flying Scotsman* which made its debut on 6th June. The trips had a creditable 81% loading factor.

Steam again appeared on Southern rails as part of the Basingstoke Rail Week celebrations. On the 19th and 20th September 6998 *Burton Agnes Hall* and 53809 were scheduled to work "The Ludgershall Limited" between Salisbury and Andover or Andover and Ludgershall, and on the following weekend a series of five round trips between Basingstoke and Ludgershall. Unfortunately on the first train on the 19th September, 6998 suffered melted axlebox bearings leaving 53809 to cope with a slightly curtailed programme of steam trips.

The second rostered engine for the "Cambrian Coast Express" was Standard class 4 No 75069, which on the 28th May is seen climbing away from Fairbourne with the 11.40 ex Barmouth for Machynlleth.

The inaugural "Sellafield Sightseer", sponsored by British Nuclear Fuels, worked from Carnforth to Sellafield on 25th April 1987 with Gresley 'A3' Pacific No 4472 Flying Scotsman. *It was a sell-out. The train is seen passing Meathop prior to its photo-stop at Grange-over-Sands where two anti-nuclear protesters handcuffed themselves to the locomotive's boiler handrail. Bulleid Pacific No 34092* City of Wells *hauled the return working.*

In the Midlands, BR's Derby Area Manager David Kirk sponsored the "Derwent Explorer" — running from Nottingham to Matlock via Derby — more as an attempt to tap the family market rather than as an out and out steam enthusiasts tour. The first trip on 21st June — hauled by 53809 — was poorly supported, struggling to break even. The second

trip on 19th July, again hauled by 53809, was much more of a success with over 300 passengers, though the engine did clip the underside of bridge 8 near Whatstandwell on the Matlock branch. Subsequent investigations revealed that reballasting had lifted the rail height beyond gauge limits. This was rectified for the third trip on 16th August — hauled by 35028 *Clan Line* in place of the withdrawn 5593 *Kolhapur* — which again was well supported. The final trip on 13th September was worked by 75069 — which had hauled a John Player Railway Club private charter from Nottingham to Tyseley the previous day. A modest profit for the overall operation was reported.

The second "Buxton Spa Express" which ran on 24th October was notable for 48151 making its main line debut in place of the failed 4472 *Flying Scotsman*. The loco gave an impressive performance hauling an 11-coach train — the tour being a sell-out. Unfortunately, in spite of the undoubted success of the two trains, plans for further trips in 1988 were in doubt due to the Department of Transport's unwillingness to allow passenger trains to run over freight only lines.

In Wales, BR sponsored a series of 12 trains titled "The Carmarthen Express" between Swansea and Carmarthen on 5/6th, 12/13th and 19/20th September. The trains were worked by 6000 *King George V* — the first recorded instance of a 'King' running west of Cardiff — and 7029 *Clun Castle*. 5080 *Defiant* had been the intended engine, but a series of mishaps resulted in *Clun Castle* being dispatched from Tyseley in 5080's place. *Defiant* which had last been seen in steam on 4th March 1967 was in the final stages of a major overhaul at Tyseley in mid-March prior to returning to the main line when the theft of the engine's left and right leading coupling rods was discovered. This put back the completion date of the overhaul, though fortunately Birmingham Railway Museum did have unrestored 'Castle' 7027 *Thornbury Castle* on site, 5080's bearings being fitted into 7027's connecting rods. This delay caused the abandonment of BRM's planned "Shakespeare Express" of the 19th July.

'A4' Pacific No 4498 Sir Nigel Gresley *approaches Weeton Tunnel with the "Scarborough Flyer" on the 2nd May 1987, en route for Leeds, Selby, Bridlington and Scarborough. The run was one of four to celebrate the engine's 50th birthday and the 21st anniversary of its ownership by the A4 Locomotive Society.*

Worse was to follow when 5080 failed on four successive running-in turns on BR metals with recurring overheating of the axle-boxes and the coupling rod bearings, causing it to miss its planned main line return with the "Carmarthen Express" on September 5th.

Of the old favourites, the "Scarborough Spa Express" barely survived in 1987 with just four days running comprising two York-Scarborough trips each day . The season started on 20th April with 34092 *City of Wells* working the two trains. The fact that 34092 was available was a minor miracle, because on a test run round the "York Circle" on the 15th April, two fusible plugs were melted thankfully with no damage to the boiler. The second trip took place on 26th July with 4472 *Flying Scotsman* in charge. The first return journey was uneventful, but *Flying Scotsman* derailed itself at York whilst getting ready for the afternoon train — the trailing bogie wheels parting company with the track. As a consequence, two Class 20 diesel locomotives hauled the afternoon train. The third trip took place on 9th August. Initially S15 No.841 — formerly named *Greene King* — was scheduled to haul the two trains. Sadly, instead of making its return to the main line with a Darlington-Hexham special to celebrate the 100th Anniversary of Darlington Bank Top station on the 5th July, it was failed by BR Eastern Region Inspector Colin Wood with driving axles and motion out of alignment and "crabbing" in the engine frames. 4771 *Green Arrow* substituted on that occasion, with 4472 *Flying Scotsman* — now recovered from its derailment — substituting on the 9th August. The fourth and last day of the season for the "Scarborough Spa Express" was the 31st August — the trains being hauled by 3440 *City of Truro*, which had already visited Scarborough on the 23rd August with the "Miss U.K. Scarborough Spa Express" private charter.

Mallard did not appear on the "Scarborough Spa Express" of 26th July as had been planned. BR had declined to pay the NRM's quoted fee of £2,000, but during 1987 the 'A4' did reach Scarborough on the 25th April with the traditional "Scarborough Spa Express" route of York-Harrogate-Leeds-York-Scarborough-York with a special run to celebrate the 10th Anniversary of the Friends of the National Railway Museum. The 12-coach train was oversubscribed and a repeat train — also full — ran the next day over the same route.

Mallard was out on the main line again with a private charter for the Royal Society for the Protection of Birds on a York-Carnforth and return trip on the 16th May. Sadly only 85 of the 414 seats were sold and a reported loss of in excess of £6,000 was made. The final tour carried out by *Mallard* on the 25th May was a York-Manchester and return trip to raise money for neurosurgical research. To increase the amount of money raised the trip was sold as two separate charters for the outward and return journey at £32 per trip. Whilst in Manchester, the engine appeared at the Manchester Museum of Science and Industry.

The other old favourite — the Fort William-Mallaig "West Highlander" — continued to prosper. In 1987 some 16,441 passengers were carried — 1,160 more than in 1986. The first engine to arrive at Fort William was 5305, by way of an SRPS-organised rail tour — the "Tyne Valley Express" — on the 14th March. Two class 27s — 27.046/049 — hauled the train from Edinburgh to Newcastle, arriving half an hour late as one of them failed on the journey. 5305 then took the train on from Newcastle to Kilmarnock in fairly poor weather, before proceeding independently to Fort William, to haul a preview "Royal Scotsman" on the 27th March and a Pullman Rail "West Highlander" private charter on the 29th

March. The other locomotive — 2005 — headed the NELPG-sponsored "Tees-Clyde Explorer" from Middlesbrough via Newcastle and Carlisle to Kilmarnock on the 13th June. Because of demand for seats, the train had to be strengthened from eight coaches to ten. Some 370 passengers were carried over 201 miles behind steam for a fare of £18.50. Perfect time-keeping was maintained throughout the trip.

A welcome innovation came with two trips respectively featuring 'Class 5' No 5305 and K1 No 2005 over the gloriously scenic West Highland main line from Fort William to Glasgow at the end of the "West Highlander's" season. 24 years had elapsed since a steam-worked passenger train last appeared on the line, and the revenue earned from the specials helped offset the movement costs of the two engines to their respective home bases. The trains were limited to six coaches, but within a few days of being advertised all 344 seats, at £24 a head, had gone. 5305 led the way with "The Jacobite" on the 17th October, with 2005 following with "The Lochaber" on the 14th November — the latter engine staying on in Edinburgh for the "Santa Specials". Happily both trips were a resounding success.

In a year when so much was happening, brief mention only can be made of some of the other interesting tours which were run.

4472 *Flying Scotsman* broke new ground with a private charter train — "The Cromwell Pullman" — which ran between Leicester and Tyseley from Monday 1st May to Friday 5th May inclusive.

4771 *Green Arrow* took part in the Tay Bridge Centenary celebrations by hauling a V.I.P. train in a two-way pass over the Tay Bridge on the 20th June, followed by a public train from Dundee to Edinburgh via the Tay and Forth Bridges. Unfortunately this latter train only attracted a handful of passengers for the 60-mile run — tickets were priced at £30. The following day saw 4771 *Green Arrow* haul an empty five-coach train from Edinburgh to York over the East Coast Main Line — many wondered why this opportunity to market a very attractive trip was missed.

On Sunday 11th October, steam returned to Whitby after an absence of 12 years when 92220 *Evening Star* hauled a trouble-free series of four trains from Grosmont to Whitby and return as part of the North Yorkshire Moors "Enthusiasts Gala Weekend".

6201 *Princess Elizabeth* was involved in a mammoth tour of 311 miles on the 24th October with "The Salopian" from Swindon to Shrewsbury. Sadly the tour was poorly supported by only 160 passengers. After hauling the "Royal Borderer" for Hertfordshire Railtours in December the locomotive was temporarily withdrawn for repair and maintenance work to the leading bogies and replacement of some superheaters, having covered 2,500 miles on railtours in the year with complete reliability.

Perhaps the saddest news of 1987 was that 6000 *King George V* had reached the end of its boiler certificate, and that its future was uncertain. Bulmers — the Hereford cider-making firm — had financed all the major overhauls on 6000 since it pioneered the "Return to Steam" on B.R. in 1971, but now found themselves unable to fund any further repair work. 6000's likely destination was thought to be the new Swindon Works Railway Museum.

"The Severn-Wye Express" was the first of four appearances for 6000 *King George V* on the main line in 1987. This was a 205-mile trip from Hereford to Swindon via Newport and Gloucester with return to Gloucester and Newport.

On the following weekend, a series of four special trains featuring 6000 *King George V* and 7029 *Clun Castle* was

GWR 'King' class 4-6-0 No 6000 King George V *accelerates away from Standish Junction at Haresfield with the "Royal Sunset" of 26th September 1987 — the 226-mile commemorative excursion from Swindon to Newport and Hereford which marked the 'Kings' final main line appearance. With the locomotive's seven-year boiler certificate having expired at the end of September, and custodians Bulmers electing not to fund another major overhaul, "KGV" appeared to be heading for a museum-based existence in the foreseeable future.*

planned to run on the Swindon-Gloucester "Golden Valley" line to mark the silver jubilee of the GWR Museum at Swindon. Coming off their Gloucester stabling point early on the morning of the 16th May, the two engines were coupled tender to tender, 7029 leading, heading for Swindon. 6000 was derailed on a three-way point in the yard causing serious damage — the left side leading driving wheel axle hornblock was fractured, together with damaged spring hangers on the leading right side driver. 7029 ran to Swindon for the 10.12 departure of the "Jubilee Express", but south of Kemble found itself in trouble as well when a superheater element started blowing. It managed to work the train to Gloucester, but the 13.35 ex Gloucester and the 15.20 ex Swindon were both diesel worked. 7029 again turned out for the 18.10 ex Gloucester, but required the assistance of two class 37s.

Overnight repairs on 7029 resulted in the engine working all four trains on the 17th without any trouble.

Meanwhile, 6000 *King George V* was in serious trouble, and initial thoughts were that the locomotive's main-line career might have come to a premature end, but help was at hand as the damaged hornblock was replaced by one removed from No 6023 *King Edward II* then undergoing restoration at Bristol. After the axlebox crown brasses had been remetalled, and the engine rewheeled, a test run from Gloucester to Newport on the 26th June confirmed that the engine was ready for the "Diamond Jubilee Express" tour on the 4th July.

6000 *King George V* hauled its last main line railtour on the 26th September — "The Royal Sunset" — a distance of 226 miles from Swindon to Shrewsbury and return to Hereford. It was an emotional day. The engine had spearheaded the "Return to Steam" in the early days, and would be sorely missed. The fact that 6024 "King Edward 1" was in the final stages of its 14-year long restoration at Quainton Road, whilst welcome and happy news, did not help dispel the feeling of sadness.

The "Pennine Limited" of the 14th November was cancelled due to lack of support. However the rostered engine — 34092 *City of Wells* — was back on the S. & C., with a well patronised and "Ethel-less" southbound Cumbrian Mountain Express on the 19th December.

The year ended with 2005 hauling "Santa Specials" on the Edinburgh suburban line on 5/6th and 12/13th December. Five trains ran per day carrying 7,000 passengers.

Once again "Christmas Specials" were operated between Marylebone and High Wycombe, with 5305 joining the pool of locomotives after new firebox stays had been fitted at Dairycoates following the engine's return from the summer season in Scotland. Two trains per day were planned for the 12/13th, 19/20th and 28/29th December — these trains being hauled by 5305 and 4498 *Sir Nigel Gresley* — and 30/31st December and 2nd January 1988 — these trains being hauled by 5305 and 35028 *Clan Line*. Whilst bookings on the pre-Christmas trains were reasonable, the demand for seats on the 30/31st December and 2nd January was so poor that they were cancelled.

So ended what turned out to be — in spite of all the fears and misgivings — a hugely successful year for steam on the main line. Not only was there a large increase in the numbers of steam specials run, but there was also the introduction of new and exciting routes with new locomotives. A feeling of optimism was in the air, though the high failure rate among the main line steam locomotive fleet was worrying. The figure given for the casualty rate in 1987 was 500 miles per casualty. This can be put in context when it is compared to the casualty rate in the Class 87 fleet which was in excess of 40,000 miles per casualty.

Looking to the future, restoration work had been started on 60532 *Blue Peter* at ICI workshops at Wilton, Teesside on 27th July, 70000 *Britannia* had been taken to Carnforth for a major overhaul to restore the loco to main line working condition, and agreement was reached between the SRPS and Steamtown, Carnforth for the overhaul and return to main line service of 44871. Other engines coming 'on line' for 1988 were 3442 *The Great Marquess* and 34027 *Taw Valley*.

Towards the end of the year — on 17th November — British Rail and the Steam Locomotive Operators Association, in the persons of David Ward and Dick Hardy, met to discuss the future of steam operations on the main line. At the end of that meeting a statement was released which laid down the plans and procedures for main line steam over the next few years, replacing the previous policy document agreed in 1982. The most comforting part of this statement for steam enthusiasts was that BR's option of another two years of steam on the main line beyond 1990 was being taken up, and thereafter the decision on further extensions

would be made annually, three years in advance. The sting in the tail, however, was that BR had set down new conditions for the continued running of steam excursions as follows:-

1. Steam operations must remain profitable to BR.

2. Administrative and staff costs have to be kept down.

3. A higher standard of locomotive reliability must be reached than has been the case in 1987.

4. Continuance will depend on BR having trained inspectors and footplate staff available, and on SLOA being able to supply reliable support teams.

In order to meet criteria 1 and 2, indications were given that "one-off" trips would become progressively rarer, and that most of the operations would be concentrated on a few main "arterial" approved steam routes. In order to try and

Frost glistens on the track as LNER 'K1' 2-6-0 No 2005 heads south out of Carlton Tunnel at Abbeyhill Junction with the 13.00 "Santa Special" ex Waverley station.

implement criteria 3, three new inspector's posts were being created at Derby — two mechanical inspectors and one boiler inspector — who would be responsible for regular six-monthly examinations of the locomotives.

There was no doubting the firmness of purpose in the planning to keep steam alive on the main line in the years ahead, and in view of some of the problems that had occurred, the document was a constructive and reasonable plan for the future. Perhaps 1987 had at last given stability to temper the enthusiasm, exuberance and excitement of the previous years.

Outlook Unsettled — 1988–1989

After the frenzied activity of 1987, the 1988 steam year started very slowly with limited activity on the main line before Easter. Indeed in the first quarter of the year only two steam specials ran.

In order to get 4498 *Sir Nigel Gresley* north to Carnforth for essential maintenance and repairs, Hertfordshire Rail Tours sponsored "The White Rose" from Marylebone to Sheffield on the 6th February.Then on 27th February Flying Scotsman Services — which now incorporated Pullman Rail — ran "The Lancastrian" from Carnforth to West Ruislip, a distance of 275 miles with No 4472 *Flying Scotsman* hauling an eight coach train containing 180 passengers, arriving at West Ruislip only five minutes down.

Following its problems on the Carnforth-Sellafield line the previous autumn, 4472 had stayed on at Carnforth for overhaul of the axle box bearings. After running-in at Carnforth with the "Mince Pie" specials, the tour was organised to get 4472 down to the old Southall MPD — now the subject of a tenancy agreement between Flying Scotsman Services and BR Property Board — so that the depot's wheel drop facility could be used to remove the driving wheels. This was carried out the following day, and the wheels were sent off to Doncaster for the fitting of new tyres. The wheels were due back in late April. In the absence of *Flying Scotsman*, it was agreed that 5305 should remain in London to cover the "Shakespeare Limited" Sunday Diner trains in the spring before the loco returned north for another years work at Fort William.

The main reason for the paucity of steam specials was the non-availability of a significant number of the larger engines in the main-line fleet. Apart from 4498 *Sir Nigel Gresley* and 4472 *Flying Scotsman* — previously mentioned — 35028 *Clan Line* had departed to the embryo Heritage Centre at Swindon to have its tyres turned, and routine maintenance carried out. 6201 *Princess Elizabeth* required attention to its superheater tubes — 18 elements being replaced — and rebushing of the inside motion, and 4771 *Green Arrow* had a cracked cylinder lining. 777 *Sir Lamiel* was still out of action and 5593 *Kolhapur* and 5080 *Defiant* were carrying out running-in turns on the Severn Valley Railway. In addition to these casualties, both 92220 *Evening Star* and 34092 *City of Wells* were rapidly approaching the end of their seven-year boiler certificates. Of the engines undergoing major overhaul, 5407 was the only likely contender for main line duties in 1988, the work proceeding smoothly at Carnforth. Of the others, the work on 5596 *Bahamas*, 44932, 44871 and 46229 *Duchess of Hamilton* (happily now purchased by the National Railway Museum from Butlins) was well advanced, but with 70000 *Britannia*, 5029 *Nunney Castle* and 60532 *Blue Peter* still some distance from completion. Indeed, non-availability and failures of steam locomotives was a problem which plagued the whole of 1988's steam operations.

Two main groups promoted 1988's main line programme. BR had taken over the marketing of the "Pennine Limited" from Pullman-Rail and was continuing to market the "Shakespeare Limited" Sunday Diner trains from Marylebone, though in limited numbers compared with 1987 — only eight "Shakespeare Limited" and nine "Pennine Limited" trains were scheduled. Flying Scotsman Services produced a package of 12 "Cumbrian Mountain Express" trains, and seven "South Yorkshireman" specials between Marylebone and Sheffield. These latter two trains were more directed at the enthusiasts market rather than BR's promotions. In the north the specials were hauled from a pool of locomotives which included (at one time or another through the year) 92220 *Evening Star*, 34092 *City of Wells*, 5305, 4498 *Sir Nigel Gresley*, 777 *Sir Lamiel* and in the autumn and winter months 48151, and 5407. The pool of locos which worked trains out of Marylebone included 35028 *Clan Line*, 777 *Sir Lamiel*, 4498 *Sir Nigel Gresley*, 4472 *Flying Scotsman*, 5305 and 7029 *Clun Castle*.

Whilst the BR-sponsored trains were generally well supported, bookings on the "Cumbrian Mountain Express" and "South Yorkshireman" were generally low — particularly in the early part of the season — with several trips failing to, or only just, breaking even. For example, the northbound "Cumbrian Mountain Express" of 28th May hauled by 4498 *Sir Nigel Gresley* carried only 200 passengers, and the return trip the following week with the same engine carried only 219 passengers. Significantly, over the three previous weekends — the 7th, 14th and 21st May, 4498 *Sir Nigel Gresley* had hauled three "Streamline Express" public charter specials for the Cambridge Railway Circle over the S. & C. — all three trains being total sell-outs. Perhaps there is a saturation point even for the S. & C.

This was by no means the whole answer as two attractive runs by 6201 *Princess Elizabeth* were cancelled due to poor bookings. The first, sponsored by Dinting Railway Centre, and booked for the 9th July was a Hereford-Newport-Chester trip which was cancelled when only 91 out of the 396 available seats were booked. The second, sponsored by the Birmingham Railway Museum on the 3rd September for a Birmingham-Marylebone and return run was cancelled when only 159 seats were sold. Compare this to two circular tours hauled by 6201 on the 21st August from Crewe via Chester and Shrewsbury thence back to Crewe. The tickets were priced at £10 and were all sold out a week before the trip ran. Poor bookings and cancelled trips were a particular worry for the locomotive owners who needed good financial returns to fund the maintenance and repairs of their locos, particularly with charges for a six month main-line certificate being increased from £750 to £925.

Also worrying was the continued string of locomotive failures or non-appearances after being booked to haul a special, particularly so given the introduction of BR's new

steam loco inspectorate at Derby. These repeated failures resulted in David Ward in mid-June describing the situation as "extremely serious", and later on in the year putting a ban on any further "one-off" trips booked after the 1st October. This ban resulted in the cancellation of 44871's debut on the S. & C. on 22nd October after major overhaul.

One locomotive more unfortunate than most was Paddy Smith's 'Black 5' No 5407, whose major overhaul was completed in April 1988. Initially due to deputise for 777 *Sir Lamiel* on the "South Yorkshireman" on 14th May and again on a private charter, the "Metro Pullman" over the S. & C. on 18th June, 5407 spent most of the year trying to overcome repeated hot box problems. Finally the problem was solved, and the locomotive re-entered service on the main line with the "Southport Visitor" on the 18th September and the northbound "Cumbrian Mountain Express" on the 1st October.

Other disappointments in 1988 included the decision by British Nuclear Fuels not to run an autumn series of "Sellafield Sightseer" trains when 4472 *Flying Scotsman* was unavailable, the absence of the Swansea-Carmarthen trains,which had been expected to run again in 1988, and the inability of all parties to find a profitable formula for the Cambrian Coast steam trains. This latter service made a reported modest profit in 1987, and it had been thought likely to have been repeated in a modified and more limited form. Some suggestions were made to introduce a Shrewsbury-Barmouth steam service on summer Tuesdays and Thursdays with a Sunday Shrewsbury-Pwllheli service. The Mid-Wales Development Board was prepared to offer a subsidy of £10,000, but the scheme was eventually turned down

mainly because the major section over Talerddig was not an approved steam route, and that there was a considerable fire risk. A more modest proposal for an Aberystwyth-Machynlleth-Barmouth service was turned down on the expectation that it would not be financially viable.

On the positive side the third year of Salisbury-based steam specials, held on 2/3rd, 9th and 23/24th July, with the special "Anniversary Pullman" commemorating the end of steam on the Southern 21 years ago running on 10th July, was a resounding success in spite of having to operate a truncated service over the first weekend due to the non-availability of one of the rostered engines — 34092 *City of Wells*. The loco suffered serious damage to the middle cylinder piston rings following a boiler priming incident on the "South Yorkshireman" of the 18th June and was not ready until the 9th July. The second locomotive should have been 777 *Sir Lamiel*, but as it was still under repair in Hull, 48151 deputised most effectively having arrived hot-foot from its triumphant return to the S. & C. with an out and back trip on the 25th June (the first appearance of an 8F on the line since the summer of 1968.) A new feature in 1988 was the inclusion of Romsey in the itinerary. Steam again appeared on the Andover-Romsey line on 25th September

As part of the celebrations commemorating the 50th anniversary of Mallard*'s world speed record run, the Friends of the National Railway Museum arranged a series of four 'Mallard 88' steam-hauled specials on Sundays in July. They were overwhelmed by demand for tickets, so the four trains were expanded to ten — and even then they were oversubscribed! The first of these excursions ran on the 9th. July 1988 when the star — Gresley 'A4' Pacific No 4468* Mallard *— ran from York to Scarborough, and is seen here leaving Malton.*

when 80080 hauled several specials during the Wino'field 150 celebrations. Sadly, with reorganisation in the Salisbury area and the departure of Gerald Daniels it was feared that this would be the last year of steam out of Salisbury.

The "Scarborough Spa Express" once again ran, but only as a pale shadow of its former self. Only four days of operation were planned, with the first three — on 14th and 21st August and 4th September — running a morning and afternoon train from York to Scarborough and return. These trains, priced at £10, were hauled by 4498 *Sir Nigel Gresley*, 34092 *City of Wells* and 3440 *City of Truro* respectively. This latter train was the only outing of the year for 3440 *City of Truro*. The fourth train on the 29th August ran from York to Scarborough via Selby and Brough. After returning to York by the direct route, it then carried on with a "York Circle" via Leeds and Harrogate. Priced at £20 this train was well patronised, as were the other three. 5407 was the rostered engine for the 29th August, but as it was still receiving attention to its axleboxes, No 92220 *Evening Star* substituted, even though its seven year boiler certificate had expired some nine days earlier — special dispensation was granted by BR.

In a troubled year the Fort William — Mallaig services did not escape without some problems. Having arrived in Fort William, 2005 worked the first "West Highlander" on the 20th March, and in doing so became the first steam loco to operate on that route with the recently installed Radio Token Block Signalling Equipment. Having worked the "South Yorkshireman" on the 9th April, 5305 returned to Hull in May prior to joining 2005 at Fort William in June only to find on examination six broken firebox side stays. Instead of working the SRPS sponsored "Nithsdale Express" from Carlisle to Edinburgh via Kilmarnock on the 11th June, and from Edinburgh to Perth on the following day,

5305 did not reach Fort William till 14th July, having worked the previous day's "Pennine Ltd" to Carlisle. In the meantime, 2005 had worked some 1,550 miles in 3½ weeks. Three steam runs in that time had to be cancelled — the "Royal Scotsman" on the 11th May and the "West Highlander" on the 15th May — because of fire risk, and the "West Highlander" of the 29th May because of sticking safety valves. It was only thanks to Gerald Boden's generosity, when he allowed the safety valves from his own engine, 'B1' No 1306 *Mayflower* to be overhauled, certified to BR standards and then used on the K1 for two months, that the steam service could be continued. Both locos again worked a charter train south at the end of the season — 5305 with "The Claymore" in deep snow on the 27th November after the initial trip on the 6th November was cancelled because of fire-risk, and 2005 on 19th November with "The Lochaber" — again in driving snow.

"The Derwent Explorer", from Nottingham to Matlock via Derby incorporating an intermediate Matlock-Derby-Matlock shuttle, survived from 1987 — David Kirk warning at the beginning of the season "If these specials are to run after this year, they have got to do substantially better than they did in 1987". He had a very positive response with an average of 400 passengers on the main section and 250 who rode on the Matlock-Derby-Matlock shuttle section. The first 11-coach train was hauled in exemplary style by 80080 on 22nd May, with 48151 also featuring both on this run and on the Derby-Hope Valley-Manchester Victoria successor to the "Buxton Spa Express". Indeed it was on the 15th October that 44932 made its return to the main line hauling "The Mancunian" from Derby to Manchester and return.

Of the "one-off" society-sponsored runs, special mention must be made of the return to the main line of 5080 *Defiant* on the 11th June with "The Red Dragon". Hauling a 12-coach train from Birmingham to Didcot and return, the engine gave a sparkling performance. The locomotive was again out on the main line on 2nd July hauling a Hereford-Newport-Shrewsbury "Welsh Marches Pullman" of 440 tons, and for a third time on the 6th August when it substituted for 4472 *Flying Scotsman* with a Worcester-Newport-Chester trip. All three runs were trouble-free and were very well received by the passengers and onlookers. 5080's stablemate 7029 *Clun Castle* was called in at short notice on the 29th May to work on the Marylebone-Stratford trains. Its final duty was the Marylebone-Banbury trip of 14th August when the return leg was worked by 4472 *Flying Scotsman* after a successful Southall-Tyseley test run on 11th August. This was the first revenue earning trip by 4472 after its overhaul at Southall with the fitting of new tyres and valve setting by Bill Harvey. 7029 itself needed new tyres, and once they were fitted, the loco was found to be out of gauge for the Marylebone-Banbury line!

Shortly after the 14th August run, 4472 *Flying Scotsman* was shipped off to Australia to take part in that country's Bicentennial festivities, being due back in March 1989.

The star of 1988 was undoubtedly 4468 *Mallard*. In May the Post Office hired *Mallard* at fairly short notice to feature in the 150th celebrations of the TPO — an 18p commemorative stamp being issued on 10th May featuring an A4. A joint film and test run from York to Harrogate and return was hurriedly organised for the 6th May, during which one of the bogie axlebox bearings ran hot. This was sorted in time for 4468 to leave York for Marylebone on the 8th May. The loco was stopped at Princes Risborough due to flash floods blocking Sudbury tunnel, and eventually had to work into Marylebone via Aylesbury, Wembley Park and over some of the 'Met' electric lines — happily arriving on the 9th just in time to be prepared for the "Postal Pullman" charter train to Banbury. Having arrived at Banbury, 4468 travelled light engine to Newton Heath, and on the following day worked the "Pennine Postal Pullman" from Manchester to York and Scarborough.

The big day for 4468 *Mallard* was the 3rd July, when the locomotive worked from Doncaster to York and return to celebrate the 50th anniversary of its world record breaking run. The "Mallard '88" Committee had organised in addition a month long series of festivities to celebrate the event. These included four trips by the loco — on the 9th July a York-Scarborough-Hull-York trip, on 16th July a York-Leeds-Settle-Newcastle-Carlisle-Eaglescliffe charter, on 23rd July an evening wine and dine train from York to Grange-over-Sands via Leeds and Carnforth, and finally on the 30th July a York-Sheffield-Manchester-Leeds-York trip. These tours were an instant sell-out, so duplicate trips were arranged for the Sundays following the original trips, together with two "Cumbrian Mountain Express" trips on 13th and 27th August. Again all the trips were fully booked. Having exceeded the 26 runs limit decided upon when the engine returned to the main line in 1986, and with the six month main line certificate expiring on November 4th, 4468 *Mallard* then retired to the National Railway Museum.

No 34092 *City of Wells* made its last run before the expiry of its seven-year boiler certificate in November when it worked a northbound private charter over the S. & C. for the Lancashire Evening Post. The loco slipped to a stop on wet leaves coming out of Stainforth Tunnel and had to obtain the assistance of a class 47 diesel loco which banked the train as far as Blea Moor tunnel.

The SRPS "Santa Specials" once more appeared on the Edinburgh Suburban Circle on 4/10/11th December, with K1 No 2005. A total of 6,500 passengers were carried. The first two trains on the 4th were composed of two sleeping cars, a BSK, two open coaches, a BG and a class 47 diesel (47.563) to provide train heating — due to the non- arrival of SRPS' own Mk1 railtour stock which was stranded by a diesel failure whilst en route back from London. More suitable stock was marshalled for the rest of the trips on the 4th, and the correct stock arrived in time for the 10th and 11th. Because of the East Coast electrification, the SRPS were told that this was probably the last time that these Santa Specials would run.

No Marylebone-High Wycombe "Santa Specials" were scheduled — indeed it was announced that the "Shakespeare Limited" would no longer run from Marylebone — BR having declared that due to Network SE resignalling and modernisation plans, Marylebone was unavailable in 1989. The last train was to have run on the 29th December, but was cancelled partly because of poor advance bookings, but also because *Ethel 3* had to be transferred to Carlisle to replace *Ethel 2* whose generator was destroyed when it self-ignited in Appleby station on 12th November whilst on a southbound Cumbrian Mountain Express hauled by 48151. Initially plans were made to move the "Shakespeare Limited" operation to Paddington. However when it was realised that no more than one train per month could be accommodated there, BR suspended the operation of these trains during 1989 on the basis that they would not be financially viable. This seemed a great pity considering how successful the trains had been — it was suggested that the decision would dissipate all the public's goodwill fostered over the past few years.

In a year bedevilled with locomotive failures, poor bookings and light loadings on many of the tours — when some influential voices were heard to predict a big reduction in the numbers of steam specials on the main line in 1989 — the last thing the movement needed was any more bad news. On the 16th May, however, there was a ministerial announcement in the House of Commons when David Mitchell — the Minister of Public Transport — said that he was "Minded to consent to BR's closure proposal for the Settle and Carlisle and Blackburn-Hellifield lines". A final decision was to be delayed till 30th November after which BR would be required to operate the line for a further four months. Hope was expressed that in the intervening time, a private buyer might come forward for the line to operate it as a private venture. Local reaction was hostile and rail enthusiasts rallied to help save the line from closure. The idea of a private individual or consortium being able to buy and then run the S. & C. as if it were a larger version of the Severn Valley Railway or the North Yorkshire Moors Railway was ridiculed.

Because of the flood of objections which resulted from the closure statement — at the end of November 28 MPs whose constituencies would be affected presented some 80,000 signatures on a petition to save the line — a two month stay of execution was granted.

After the euphoria of 1986 and 1987, the cold clammy hand of reality had well and truly clamped down on the main line steam preservation movement in 1988, and 1989 — though promising much initially — turned out to be one of the gloomiest years on record since 1971.

Initially the portents for 1989 were good. An attractive programme of tours with several new routes sponsored by BR and Flying Scotsman Services was announced. The jewel in the crown was to be the Railway Heritage Centre at Crewe, where a pool of locomotives, including 4498 *Sir Nigel Gresley*, 35028 *Clan Line*, 34027 *Taw Valley* and 5407 were to be based to work the 30 new BR-sponsored Crewe-Holyhead trains on three days a week — Tuesdays, Wednesdays and Sundays from June 27th to September 3rd. These would be followed on 7th October by four "Ynys Mon Express" — Flying Scotsman Services' version of the "North Wales Coast Express". Two new trains also originating from Crewe were the "West Mercian" — with steam haulage from Crewe to Hereford and return by way of Whitchurch and Shrewsbury — and the "Cheshire Cheese" which would involve a round trip from Crewe via Chester, Shrewsbury and Whitchurch. Four tours on each route were planned, with the "Cheshire Cheese" having two circuits of the Crewe triangle each day.

Two other new routes were proposed — a series of four "Lincolnshire Poacher" trains from Nottingham to Lincoln via Newark, and the "Peaks Express" which would run on four Bank Holiday Mondays starting on 27th March from Marylebone to Derby via Banbury and return, hauled exclusively by 4498 *Sir Nigel Gresley*. The old favourites were to continue, these being a series of four "Scarborough Flyer" trains commencing on 25th June, four "Welsh Marches Express" on the Shrewsbury-Hereford-Newport-Hereford route, commencing on the 15th April and a series of eight "Cumbrian Mountain Express" trains culminating in 4771 *Green Arrow* hauling the southbound train from Carlisle to Hellifield on 13th May, the last day of BR ownership of the line as things presently stood. The sting in the tail for these trips was that BR decided to cash in on the "Final Train Mania" by raising its charter fees to Flying Scotsman Services. The consequences were that the trains on the 1st and 8th May were priced at £38 a head with the last train on the 13th May being priced at £50.

The season started quietly and confidently with two "Cumbrian Mountain Express" trains in January hauled by 35028 *Clan Line* and two in February hauled in atrocious weather by 4771 *Green Arrow*. These latter two trains comprised 11 coaches, a support coach and an "Ethel". Both trains were fully booked, and 4771 *Green Arrow* in particular, gave a sparkling performance.

On the 13th January 5080 *Defiant* worked into Birmingham Snow Hill station in disguise, wearing former GWR 'City' class 4-4-0 *City of Birmingham* nameplates with a "Victorian Train" as part of the city's celebrations of the centenary of its charter being granted by Queen Victoria. The following day No 35028 *Clan Line* worked a 12-coach press and test train (plus *Ethel 3*) from Crewe to Llandudno and Holyhead. The trip was a proving run for the summer's "North Wales Coast Express" and passed off uneventfully. It marked the return of steam to the line after an absence of 20 years.

Flying Scotsman Services programme for 1989, "Steam '89 on the main line" commenced in earnest on Good Friday, the 24th March, when 5407 hauled "The Lancastrian" from Carnforth to Crewe via Blackburn, Manchester and Chester to position itself to work the inaugural run of the "Cheshire Cheese" on 28th March — the beginning of the year's steam operations from Crewe. The run itself was well supported, and trouble-free. Unfortunately it marked the beginning of a traumatic, difficult and exasperating year of problems for all connected with main line steam preservation.

4498 *Sir Nigel Gresley* was the first casualty, suffering a bent left eccentric rod on March 27th whilst working the return leg of the inaugural "Peaks Express". The damage was probably caused by slipping as the train left Princes Risborough, and the locomotive had to be taken off at High Wycombe. With the A4 officially stopped for a detailed investigation by Derby DM & EE the May 1st "Peaks Express" had to be cancelled. The following day saw 5407 complete two circuits of the Crewe-Chester-Shrewsbury-Crewe triangle. There were no mechanical problems, but only 400 of the available 900 seats were sold. Worse was to come when on 15th April double trouble struck the "Welsh Marches Express" which was to have been hauled by 5080 *Defiant*. The tour only attracted 160 passengers, and the pre-run loco inspection discovered a fractured oil feed pipe to the front left driving wheel axlebox resulting in a last minute withdrawal of the loco. A diesel loco was hurriedly made available, but later in the tour it also failed!

The slump continued when the first "Lincolnshire Poacher" — hauled by 44932 — ran on 22nd April with only 180 passengers. On the following day the third main line failure of the year occurred when 3440 *City of Truro* had to be taken off its Derby — Didcot "Western Venturer" at Dorridge with melted tender axlebox bearings — 47.662 substituting. Then on the 29th April when No 6201 *Princess Elizabeth* worked the "Wye-Dee Express" , a positioning train to move the 'Princess' up to Crewe for use on the "North Wales Coast Express", only 195 seats were sold. Disaster struck when society member Jack Street, a former Crewe works boiler foreman, collapsed and died on the footplate at Onibury. As a mark of respect, the headboard was reversed for the remainder of the run.

Meanwhile, Michael Portillo, now the Transport Secretary, told the House of Commons on the 9th March that because of the weight of new evidence which had been presented in favour of keeping the Settle & Carlisle line open, and also because he was considering proposals from private bidders hopeful of taking over the line, the S & C would

remain open until mid-October. An all-party Settle-Carlisle group was formed in the Houses of Parliament with the object of keeping the minister aware of the strength of public opinion about the proposed closure of the line, and to seek to keep the line open as part of the national railway network. As a consequence, Flying Scotsman Services announced a further series of ten "Cumbrian Mountain Express" tours between 13th July and 30th September, to be hauled by 4771 *Green Arrow* and 45596 *Bahamas*. Only a month later the Secretary of State for Transport announced on the 11th April to the delight of all enthusiasts that he had refused to allow BR to close both the S. & C. and Blackburn-Hellifield lines.

In the midst of all the doom and gloom for the railtour operators, some tours did prosper — mostly privately sponsored tours for individual loco-owning groups. Amongst these were 48151 on the 6th May on what was promoted as the last steam working over the former Midland Railway Trans-Pennine route from Derby to Manchester, BR having decreed that the Hope Valley route was now too busy to path steam trains. After its successful test run from Derby to Sheffield and return on the 19th May, No 45596 *Bahamas* worked an excursion from Derby to Didcot and return on the 27th May.

Elsewhere the passenger slump continued. On the 27th May "The Lancastrian", hauled by 35028 *Clan Line* from Carnforth to Crewe via Blackburn and Manchester, only carried 120 passengers, and on the same day the first working of the "West Mercian", with No 34027 *Taw Valley,* only

sold 118 seats out of the 400 available. Worse was to follow when the "Lincolnshire Poacher" of the 3rd June, with 80080 ran with less than 100 passengers, and 6998 *Burton Agnes Hall* weighed in as another big loss-maker when the "Welsh Marches Express" of the 10th June carried only 125 passengers.

With only 40 seats booked on the "Cheshire Cheese" for 17th June, it came as no surprise when Flying Scotsman Services announced the cancellation of all of its Crewe-based steam tours until the end of August,with the exception of the "Capitals United" on the 26th August. These included the "Cheshire Cheese" tours of 17th June and 1st and 29th July, and the "West Mercian" tours of 15th July and 5th August. In addition, the "Scarborough Flyer" tour of 25th June was also axed because of poor bookings. A Flying Scotsman Services spokesman commented "There may be too many trains in the 1989 main line programme".

Matters were not helped when on the 20th June, on the inaugural run of the "North Wales Coast Express", 34027 *Taw Valley*, itself deputising for the rostered engine No 5407 which had failed on a test run with cylinder valve problems and a bent radius rod, itself suffered a lubrication failure at Flint causing the right-hand piston valve to seize. The engine was nursed to Llandudno, and 35028 *Clan Line* was hastily summoned from Holyhead to take over the train.

There is no doubt that when you are down, fate likes to add a few judicious kicks of its own. The first came when 4498 *Sir Nigel Gresley* was undergoing a routine check at Didcot in late June. Serious cracks were discovered round the throat-plate washout plug. As a consequence the A4 Locomotive Society decided to bring forward by two years its full seven-year overhaul at Carnforth. The loco was towed from Didcot to Carnforth on 17th July. This was a big blow for the society, as it not only meant that the loco could not take its place in the loco pool for the "North Wales Coast Express" trains, No 6201 *Princess Elizabeth* substituting, but it also missed out on the four "Peaks Express" tours and the "Capitals United" tour to Marylebone on 26th August. This latter duty was taken over by 35028 *Clan Line*, though fate was again unkind when the loco stalled on Sapperton Bank and required assistance from a diesel — some delay occurring.

The second blow fell with the onset in mid-summer of a BR-NUR industrial dispute. Whilst this did not affect the running of the trains directly, it did create an atmosphere of uncertainty in the minds of passengers contemplating booking a trip. Because of the uncertainty the July trips over the S. & C. were cancelled.

The third blow came in late July when, as a consequence of glorious summer weather, several trains were cancelled because of fire risk. These included the two trips organised by the Great Western Society with No 6998 *Burton Agnes Hall* from Didcot to Worcester and the S.V.R. on the 22nd and 29th July. On the first trip, steam was banned only 2½ hours before departure — ironically all seats on the train had been sold. A diesel locomotive substituted, running through to Kidderminster. The "Peaks Express" of 28th August hauled by 35028 *Clan Line* was another casualty — being diesel-piloted between Banbury and Marylebone.

The "Scarborough Flyer" of the 23rd July, headed by 3440 *City of Truro*, did run, but with only 130 of its 350 seats sold, incurring a loss of £5,000. The proposed trip by 'K1' No 2005 on 15th July to Scarborough via Selby and Hull to mark the loco's 40th Anniversary was cancelled only 14 days before the run with more than 100 of the 367 seats on offer unsold. A loss of some £3,000 was estimated.

As a result of continued poor bookings, Flying Scotsman Services cancelled the "Lincolnshire Poacher" of 12th August, the "Welsh Marches Express" of 19th August — when 75069 was due to make its return to the main line — and the "Scarborough Flyer" of 20th August, which at the beginning of August had only 15 seats booked.

Calls were made to reduce the size and variety of steam tours on the main line — to make a steam trip on BR a special occasion rather than the norm. The "scarcity factor" argument once again appeared, and serious questions were asked as to whether the movement was pricing itself out of the market — a £35 ticket for 82 miles of steam-hauled running on the "Scarborough Flyer" was considered by some to be excessive.

By and large the "Cumbrian Mountain Express" tours were a success, with good loadings. The pick of the runs was arguably that of 45596 *Bahamas* southbound on the 31st August — a green engine and a complete set of maroon coaches. The trip was capped by 45596 hauling the train tender first on the Hellifield-Carnforth leg when the ros-

tered diesel failed. Earlier in the season — in June — the same loco appeared with 80080 in a highly successful series of shuttle trains between Nottingham and Derby to celebrate the Midland Counties Railway's 150th anniversary, and broke new ground with a rare "Cumbrian Coast Express" trip on the 8th July. On the 17th September 45596 *Bahamas* became the fifth engine in five years to appear on the "Southport Visitor". On this occasion, two return trips between Manchester and Southport and one Southport-Wigan shuttle proved to be a winner for the Southport Visitor sponsored "Festival of Nostalgia".

For the sixth consecutive season the "West Highlander" ran in Scotland. The price of a ticket was £10 — a rise of only 10p in two years. The loadings were so heavy that there was need of seven coaches on a daily basis — perhaps there is a lesson to be learned somewhere there. Trains ran on Sundays, Mondays, Tuesdays and Thursdays from Thursday 18th May, with the "Royal Scotsman" running on Wednesdays. The rostered engines were 'Black 5s' Nos 44871 and 5305.

No 44871 duly arrived in Fort William on 21st April, well in time for the start of the season. No 5305 was due to work a special charter train promoted by BR East Midlands from Hellifield to Carlisle on the 1st June en route for Fort William, but delay in completing the replacement of more than 800 firebox stays at Dairycoates Restoration Centre, Hull caused the cancellation of the tour, with 5305 being further delayed when a faulty brake valve was discovered at Carlisle whilst en route to Fort William on the 24th June. In the meantime 44871 valiantly soldiered on, and in the season hauled 46 trains with a grand total of 3,772 miles run without any problems!

In a surprise move, 'K4' No 3442 *The Great Marquess*, after a successful test run on 30th June, hauled "The Mancunian" railtour from Hereford to Stockport on the 8th July, and the "Pennines Express" from Skipton to Carlisle the following day as a means of getting the loco up to Fort William for a two week stay. 3442 hauled its inaugural train — Lord Lindsay's private charter — on the 15th July — and worked a further ten scheduled trains during its short stay. Plans were made for a Perth-Stirling-Glasgow-Kilmarnock-Dumfries return trip on the 30th July, but these had to be cancelled due to engineering work on the line on that day. On Saturday 5th August, the K4 worked a Carlisle-Blackburn "Pennines Express" and on the following day a Stockport-Hereford "Lochaber Envoy" before returning light-engine from Hereford to Kidderminster on the 7th August. Happily all of 3442's trains were well supported.

4472 *Flying Scotsman* meanwhile was experiencing a huge commercial success during its stay in Australia. As a result, its departure date for Tilbury was initially put back to the first week in September and then to 4th November — finally arriving back at Tilbury on 14th December. As a consequence of its absence the planned autumn series of "Sellafield Sightseer" trains had to be cancelled.

In this country steam-hauled railtours continued on their topsy-turvey way. On the 10th July 6201 *Princess Elizabeth* made its debut on the Crewe-Holyhead line, hauling the "Inaugural Steam Charter Train" — which was sponsored by the Royal British Legion. More than 200 passengers were turned away! The loco performed well — doubts about its tender water capacity were well and truly laid to rest. On the 28th August 6201 was due to make its debut on the "North Wales Coast Express" but its BSK support coach was derailed in the Heritage Centre bending 6201's drawbar. The train was delayed for two hours, finally leaving Crewe

Brel Ewart's Butterley-based BR Standard 'Class 4' 2-6-4T No 80080 bursts out of Nottingham (Midland) station at the start of its run to Derby and Matlock with the "Derwent Explorer" of the 22nd May 1988. Spirited running by 80080 at the head of 11 coaches carrying over 400 passengers resulted in the special having to wait for "time" on several occasions during the day. The former Midland Railway goods warehouse on the left was completely demolished a few days after this picture was taken.

behind two Class 31 diesel locomotives. 'Black 5' No 5407, which had worked the previous day's train, was quickly fired up and sent off to Holyhead to haul the return working. Following repair and ultrasonic testing of the drawhook, 6201 *Princess Elizabeth* finally took up her duties on the "NWCE" on the 29th August. Amongst its other duties, 6201 *Princess Elizabeth* worked the "Jack Street Memorial" train on 10th September from Crewe to Holyhead.

The late autumn and winter programme of steam tours on the main line was probably the most successful of the whole year, though Flying Scotsman Services had to cancel the last four "Ynys Mon Express" tours. The first two, on 7th October (hauled by 6201 *Princess Elizabeth*) and the 28th October (hauled by 5407), were well supported. Cancellation occurred because there were no steam locomotives available at Crewe to work the trains! The problem was the six month main line certificate required for any locomotive working on the main line. With the cost being £925, many locomotive owners were unwilling to pay this sort of money when there was a reduced amount of main line work in the winter months. 35028 *Clan Line* had already left Crewe with the "Capitals United" on the 26th August, and did actually work a private charter on 7th October from West Ruislip to Stratford and return two weeks after its main line certificate had expired — special dispensation having been obtained from BR — prior to retiring to Southall for essential winter maintenance. 6201 *Princess Elizabeth* also had an expired main line certificate, and 5407 had returned to Carnforth. "Cumbrian Mountain Express" trains were substituted on 25th November, and 9/27th December with 5407 being the rostered engine. Because of track alterations, the change over point from diesel to steam was moved from Hellifield to Blackburn.

Elsewhere, taking advantage of 44871's return from Scotland, a special trip was organised on the 7th October from Dundee to Keighley with the steam section being from Carlisle to Keighley. This was 44871's first revenue-earning trip over the S. & C. since the 15-guinea Special of August 1968. The last of the year's "Welsh Marches Express" was run on 21st October with 6998 *Burton Agnes Hall* hauling the train — some compensation for the disappointments of the summer "fire-risk ban". 34027 *Taw Valley* worked a Nottingham-Derby-Marylebone special — the "Sherwood Forester" — on 11th November as a positioning run to enable it to work two proposed "William Shakespeare Pullman" trains out of Marylebone on 2nd and 30th December.

The 29th October 1988 was one of the clearest, crispest days of the year and coincided with the northbound "Cumbrian Mountain Express" headed by David Smith's beautifully restored Stanier 8F 2-8-0 No 48151. As the sun sets, 48151 leaves Appleby on the last leg of its trip to Carlisle.

In Scotland, 5305 broke new ground by working a four-coach private charter train from Fort William to Crianlarich on 23rd October, and during the month of November worked a series of crew-training runs between Fort William and Mallaig hauling four condemned coaches and a support coach. After a four week course three men passed out as fully qualified steam locomotive drivers — the first for 25 years. On the 9th December 5305 worked south to Edinburgh, and on 10/16/17th December was allowed to work the SRPS "Santa Specials" round the Edinburgh suburban line since the electric cables on the recently completed section between Portobello Junction and Waverley station were not being energised till after Christmas.

As a consequence of all the problems of 1989, BR announced that they would only be operating two steam-hauled services on a regular basis in 1990. These were the "West Highlander" between Fort William and Mallaig and the "North Wales Coast Express" between Crewe and Holyhead. Though the loadings on the early trains on this latter route had been disappointing, with passenger levels at times only 50% of seats available, once the NUR/BR dispute had been settled and the school holidays had started, loadings improved with three trains having to be strengthened to 12 coaches. BR considered the results sufficiently encouraging to plan for a series of 31 trains running between July and mid-September. Flying Scotsman Services announced that because traffic on other routes had proved to be very disappointing, they would be confining their operations to three main routes — Marylebone-Stratford-Tyseley, the S. & C. and the North Wales Coast route, though they would consider private charter bookings for other routes on their merits.

1989 was a very difficult year for all concerned with the running of main line steam services — probably the most difficult and worrying since the return of steam to the main line in 1971. With locomotive failures continuing to be a problem, and public support apparently waning for the various tours — particularly in the first nine months of the year — doubts were being raised as to the continuing viability of steam tours on the main line. Questions were being asked. Was the current economic situation to blame? Were the tours overpriced in the minds of the travelling public? Were the right sort of tours being promoted — should the operators concentrate more on short family-orientated trips? Was there still a place in the leisure market for steam-hauled main line tours? Should a scarcity factor be introduced?

1990 was looked forward to with some trepidation.

On the 28th March 1989, ex LMS Class 5 4-6-0 No 5407 worked the first of the years new "Cheshire Cheese" specials around the Crewe circular route via Chester and Shrewsbury. Sadly due to poor loadings and a slump in passenger bookings, it turned out to be the only working in the year. Paddy Smith's 'Black 5' is in fine form as it rushes through Haughton with the afternoon train.

The "Cumbrian Mountain Express" of 1st April 1989 was hauled northbound by 'Merchant Navy' No 35028 Clan Line. The train runs through glorious scenery at Baron Wood on the last leg of its trip from Hellifield to Carlisle.

The southbound "Cumbrian Mountain Express" of the 30th September 1989 was run in almost unbroken sunshine. LNER 'V2' 2-6-2 No 4771 Green Arrow *produced a memorable performance, the highlight being a storming run up to Ais Gill summit. The train is seen here crossing Ais Gill viaduct in fine style.*

Below:
The 25th November 1989 saw LMS 'Black 5' 4-6-0 No 5407 head a northbound "Cumbrian Mountain Express" from Blackburn to Carlisle. With 9 coaches and an 'Ethel' the 'Black 5' produced some pyrotechnics on its climb past Sheriff Brow en route for Blea Moor.

The centenary of the Forth Railway Bridge was celebrated on the 4th March 1990 when Gresley 'A4' Pacific No 60009, now named Osprey so as not to offend any anti-apartheid campaigners, majestically headed south over the bridge with a special train of V.I.Ps including BR chairman Sir Robert Reid, heading for Edinburgh. Later in the day Osprey picked up an 'Ethel' train-heating unit at Edinburgh and departed back for the bridge with the afternoon public run of "The Forth Centennial" to Perth and back. (Brian Morrison)

Right:
Perhaps the only thing spoiling this picture of 'Jubilee' No 45596 Bahamas heading south at Smardale with the "Cumbrian Mountain Express" of 14th July 1990 is the support coach marshalled behind the locomotive. With the old paintwork stripped down, and just one end panel bearing the maroon livery, the coach provides an interesting contrast to the Pullman and Intercity liveries elsewhere in the train.

Birmingham Railway Museum's "Shakespeare Express" service over Easter weekend in 1990 saw two Great Western 4-6-0s working an intensive service of 16 trains between Tyseley and Stratford-upon-Avon on April 15th and 16th. On the 15th, 'King' No 6024 King Edward I majestically powers up to Wood End Tunnel with the 17.05 ex Stratford for Tyseley, becoming the first member of its class ever to work over the North Warwickshire line. These runs on the "Shakespeare Express" were the comeback runs of the 'King' after its long period of restoration at Quainton following its purchase from Barry scrapyard in 1973.

Below:
The reward for braving icy winds and sleet and snow showers on the 16th April was this action-packed picture of 5080 Defiant powering through Danzey with the 11.05 ex Stratford.

Following its return to the main line in 1990, BR Pacific No 71000 Duke of Gloucester *made several powerful and notable main line runs, particularly over the S. & C. line, culminating in its record breaking run on the southbound "Cumbrian Mountain Express" on the 20th July 1991 when it ran from Appleby to Ais Gill summit in 21 minutes and 11 seconds, thus beating the record set by* Duchess of Hamilton *seven years previously by 1 minute and 15 seconds. Seven weeks earlier — on the 1st June 1991 — the 'Duke' bursts out of Birkett tunnel on the southbound "Cumbrian Mountain Express".*

The long-awaited return of BR Pacific No 70000 Britannia *to the main line took place on the 27th July 1991 when it ran out of Crewe to Chester and Shrewsbury with the "Britannia Phoenix". On the 7th September 1991 it made its debut on the "Cumbrian Mountain Express", hauling a train from Carlisle to Blackburn. On a sunny day it made a spectacular sight as it reached Ais Gill summit — Wild Boar Fell is in the background.*

The Drummond Locomotive Society — the owners of M7 No 30052 — must have been delighted to see their locomotive out on the main line on 28th June 1992 — albeit in the guise of former Salisbury station pilot No 30673. It is seen leaving Eastleigh with the stock for its Laverstock shuttles.

Indian Summer — 1990–1992

After the roller-coaster ride of 1989 it was generally agreed that a crossroads had been reached. If steam was to continue on the main line, some hard decisions had to be made, where the head for once should rule the heart. It was no surprise, therefore, when at a tri-partite meeting between BR, SLOA and Flying Scotsman Services, certain fundamental guidelines were established. The basic premise was that in 1989 an attempt was made to run far too many trains. Therefore for the 1990 season the number of steam-hauled excursions had to be reduced, and a firm decision was made to run only one steam programme on any day. Just as important in the battle to cut costs was the need to reduce the number of movements in running the trains. Therefore a firm basic programme that could be advertised widely and beyond the enthusiast market was considered essential using a limited number of well-proven routes with large engines and heavy trains. Some one-off charters would be considered on their merits. In an attempt to reduce the numbers of locomotive failures, a pool system of locomotives at certain depots which would cover the runs in that area was planned, and this worked very well.

The success of these measures was dependent upon several imponderables — notably the economic situation, with the inexorable rise in interest rates, and the introduction of the Community Charge. On the other hand, no less than seven high profile and powerful locomotives were due to return to the main line in 1990. These were 777 *Sir Lamiel*, 46229 *Duchess of Hamilton*, 71000 *Duke of Gloucester*, 6024 *King Edward I*, 60009 *Union of South Africa*, 4472 *Flying Scotsman* and 46203 *Princess Margaret Rose*. With these attractive locomotives to add to those already with a main line ticket like 6201 *Princess Elizabeth*, 45596 *Bahamas*, 35028 *Clan Line*, 34027 *Taw Valley*, 4771 *Green Arrow* and 5080 *Defiant*, and the smaller locomotives such as 3442 *The Great Marquess*, 5407, 44932, 44871 and 53809, hopes were high that with an attractive programme the year would be a very successful one.

Flying Scotsman Services — their programme entitled "Nostalgic Steam Days Out" — started the year off on 20th January with 34027 *Taw Valley* hauling a "Robin Hood" from Marylebone to Nottingham and return.

Attention was focussed in February on the return of 60009 *Union of South Africa* to the main line after major overhaul on the SVR at their Bridgnorth works. The loco-motive was scheduled to work four trains in February prior to returning to Scotland to haul the special commemorative train over the Forth Bridge on the 4th March to celebrate the centenary of the bridge. In the event, though 60009 moved under its own power for the first time on 30th January, it was not ready for its debut train — a "White Rose" from Marylebone to Sheffield — on the 17th February, nor

the "Pennine Limited" from Leeds to Carlisle on the follow-ing day. Both these trips were impressively hauled by sub-stitute loco 3442 *The Great Marquess*. After a test run on 22nd February, 60009 — without nameplates — completed a trouble-free run from Carlisle to Skipton with the "Citadels Express" on 24th February. However, at Skipton a serious problem was noted with weeping from the firebox lap joint. This was attributed to a white hot fire on the climb to Ais Gill summit and acidic water taken on at Garsdale. The locomotive was taken to Carnforth for caulking of the affected seam, and 3442 *The Great Marquess* was called on yet again to haul the 25th February train which was altered at the last minute from a northbound to a southbound "Pen-nine Limited" since 3442 was at Carlisle.

Repairs duly carried out, 60009 — now carrying the polit-ically correct nameplate of *Osprey* instead of *Union of South Africa* in an attempt to defuse any problems from anti-apartheid protesters — hauled "The Forth Centennial" from Edinburgh to Perth and return on the 4th March before entering a month-long charter with BR for crew-training runs for Scotrail.

Three other noteworthy trains ran in March. On the 10th, 777 *Sir Lamiel* returned to the main line hauling a fully-booked 500+ ton train from Blackburn to Carlisle in impressive fashion. A fortnight later as a consequence of the sterling performances put in whilst substituting for 60009, No 3442 *The Great Marquess* hauled an extra CME from Carlisle to Blackburn, and on the 31st March 34027 "Taw Valley" worked an amended "White Rose" from Marylebone to Nottingham and thence to Saltley. 34027 then proceeded to the SVR for routine maintenance, whilst the train was diesel-hauled back to London. This was the last train in the winter series, and was poorly loaded.

The summer — April to October — season began with a bang. First out with a society members' only trip — "The Red Dragon" — was 71000 *Duke of Gloucester* with a Great Western Society sponsored run from Didcot to Derby and return on the 7th April after completion of the £25,000 work on its boiler and chassis. Priced at £39.50, the train was fully booked by mid-February so a relief train was run on 29th April. This train was followed by the "Mid-Day Scot" on 21st April from Marylebone to Nottingham and return, a fund-raising exercise for the Douglas Bader foundation. On this trip, 71000 was said to have "Run like a bionic grey-hound"! On the 30th June, 71000 *Duke of Gloucester* hauled a Swindon-Gloucester-Newport-Shrewsbury-Crewe posi-tioning train and then worked the first "North Wales Coast Express" of the season on 1st July.

Next out on the main line was 46229 *Duchess of Hamil-ton* on the 13th April after its £225,000 overhaul and refit. The Friends of the National Railway Museum "members'

Gresley 'K4' No 3442 The Great Marquess *won itself an army of new friends on the 18th February 1990 when it hauled a train of no less than 540 tons (12 loaded Mk1 coaches and an 'Ethel') up the "Long Drag" without ever losing control. The 2-6-0, which maintained a rock-steady 20-25 miles per hour all the way with the "Pennine Limited", was standing in for 'A4' Pacific No 60009* Union of South Africa *after the latter's test run failed to be completed in time. It is seen here heading north at Horton-in-Ribblesdale.*

only" train — the "Duchess Pullman" of 14 coaches — ran from York to Carlisle and return, being double-headed with 47.555 under the overhead electric cables from York to Leeds. A sparkling performance was given by the loco.

The fifth new engine to appear on the main line was 6024 *King Edward I* along with its stable-mate·5080 *Defiant* on Birmingham Railway Museum's series of "Shakespeare Express" trains over the weekend of the 15th and 16th April. Four trains ran each day between Tyseley and Stratford — a ticket costing £12. No 6024 had required no less than three test runs to sort out problems with melting of the white metal on the crosshead bearings, the last run being on the 5th April. All went well on the weekend, with good public support.

To end an exciting April, 35028 *Clan Line* returned from winter maintenance to haul the inaugural "White Rose" charter train for the Risborough and District Railway Society from Marylebone to Derby and return, with 44932 working the optional Derby-Sheffield train. This was the last steam train to operate out of Marylebone for some considerable time due to crew shortages and engineering work on the Chiltern line.

The 2nd May saw 4472 *Flying Scotsman* return to the main line after its absence in 1989 in Australia, with the "FSS Executive". This six-coach train plus support coach ran from Didcot to Banbury, and thence 4472 headed for Carnforth with the support coach. There it was in position for a month of "Sellafield Sightseer" excursions from Carnforth to Sellafield, sponsored by British Nuclear Fuels. Its first of five revenue-earning runs was on the 7th May with the train originating from London Euston. Other trains on 12th, 19th and 28th May, and 6th June originated from Rugby, Bristol via Newport, Edinburgh via York and London Euston respectively. All the trains were well supported. On 16th

June, 4472 *Flying Scotsman* made its debut on the North Wales coast line hauling a "Ynys Mon Express".

The seventh new engine to appear on the main line in 1990 was 46203 *Princess Margaret Rose* which after a successful loaded test run on 17th May, hauled the "Richard Levick Memorial" train twice round the Derby-Sheffield circuit on the 2nd June. This trip was in memory of the Midland Railway Centre's Mechanical Engineer who died in an industrial accident in 1989.

A reminder that running steam trains on the main line can be a dangerous pastime came on 23rd June when 44871 was making its way from Carnforth to its new home with the SRPS at Bo'ness. The plan was that 44871 would haul an ARPS/FSS sponsored Leeds-Appleby train — the "Middleton Pioneer" — on the 23rd and on the following day haul an SRPS sponsored Carlisle-Kilmarnock train. Whilst running from Carnforth to Leeds, a boiler washout plug behind the right-hand side trailing driving wheel was blown from the firebox at Eldroth. Steam was deflected off the driving wheel into the cab badly scalding the fireman, Keith Wyatt. The fire was immediately dropped and the loco eventually hauled back to Carnforth. The special was diesel hauled with the following day's special being cancelled.

In the summer season Flying Scotsman Services promoted three standard package steam trips. The first was the "Ynys Mon Express", FSS's version of BR's "North Wales Coast Express" from Crewe to Holyhead. The initial loco roster included 71000, 4472 and 34027, with 60009, 6201 and 5407 being added to the list later in the season. The first train ran on 16th June hauled by 4472 *Flying Scotsman*.

The other two packages reflected the degree of thought and planning which had gone into 1990's steam programme. The "White Rose" was originally rostered to start at Marylebone, but with the difficulties previously mentioned, the train was diesel-hauled from Paddington to Didcot and then steam-hauled to Derby. Passengers had several options for their day out — they could alight at Warwick for a visit to either the Castle or Stratford-on Avon, or at Derby for a visit to Chatsworth House, Derby Pottery or Crich Tramway Museum (buses being laid on), or they could opt to stay on the train for a Derby-Sheffield circuit hauled by a second loco. If seats were available passengers could purchase tickets at Derby for the second part of the tour only. The first train from Paddington ran on the 7th July with 35028 *Clan Line* on the Didcot-Derby leg and 53809 on the Derby-Sheffield circuit. Apart from changing its point of origin, the service was dogged by bad luck. Because of very hot weather, four trains in July and August were cancelled due to the fire risk. As time went on fewer passengers re-booked on subsequent trains, so Flying Scotsman Services cancelled the remaining trains after the 6th October tour.

The other package promoted by FSS was a re-vamped "Cumbrian Mountain Express" with one loco hauling the Leeds-Appleby section and a second loco hauling the return leg. The first of these 2-locomotive CME's ran on 26th May with 45596 *Bahamas* on the northbound leg and 777 *Sir Lamiel* on the southbound leg. The pool of locos for this service included 46229, 6201, 4771, 5407 and 60009 in addition to the above two locos. The trains were very well patronised, being fully booked several weeks before they ran. Some problems inevitably arose — mainly in the autumn with problems of adhesion. After diesel assistance had to be summoned on four occasions in five weeks — 20th October with 45596, 27th October with 6201, again 27th October on the reverse leg with 46229, and 17th November with 6201 — reduced loads were introduced on all trains till 31st March

1991. Class 7 and 8 locomotives were restricted to 11 coaches or the equivalent, whilst Class 5 and 6 locomotives were limited to nine coaches. The double problem with adhesion on the 27th October train was compounded when the booked class 47 loco failed south of Skipton — the train arrived back at King's Cross at 1.30am! An extra CME was arranged for the 8th December to cope with the displaced bookings where train loads had to be lightened to cope with the slippery conditions. As luck would have it, this train had to be curtailed and turned back at Leeds after attempts at keeping the S. & C. line open in snowstorm conditions proved fruitless.

BR only operated two steam hauled packages on a regular basis in 1990. The first was the evergreen "West Highlander" from Fort William to Mallaig which started in mid-May. The rostered engines were K1 No 2005 and 'Black 5' No 5305. The K1 started the season by hauling the first "Royal Scotsman" on the 18th April, and the second luxury train — the "Queen of Scots" — on the 20th April. During the period May to July, two "West Highlander" trains and three "Queen of Scots" trains were not steam hauled due to the fire risk, but otherwise the season was uneventful. When 2005 headed south on 5th November, the loco had run 58 trips and amassed a total of 5,343 miles run without any problems. 5305 followed south with a fully booked SRPS sponsored trip — "The Lochaber" from Fort William to Glasgow — on the 10th November.

The "North Wales Coast Express" — BR's second package — operated from 1st July to 16th September, running on Sundays, Tuesdays and Wednesdays. Again, good loadings were experienced on all the trains, though persistent lineside trespassing caused considerable problems, with threats being made that if it persisted, the whole main-line steam programme might be put in jeopardy. Q-trains were run by the BR Police with some 40 trespassers being cautioned and two charged. The Q-train did, however, cause more problems than it cured, on one occasion delaying the steam special on so many occasions as to bring complaints from the travelling passengers. A proposal to run some enthusiasts' specials at speeds of up to 75 mph never occurred — the station platforms and tunnels could not be adequately surveyed in time. On the 4472 *Flying Scotsman* hauled train of the 18th July, tragedy struck when a passenger who was looking out of an open window hit his head on a rocky outcrop whilst the train was travelling through Penmaenbach Tunnel and was killed instantly.

Having relocated itself at Didcot, 6024 *King Edward I* was out on the main line on the 24th November with a GWS sponsored private charter — "The Royal Venturer" from Didcot to Derby and return. Two weeks earlier, 46203 *Princess Margaret Rose* ran a private charter for the John Player Railway club of Nottingham from Nottingham to Didcot and return. After this trip, the locomotive went into the workshops at Butterley and its height was reduced by 2½-inches to give it better route availability — notably on the S. & C. route.

The year ended with continuing success for the "Ynys Mon Express", No 35028 *Clan Line* hauling 14 coaches plus an "Ethel" — 580 tons — on 1st December, a record for a preserved locomotive. 71000 *Duke of Gloucester* completed the year on the North Wales coast with the final "Ynys Mon Express" on the 29th December.

After all the problems of 1989, 1990 was a resounding success, proving the wisdom of the actions taken by BR, SLOA and FSS. Most trains were very well supported, and locomotive failures were at a minimum. It was not surprising, therefore, that Flying Scotsman Services continued to promote the two-engine CME and the popular "Ynys Mon Express" in 1991. Indeed, in December of 1990, many bookings for the CME had been received for these tours up to the 11th May tour! In addition, FSS announced that they were promoting four "Welsh Marches Express" package tours from Crewe to Hereford via Chester and return via Whitchurch involving the use of two locomotives, and the return after an absence of five years of the "Cumbrian Coast Express" in place of the "Sellafield Sightseer". This train would be steam-hauled from Carnforth to Workington. The engine would then proceed light engine to Carlisle,to be used on a subsequent CME(S) working. At Workington, a second locomotive would be attached for the return trip to Carnforth. The first train ran on 25th May, and the season ended on the 5th October. Gone, however, was the "White Rose".

In an attempt to cut costs, a new series of trains — The Steam Locomotive Positioning Trains — were announced. These were to run on Mondays or Fridays at a flat rate of £31 per ticket, and were intended to provide some income from the necessary movement of locomotives from one area of operations to another. Three separate packages were announced — the "Red Rose" with a series of eight trains from Carnforth to Crewe or reverse, the "South Yorkshireman" with three trains from Didcot to Derby or reverse, and the "West Mercian" with two trains from Didcot to Hereford or reverse. These trains were never expected to do very well, but at the end of the day bookings were disappointing with an average of 120 passengers per train.

Early in the year — on the 9th and 23rd February — two "William Shakespeare Express" trains were planned to run from Marylebone to Stratford. Surprisingly they were poorly booked and were finally cancelled when engineering work to upgrade the Chiltern Line got behind schedule and heavy weekend possession of the line was required. FSS let it be known that they regarded steam out of London as having come to an end in the foreseeable future. The two trips were re-scheduled as "Welsh Marches Express" tours with the 9th February trip causing quite a stir as it would feature two Bulleid Pacifics working the two legs of the trip for the first time on a modern BR special. Sadly it was not to be, the tour having to be cancelled at the last minute due to adverse weather conditions.

The first six months of the 1991 steam programme proceeded very smoothly with several highlights. The "CME" of the 5th January was run in appaling weather conditions with 4771 *Green Arrow* and 6201 *Princess Elizabeth* performing heroics. On the 12th January 6024 *King Edward I* worked the "Derby Sovereign" from Didcot to Derby and return for Pathfinders Tours. Following this 71000 *Duke of Gloucester* worked the "Ynys Mon Express" of the 19th January, notable for it being the last working which used the universally disliked "Ethel". On the 2nd February the new generator brake van — which cost some £75,000 — was in operation for the first time on the "CME". 60009 *Osprey* was in charge of the steam section of the "North Briton" from Edinburgh to Aberdeen over the weekend of the 8th to 10th March. The Great Western Society sponsored a "White Rose" itinerary with 35028 *Clan Line* and 53809 on the 17th March, and on the 23rd March 60009 *Osprey* was again in action with an SRPS train from Perth to Carlisle, enabling the locomotive to work the southbound leg of the "CME" on the 30th March and the "Ynys Mon Express" on the 1st April. Appleby was the place to be on 22nd June, when 6201 *Princess Elizabeth* handed the "CME" over to 46203 *Princess Margaret Rose*.

BR's plans for 1991 involved the ever-popular "West Highlander", the previously successful "North Wales Coast Express", and in a surprise move a limited return to steam on the Cambrian Line. The "Cambrian Limited" initially worked from Shrewsbury to Barmouth and return on the 16th and 23rd June, with 75069 and 7819 *Hinton Manor* providing the motive power on a seven coach train. Repeat runs were made on the 22nd and 29th September, though they were diverted from Barmouth to Aberystwyth after a class 37 locomotive derailed all of its wheels on a bridge north of Dovey Junction. These last two trains were fortunate not to be stopped by the very dry hot weather. All four trips were a sell-out, and thoroughly enjoyed by the tour passengers.

44871 and 44932 were the rostered locomotives for work on the Fort William-Mallaig line in the summer. Because of the Gulf war — and the subsequent lack of American tourists — the "Queen of Scots" luxury tour train did not operate in 1991. Nevertheless, in addition to 63 service trains, 20 "Royal Scotsman" trains were booked for the season. 44871 arrived in early May to work the first part of the season, and was joined in Fort William a month later by 44932. Unfortunately 44932 failed with leaking superheater tubes and a weeping firebox lap plate whilst hauling the "Royal Scotsman" of the 7th August and had to be hauled south for repairs. 44871 held the fort for two weeks before being joined at short notice by 5407. 44871 returned south on the 21st September at the head of an SRPS-sponsored train to Glasgow on a day of torrential rain and poor light, and 5407 returned south with "The Claymore" on the 23rd November.

The "North Wales Coast Express" commenced its season on the 30th June with 46229 *Duchess of Hamilton*, and ran through to the 15th September, the last train being hauled by 45596 *Bahamas*. After a quiet but steady opening to the season, bookings began to drop off. It soon became quite clear that loadings only rose to acceptable levels with the introduction of new motive power, and that the holidaymakers on the North Wales Coast were not being attracted to travel on the steam train. BR expressed some doubts as to whether they would be justified in promoting the train in 1992.

Elsewhere, several interesting initiatives appeared. David Smith from Carnforth promoted a series of excursions titled the "West Cumbrian" from Carnforth to Sellafield each Thursday from 25th July to 29th August. A return ticket cost only £19.75 and compared very favourably to the cost of the FSS-sponsored "Cumbrian Coast Express". 'Black 5' No 5407 hauled the first train. Also promoted by Carnforth were a series of three shuttles per day on the 8/9th June between Carnforth and Barrow hauled by 48151 at £7.50 a head. The public's response was measured by an 80% loading factor.

Network SouthEast arranged two interesting steam spectaculars. On the 12th and 13th September, 34027 *Taw Valley* banked by 80080 hauled a series of shuttle trains up the 1 in 30 harbour branch at Folkestone. The trips started at 2pm, and ran every 45 minutes. Then on the weekend of the 19th and 20th October the Cambridge steam gala saw 4472 *Flying Scotsman*, 34027 *Taw Valley* and 70000 *Britannia* run a series of shuttle trains between Cambridge and Kings Lynn at £15 per head. All the trains were a complete sell-out with some 4,000 people travelling, generating some £51,000.

John Davies — Regional Manager for BR in Wales — also produced an innovative programme of steam-hauled trips with 80080 hauling a six-coach train from Cardiff Central to

The "Robin Hood" excursion train of 31st March 1990 was headed by Ex SR 'West Country' class 4-6-2 No 34027 Taw Valley — *seen here near Bicester on the outward run.*

various of the Cardiff Valley lines on 6/20/27th October. It gives an interesting insight into the pressures produced in sponsoring this kind of tour when one ponders John Davies' words after the event — "This will almost certainly be a one-off as we did not realise what we were taking on. The cost of making all the arrangements has been horrendous and imposed a big work-load on all the staff. We could not afford the staff to make it a regular operation."

Only three new engines returned to the main line scene in 1991, with varying fortunes. 5029 *Nunney Castle* was the first, successfully negotiating a loaded test run from Derby to Sheffield on 7th March. Its first run was at the head of the "VIP Intercity Special" on 8th June from Didcot to Great Malvern and return, and this was followed by a Didcot-Stratford "William Shakespeare Express" on 6th October (postponed from 14th September because of the fire risk.) The engine performed immaculately. On the 9th November 5029 became the first steam locomotive in a decade to haul a train out of Paddington station when it ran a fully loaded 11-coach "William Shakespeare Express".

The second engine was 70000 *Britannia*. The locomotive was steamed at Carnforth for the first time in four years on New Year's Day, but had to wait till 27th July for its return to the main line on the "Britannia Phoenix" run by the Britannia Locomotive Society from Crewe to Hereford via Chester with return via Whitchurch. This trip very nearly had to be cancelled, the loco failing its loaded test run on 25th July on the Crewe-Chester-Shrewsbury triangle with failure of the right-hand side con-rod big-end. Thanks to a concerted effort by BR, BREL and SVR engineering staff the bearing was remetalled and fitted in time for another test run at 1.30p.m. on the 26th July on the same route. Again the bearing ran hot, but the loco was passed for the following day's excursion, which itself was a triumph. 192 passengers were on the train paying £49 a head for the privilege of being a part of the comeback celebrations. Following the tour, scuff marks were noted on the leading driving wheel tyres. The loco was taken to Liverpool for full examination and missed its rostered turn on the CME of 10th August, 4472 *Flying Scotsman* substituting. The loco did make its return to the CME with a southbound run on 7th September.

The third locomotive to make its main line debut was SVR's 8F No 8223. A Derby-Sheffield loaded test run on 12th September passed uneventfully, and the loco made its debut on the north-bound leg of the "Welsh Marches Express" on the 21st September. At the end of the run it was noted that the rivets securing a driving wheel balance weight were rubbing against a patch on the frame causing bruising of the frame. The loco was failed and taken to Bridgnorth for axlebox repair to cure the problem. Unfortunately the loco missed its positioning run with the "Red Rose" of 30th September, and so missed out on its booked turn on the CME of 26th October — which it would have worked with its sister 8F No 48151.

Bookings for the first nine months of the year had been fairly stable considering the country's economic climate. Bookings on the "Cumbrian Mountain Express" averaged 335 passengers per train, with the "Cumbrian Coast Express" trains showing an average of 275 passengers per train and the "Welsh Marches" some 255 passengers per train. Overall in the October figures, average loadings were 70% — just on the break-even borderline. At its meeting in October, SLOA suggested that 1992 would be the last year with a programme on the present scale.

As the winter progressed and the recession bit even deeper, there was a dramatic downturn in bookings. In mid-December Flying Scotsman Services cancelled three trains which had failed to attract even a third of their 388-seat capacity. These were the "West Mercian" of the 27th December with 71000 *Duke of Gloucester*, the "Ynys Mon Express" of 30th December again with 71000 *Duke of Gloucester* and the southbound "Cumbrian Mountain Express" of the 11th January with 34027 *Taw Valley*. It was only a year earlier that extra coaches had to be put on the "Ynys Mon Express" behind 71000 *Duke of Gloucester* on the 29th December 1990 — but a year is a long time for preserved steam on the main line.

Worse was to come when the slump in bookings continued after Christmas, and 11 more main line steam excursions were cancelled by Flying Scotsman Services. These included all five of the Friday "West Mercian" Swindon-Hereford positioning trains, two "Welsh Marches Express", two "Ynys Mon Express" and two "Cumbrian Mountain Express" trains. Even the appeal of 5029 *Nunney Castle* on the North Wales Coast route on 29th February sold only 160 of the train's 394 seats. The route was changed to a "White Rose" itinerary, but the locomotive unfortunately failed on the return journey at Derby with the big end running warm, the train being hauled back to Paddington by 47.975, arriving 88 minutes early. The February 22nd "Welsh Marches" tour with 5029 *Nunney Castle* and 34027 *Taw Valley* fared even worse with only 66 bookings. Not all the excursions were so badly affected — 5407 ran on the 18th January with a 10-coach positioning special from Carlisle to Farrington Junction with all seats full. Other casualties in the winter and spring programme were 777 *Sir Lamiel*, whose Didcot-Sheffield trip for the Humberside Locomotive Preservation Group was cancelled because of insufficient bookings, and the "North Briton" of the 14th and 15th March which was cancelled because of pathing problems.

In a truncated winter and spring programme, 8233 — now running as 48773 — finally got back on the main line with "The Lancastrian" from Shrewsbury to Blackburn on 1st February prior to its seven year boiler certificate expiring. 6024 *King Edward I* appeared on the "William Shakespeare Express" from Paddington to Stratford on 2nd February and again on 22nd March. On the return trip on this latter excursion, the brass safety valve cover on 6024 struck the lower flanges of a steel beam supporting Ladbroke Grove overbridge. A fixing stud was sheared off, and the valve assembly projected itself into the underside of the bridge. Only quick thinking and action by the driver prevented a serious accident. Happily the locomotive was repaired in time for the Bristol Evening Post-sponsored runs from Bristol to Newport and return on the 4th May. On the 16th February, 60009 *Union of South Africa* (disguised as 60004 *William Whitelaw*) ran from Edinburgh Waverley to Glasgow Queen Street with a special commemorating the 150th anniversary of the NBR route between the two cities.

In the midst of the winter doom and gloom, two events brightened the main line steam scene. The first was the return to the main line of 60532 *Blue Peter* on the 7th March with "The North Eastern" which ran from Manchester Victoria to Carlisle. This was the first time it had hauled a passenger train on BR since 1966. The engine had been handed over to the North Eastern Locomotive Preservation Group on 11th November 1991 at Wilton, and had worked service trains on the North Yorkshire Moors Railway for several weeks before its loaded test run on 27th February. During this run it melted its big-end bearing on the right side. After re-metalling at Butterley, it worked five service trains on the 1st March before being passed for the 7th March run. Not surprisingly this was a fairly lack-lustre affair. However on the 21st March on a southbound CME to Bradford Forster Square, the engine was only seconds outside the "Blue Ribbon" time of 71000 *Duke of Gloucester* for the climb from Appleby to Ais Gill summit, a result affected by the need to ease the regulator when the injectors could not maintain the boiler water level. Needless to say both trips were a complete sell-out. During the summer season the engine worked eight trips over the Settle and Carlisle line.

The second bright spot was Network South-East's avowed intention to encourage steam operations on their sector wherever and whenever practicable. Their season started on 29th February with 6998 *Burton Agnes Hall* running a shuttle service between Didcot and Oxford in connection with the 100th Anniversary of the Cholsey and Wallingford "Bunk" — when a GWR loco was uncoupled from its train by a couple of pranksters and left its train behind in the station when the guard whistled it away. Next, on the 25th April on the occasion of the Gala Day celebrating the opening of Aylesbury's new servicing depot and the introduction of the class 165 diesel turbo units to the Chiltern Line, 44932 ran four return shuttles between Princes Risborough and Aylesbury. On the 6th and 7th June, in connection with Ashford 150 celebrations, 34027 *Taw Valley* ran four Ashford-Hastings shuttle services on the Saturday, with 75069 repeating the programme on the Sunday. Some 200 enthusiasts who took the opportunity to return to London Bridge station on the Sunday night on a relief train with "unusual" motive power were rewarded when this turned out to be 34027 *Taw Valley*. This was the first run by a steam locomotive over the energised third line since the early 1970s when flagrant trespassing by photographers nearly resulted in a number of fatalities, and the first appearance of a steam locomotive at London Bridge station since 1964. The run was significant in that it opened the possibility of steam runs over energised third rail tracks after dark.

Perhaps the most spectacular of the Network South-East's steam programme was the running on 21st and 28th June of steam specials between Eastleigh and Exeter, with three shuttle services per day between Eastleigh and Salisbury. 75069, 777 *Sir Lamiel* and 34027 *Taw Valley* were the locos involved with restored 'M7' No 30053 (masquerading as 30673) performing pilot duties at Salisbury station. Further Network South-East initiatives included 6024 *King Edward I* and 5029 *Nunney Castle* running an hourly passenger service between Quainton Road and Aylesbury on the 30/31st August in connection with the celebrations marking the centenary of railways in Aylesbury, the Twyford-Henley branch line shuttles with 46521 on 1/8th November, and Marks Tey-Sudbury branch line shuttles with 69621 on the 27/28th December. Pride of place, however, must go to the after dark special which ran with 34027 *Taw Valley* from Waterloo to Bournemouth on Friday 11th September, the

'A2' Pacific No 60532 Blue Peter **worked its first train in 25 years since withdrawal from BR service when after extensive overhaul and rebuilding it made a highly successful test run from Grosmont to Pickering on the 15th December 1991.** Blue Peter **hauled its first main 'line tour — the "Blue Peter Express" from Blackburn to Carlisle via the S. & C. line on 7th March 1992. The locomotive is seen here on the return working at Ais Gill summit on 21st March 1992 with the "North Eastern".** (John Cooper-Smith)

first steam train out of Waterloo station since 1967.

The summer programme presented jointly by SLOA, BR and Flying Scotsman Services featured 73 trains with 18 different locomotives. The bulk of the trains were rostered for the Settle-Carlisle line, with the "Cumbrian Mountain Express" originating in London Euston, and travelling via the West Coast Main Line with the steam section being Carlisle-Farrington Junction or reverse. A second train — the "Cumbrian Mountain Limited" — originated from London King's Cross and took the East Coast Main Line route. The steam section was from Bradford (Forster Square) to Armathwaite or reverse with a return diesel-hauled run over the S. & C.

Two imaginative new services were proposed. The first was a resurrection of the "Cambrian Coast Express" though in a modified form. The plan was for 80080 to haul a Crewe-Towyn-Crewe special — running bunker-first in one direction — on 27th May with a repeat run featuring sister engine 80079 on 20th August. The trains were sell-outs, with 80080 outperforming 7819 *Hinton Manor* and 75069 on the climb from Machynlleth to Talerddig summit. Problems arose however when BR's civil engineer would not pass 80080 for the Machynlleth-Towyn section due to doubts as to the tank's suitability to traverse the Dovey Estuary curves,

so the special terminated at Machynlleth. The second problem was the unavailability of 80079 — 80080 substituting. The trains were a great success, with repeat runs on 13th and 20th September.

The second initiative — four Crewe-Llandudno specials to be hauled by 80080 and 80079 in July and August, alternating on Wednesdays with the North Wales Coast Express — never got off the ground due to poor bookings. With no more than 70 bookings being taken for any of the trains the break-even point of 200 passengers was never reached.

The weather took a hand in the summer when a steam ban was imposed on the North Wales Coast line after 5305 was alleged to have started a lineside fire on the Crewe-Chester section on the 19th July — the train being diesel-piloted from Llandudno. Four excursions were affected with the NWCE on the 22nd July being re-scheduled as a CME with a diesel pilot as far as Kirby Stephen. Two other trains were either re-scheduled to a different date or to a different route. SLOA had to field some very vitriolic letters from disgruntled passengers.

In Scotland, Intercity's Fort William-Mallaig specials — "The Lochaber" — featured 5407 and 2005. No 5407, making its fourth appearance at Fort William in nine seasons, was first to Fort William, hauling a Blackburn-Carlisle-Kilmarnock positioning special on May 4th, arriving in Fort William on the 5th in time to haul the first "Royal Scotsman" charter train on the 6th May. Unfortunately the loco was withdrawn from service on 26th July due to excessive wear on the driving wheel flanges, so 2005 had to soldier on alone for the rest of the season with over 30 main line trips. 5407 was able to return south with "The Claymore" on the 24th October, though again the engine failed — this time at Rhu with the loss of a small retaining pin in the linkage to the regulator valve inside the dome (a most unusual event).

With the last two "Royal Scotsman" trains cancelled, 2005 returned south with a fully booked train on the 7th November — though not without problems when the locomotive slipped to a standstill on the tree-lined five-mile climb at 1 in 67 from Arrochar & Tarber to Glen Douglas with the southbound "The Claymore" on November 7th, arriving 90 minutes down.

Though the "Northern Belle" had been running in Scotland for eight years, John Begg — its mentor — realised a dream on 2nd August when the train left Aberdeen for Elgin with 'Black 5' No 44871 *Sovereign* at its head. Scheduled to run every Sunday to September 6th, two trains were cancelled due to poor bookings. However more than 1000 passengers were carried, with the final train running through to Inverness.

Five locos retired from the main line in 1992 at the end of their seven-year boiler certificate. First to go was 44932 after appearing on the Princes Risborough-Aylesbury shuttles on 25th April. 3440 *City of Truro* soon followed in rather sad fashion. The loco's last scheduled run was to have been on the 10th May from Ealing Broadway to Derby, but this train was cancelled because of poor bookings. Its last run was therefore the previous week from Derby to Paddington. 'Black 5' 5305 was next to go after its less than satisfactory "Ynys Mons Express" trip on the 19th July when it was diesel piloted after starting a lineside fire. The "Ynys Mon Express" of the 2nd August was scheduled for its final run on the main line but this was a casualty of the steam ban due to fire risk. The very popular 4771 *Green Arrow* hauled its last train — the Armathwaite-Bradford Forster Square "Cumbrian Mountain Limited" — on the 1st August, whilst the even more popular 4472 *Flying Scotsman* signed off with the "William Shakespeare Express" of 25th October with plans to undertake a tour of preserved lines. Prior to 4472's retirement, however, the engine had a very busy schedule enhanced by having to substitute for 4498 *Sir Nigel Gresley* on the 5th and 12th September.

The A4 was withdrawn from traffic on 17th July 1989 with a series of hairline cracks in the firebox, and was due to return to the main line on 30th August hauling the "Furness Flyer" shuttles from Carnforth to Barrow. The main line test run on 27th August from Derby to Sheffield was marred by a strange "bump" during the run. On checking the engine on its return to Carnforth, a cracked bogie axle-box horn cheek was discovered — ruling out the engine's return to the main line on the 30th. This was soon rectified by the Severn Valley Railway, but fate struck again when on the 5th September — the morning of its comeback run over the Settle and Carlisle line from Farrington Junction to Carlisle with the "Gold and Silver Jubilee Express" celebrating the 25th anniversary of the A4 society and the 50th anniversary of Ian Allan Ltd — the engine was derailed in Carnforth yard. 4472 *Flying Scotsman* substituted on that trip and on the reverse trip the following week — the Cambridge Railway Society sponsored "Cam-Eden Express". Following a three-week visit to the Severn Valley Railway where it worked on normal service trains, 4498 *Sir Nigel Gresley* finally returned to the main line on the 21st November with a "Cumbrian Mountain Limited" from Bradford Forster Square to Carlisle.

One summer service which again prospered was the highly acclaimed Carnforth-Barrow shuttles on the 6/7th June and each Sunday in August. Motive power was provided by 8F 48151, and with an adult return ticket costing just £8, this must have been the steam bargain of the year.

The winter season featured a crop of Society specials. First on Sunday October 4th was "The Silver Jubilee" — steam-hauled throughout from Oxenhope on the Keighley and Worth Valley Railway to Carlisle and return by 45596 *Bahamas* to celebrate the 25th anniversary of the Bahamas Locomotive Society. On the same day, 71000 *Duke of Gloucester* hauled a Northampton & Lamport Railway Society special from Crewe to Hereford. Perhaps the most spectacular was the "Great Central Enterprise" which ran from Leicester to Didcot and return with 46203 *Princess Margaret Rose* on the Derby-Dorridge leg and 6024 *King Edward I* between Didcot and Dorridge. The special was chartered to promote the Great Central Railway's £2 million share issue with seats at £10 a head!

SLOA's winter programme was fairly sparse — promoting no CME's or CML's between 10th October and 21st November in an attempt to avoid problems with slipping on fallen leaves ·in the notorious Stainforth gorge. Problems still arose. 46229 *Duchess of Hamilton* was in trouble with slippery track on the northbound CME from Farrington Junction to Carlisle on the 3rd October, whilst on the 7th November 71000 *Duke of Gloucester* came to a standstill on Church Stretton Bank whilst hauling a Crewe-Gloucester "Welsh Marches Express". The train reached Hereford some two hours late — the steam locomotive being substituted there by a diesel. Other more successful trips were a Workington-Bradford Forster Square version of a Cumbrian Coast Express on 10th October with 46229 *Duchess of Hamilton* and an Ealing Broadway-Stratford trip with 70000 *Britannia* on 20th December.

After the return of steam on the Waterloo-Bournemouth line with 34027 *Taw Valley* on 11th September, hopes ran high that this might mean the relaxation of the steam ban over "third rail" tracks in the densely populated south-east of England. Suddenly proposals which seemed unthinkable even 12 months previously began to appear. Two exciting runs were proposed for December — Waterloo-Salisbury and return with 34027 *Taw Valley* on 4th December and Waterloo-Eastleigh and return on 18th December with 777 *Sir Lamiel*. Sadly both these trips fell victims to an overtime ban by train crews on the former LSWR and were cancelled — though hopes were expressed that they might re-appear on the list of 1993 trips.

Santa specials abounded on the main line in 1992 with 44871 hauling two SRPS Santa Special trips between Edinburgh and Dunfermline on the 5th December. 46203 *Princess Margaret Rose* and 6024 *King Edward I* hauling four "Evening Mail Santa Special" shuttle trips between Hall Green and Stratford-on-Avon on 6th and 13th December and 46521 hauling a Didcot — Morton-in-Marsh — Worcester — Kidderminster "Ivatt Christmas Special" on 12th December.

In 1992 the recession was biting deeply, and main line steam excursions — particularly in the first few months of the year — were hard hit. In March, David Ward went as far as to suggest that there were probably only six more years of main line steam running left. SLOA themselves were deeply worried, and decided to set up a three man Strategy group independent of the Sales and Publicity group to produce a radical re-think of the main line steam programme. The possibility of running main line steam excursions out of London termini — "new" steam routes to "new" destinations — raised everybody's hopes only to be dashed at the last minute. What would the shape of things to come be in 1993?

Rip Tide — 1993–1994

The return of steam to the Waterloo-Bournemouth road in September 1992 seemed to be the high water mark of the 21 year main line steam revival. It soon became clear that it was only the catalyst for Network SouthEast to promote a mouth-watering programme for the beginning of 1993. Five exciting trains were scheduled starting with 34027 *Taw Valley* on a London Bridge-Hastings and return trip on 3rd January. 70000 *Britannia* (as 70004 "William Shakespeare") would head a Victoria-Dover charter on 29th February, with 777 *Sir Lamiel* hauling a Waterloo-Portsmouth excursion on 12th February and a Waterloo-Southampton charter four weeks later on the 12th March. Finally 34027 *Taw Valley* was scheduled to run on the 4th April with a London Bridge-Margate train. No sooner was the cup filled than it was dashed from enthusiast's lips with the cancelling of the first two trips, partly because of engineering work, and partly because a 60mph path could not be found on the line, and the remainder because of an industrial dispute affecting train crews.

A major milestone in the history of preserved steam on the main line was reached, however, when on the 20th January No 70000 *Britannia*, disguised as 70004 *William Shakespeare* and in full "Golden Arrow" regalia, headed an after dark special charter from Dover to Victoria. The occasion was to mark the retirement of SLOA Chairman Dick Hardy and Chief Mechanical Engineer John Peck.

BR Intercity/FSS/SLOA announced a busy winter/spring programme starting with a southbound CME hauled by 4498 *Sir Nigel Gresley* on the 1st January. Highlights of this programme were the announcement that there would be regional starting points for some CME's — including Bristol, Cardiff and Peterborough — and that steam in the form of 80080 would return to the Nottingham-Skegness line after a gap of 30 years on the 10th April with the "Jolly Fisherman".

Continuing claims that main line steam excursions were too expensive were answered with the introduction of a £30 standard class fare, with genuine half-fare children's tickets, and the introduction of family tickets. By mid-January with bookings described as "encouraging", these steps appeared to be justified.

Several private charters ran in the early part of the year, notably the Didcot-Oxford shuttles organised by the Great Western Society using 6998 *Burton Agnes Hall* on the 2nd January, and the double run over the S. & C. by 60532 *Blue Peter* for the NELPG on the 6th March. The biggest surprise of the winter was, however, the appearance of 80080 at the head of a twice-daily Monday to Friday stopping passenger train service between Carlisle and Kirkby Stephen for a three-week period in February and March devised around a new BR steam crew-training initiative.

Two 'one-off' trains captured the headlines in the early spring. On 28th March, NELPG organised two special charter trains headed by 62005 which ran from Darlington Bank Top station to Eastgate over the freight-only section of the Weardale line from Bishop Auckland to Eastgate which was under the threat of closure. Though the promoters had only four weeks to organise the runs, all went well on the day and over 1,000 passengers were carried. Then on the 13th April, the long-awaited and much changed meeting of the "Big Three Red Engines" took place. Originally planned as a series of Nottingham-Sheffield shuttles, it was revised as an "Ynys Mon Express" with each of the Stanier Pacifics — 46229 *Duchess of Hamilton*, 6201 *Princess Elizabeth* and 46203 *Princess Margaret Rose* — taking a leg and all three meeting up at Llandudno Junction. The event was a great success and much acclaimed.

The core of the BR InterCity/FSS/SLOA summer programme in 1993 was centred on the S. & C. line with CMEs or CMLs running on no less than 25 consecutive Saturdays from April 17th to October 2nd. Even though the loco pool contained 71000 *Duke of Gloucester*, 60532 *Blue Peter*, 46229 *Duchess of Hamilton*, 6203 *Princess Margaret Rose* and 4498 *Sir Nigel Gresley*, fears were expressed that the number of trips proposed (plus several other "one-offs") would result in "burn-out" for the route.

The high spot of the summer programme was that steam — the first since September 1964 — would return to the Central Wales line to commemorate the 125th anniversary of the former LNWR/GWR line. The first train, hauled by newly rebuilt 80079, was a Shrewsbury-Carmarthen "stopper" which ran on Sunday 16th May. One week later, on the 23rd May, 'Black 5' No 44767 *George Stephenson* ran a non-stop Shrewsbury-Carmarthen charter. Whilst in South Wales both engines were in action over the May Bank Holiday, the 30th and 31st. On both days, 44767 *George Stephenson* ran a Swansea-Carmarthen and return trip, with 80079 taking over at Carmarthen for a return trip on the 30th to Pembroke Dock and Fishguard, and on the 31st to Milford Haven. Finally on 6th June the engines worked double-headed over Sugar Loaf Summit with the return Carmarthen-Shrewsbury working.

Elsewhere in Wales the situation was much less happy. Because of indifferent passenger loadings in 1992 both the "North Wales Coast Express" and "Ynys Mon Express" had been removed from the summer programme — as had the "Welsh Marches Express". Three "Cambrian Limited" Crewe-Tywyn charter trains had been scheduled to run in June, July and August, hauled by 'Standard 4' tank No 80080, but these were also axed when BR's track inspector would only allow the trains to run to Aberystwyth.

In Scotland the Fort William-Mallaig service, now titled "The Lochaber", ran for the ninth consecutive year with 'Black 5s' Nos 44871 and 44767 *George Stephenson* as the motive power. The number of service trains was increased from the 45 in 1992 to 53 with an adult return ticket costing £15. 44871 rather disgraced herself by stalling on Beasdale Bank with an SRPS charter on 29th May, having to split the train and taking one portion forward to Arisaig before returning for the remaining coaches.

Sadly the promoters of the Aberdeen-Elgin steam tours — the "Northern Belle" — abandoned all hope of a repeat series in 1993, being discouraged by BR's charges of £10,000 per train, and the absence of any subsidy from Scottish tourism agencies. After the success of 80080 on the crew-training passenger trains on the S & C line, Scotrail chartered A4 No 60009 *Union of South Africa* for a four week period from 8th June to 13th July to work a similar five days a week Perth-Glasgow passenger service which would incorporate crew-training. Unfortunately on the very first run, a high pressure steam joint in the cab of the locomotive failed, filling the cab with steam and severely scalding Senior Traction Inspector Lachie Duncan. The programme was promptly abandoned. A similar and very successful programme did run, however, using 60009 *Union of South Africa* during the month of October.

Inevitably during the summer there were high and low points. On the debit side, Bulmers announced that its railway centre — the focal point of the historic 1971 "Return to Steam" programme — would close in June with 6000 *King George V* going to Swindon Railway Museum as a static exhibit. Another door to close was that of the former Great Western and Great Central Joint "Chiltern Line" over Saunderton Bank to steam operations from May 17th, as a result of the introduction of "Driver-Only Operation" on the line. The last "Shakespeare Express" from Ealing Broadway to Stratford-on-Avon ran on the 9th May hauled by 71000 *Duke of Gloucester*. Perhaps it was symptomatic that the locomotive failed at Tyseley with water seepage from six superheater flue tubes.

On the credit side, the Bishops Stortford-Ely shuttles of the 17th and 18th April with 70000 *Britannia* and 71000 *Duke of Gloucester* were a sell-out, and on the 2nd May 6998 *Burton Agnes Hall* had its main line final fling with a series of short-haul shuttles between Didcot and Oxford before being withdrawn to its new home on the East Lancs Railway. Steam successfully returned to Scarborough on the 2nd May after an absence of four years with the "Scarborough Flyer" — an SRPS charter train from Edinburgh — headed by 60532 *Blue Peter*. Ivatt Class 2 No 46441 also returned to the main line on the London Underground Metropolitan shuttles to Amersham on the 22nd and 23rd May, and then on the 24th July hauled a Carnforth-Oxenhope and return private charter. No 6201 *Princess Elizabeth* had its final run on the main line on the 13th June before the expiry of its boiler certificate, hauling a packed train in great style from Crewe to Worcester via Chester, Shrewsbury, Hereford Newport, and Gloucester — a trip of over 200 miles.

A new train — the "Cotswold Venturer" — was introduced during the summer as a replacement for the "William Shakespeare Express" charters, and proved extremely popular. Running in a clockwise direction from Swindon via the "Golden Valley" to Worcester, Evesham, Oxford and Didcot it featured 5029 *Nunney Castle* on the 27th June, 70000 *Britannia* on 25th July, and 6024 *King Edward I* on 22nd August. It proved so popular that a fourth train — headed by 34027 *Taw Valley* — ran in the reverse direction on 29th August.

Undoubtedly the train which caused most heartache for the planners in 1993 was the re-creation of the "Fifteen Guinea Special" on the 11th August — commemorating the 25th anniversary of BR's 1968 steam finale. Attempts were made to return 70013 *Oliver Cromwell* to the main line for the charter. The initial plan was that 44932 (substituting for 45110 presently out of service) would take the special on the first leg of the trip from Liverpool Lime Street to Manchester where 70013 would take over for the run to Carlisle. 44932 meanwhile would run light engine to Carlisle and there join forces with 5407 for the return run south over Ais Gill. In spite of an energetic campaign Bressingham would not release *Oliver Cromwell*, and first Manchester then Liverpool Lime Street were ruled out. Problems arose with the participating engines, and the last straw was the prohibition on all locomotive hauled workings over the Blackburn-Hellifield line late in July. The end result was a much altered "Cumbrian Mountain Limited" which ran from Leeds to Carlisle with 46229 *Duchess of Hamilton*. The return trip was double-headed by 45596 *Bahamas* and 44871.

Steamtown's "Furness Flyers" on August Sundays at £10 a return adult ticket again proved popular. 48151, 46441 and 45596 *Bahamas* provided the motive power. 48151 was out on the main line again on 25th September with a Carnforth-Scarborough and return private charter.

As autumn approached it was generally agreed that 1993 had thus far been very successful, with good loadings on most trains, and with the travelling public welcoming and supporting the new routes. It was, therefore, with some confidence that Network SouthEast announced what was described as a "sizzling September package" involving five trains over the Waterloo-Exeter line.

The first train on August Bank Holiday — the "Royal Wessex" featuring 34027 *Taw Valley* on an Eastleigh-Yeovil Junction-Poole itinerary — was cancelled due to poor bookings, whereas the "Rougement" on 5th September with a pair of '50s' from Waterloo to Exeter and 34027 *Taw Valley* on the return journey was sold out. The "Hardy Explorer" booked to run from Eastleigh to Waterloo on the 12th September saw the return to the main line of Maunsell S15 2-6-0 No 828 which deputised for the booked locomotive No 777 *Sir Lamiel* which had failed. The train was only moderately well loaded. The fourth train — the "Sarum Limited" on 19th September — had a Bristol starting point and featured 34027 *Taw Valley* on the Exeter St. David-Salisbury-Waterloo leg. Surprisingly the train was only poorly supported. The final train — the "Maunsell Limited" on an Eastleigh-Yeovil Junction-Eastleigh-Basingstoke tour — was advertised as featuring Nos 828 and 777 *Sir Lamiel* double-heading and was much better supported. However because of 777's continuing absence 34027 *Taw Valley* substituted. The surprisingly patchy support levels resulted in some voices being raised asking if the market in that area was being over-saturated. Fears were expressed for the success of the proposed four round shuttle trips a day between Eastleigh and Salisbury planned for the 9th and 10th October with No 828 and No 70000 *Britannia*, but were ill-founded. Even though boiler problems kept *Britannia* off the first train on the 9th the weekend turned out to be a huge success.

The surprise of the year came when it was announced that the "Dorset Phoenix" Weymouth to Waterloo run on 13th November by No 34027 *Taw Valley* was to take place during daylight hours. This relaxation of the ban on running steam in daylight hours over electrified third-rail track was a one-off experiment to see if enthusiasts could be trusted to

LMS 'Coronation' Pacific No 46229 Duchess of Hamilton **heads north just south of Ribblehead station with the "Cumbrian Mountain Express" of the 17th March 1993. An authentic "Royal Scot" headboard enhances the scene.**

(John Cooper-Smith)

behave responsibly. Happily all enthusiasts behaved impeccably. Not surprisingly the train was a sell-out.

Encouraged by the buoyant summer market, promoters presented an attractive autumn programme of steam tours in Scotland. No 60532 *Blue Peter* returned to some of her old stamping grounds on 18th September with "The Fair Maid" — a trouble-free railtour organised by NELPG, with 280 miles of steam, all for a fare of just £32. The route took the train from Carlisle to Glasgow via Kilmarnock, and included Stirling, Perth and a run over the Forth Bridge to Edinburgh Waverley. History was made in that no diesel-pilots were used under the wires at Carlisle, Glasgow or Edinburgh.

Expectations were high for the steam feast provided for the weekend of 16/17th October, with 44871 returning from Fort William to Glasgow with "The Lochaber" on the Saturday and 60532 *Blue Peter* on the "Aberdonian" from Edinburgh to Aberdeen on the Sunday. Sadly on both days almost everything that could go wrong did. On the Saturday, delays in the diesel journey to Fort William and at Fort William meant that the steam special was an hour down by the time it reached Corrour. Further delays occurred at Tulloch where the train was held for a 'down' sprinter. Finally in failing light and increasingly treacherous track conditions, 44871 slipped to a halt on the 1 in 57 climb from Arrochar to Glen Douglas, and had to split the train into two portions for two ascents of the climb up to Glen Douglas. Worse was to come when a further hour was lost in watering and shunting at Glasgow, and the final straw came when the train was diverted on to the Edinburgh Suburban line instead of running straight into the Waverley station slipping to a halt at

Morningside. The 270 hapless passengers finally reached Waverley station at 2.45am, some 19 hours after starting out, all having missed their connections!

Worse was to follow on the Sunday with the late start of "The Aberdonian" being compounded by the locomotive slipping to a stand on the 1 in 74 climb into Dunfermline at Townhill after a signal check. A diesel pilot was summoned and eventually the train — with pilot — reached Perth some three hours down, having travelled only 50 miles! A conference was hurriedly called between ScotRail and NELPG, and a decision was made to terminate the tour at Perth. More problems arose when ScotRail suggested the train wait at Perth till 7pm when it could regain its booked path. This was too much for the long-suffering passengers, some of whom had been on the previous day's train. Passenger-power prevailed and the train left Perth at 3.53pm. The problems were not yet over, and a combination of steaming problems and signal checks resulted in the train arriving in Edinburgh at 6.25pm. After all the anger and disappointment had died down, the one remaining impression in the minds of BR managers must have been that the running of steam excursions poses problems. The one thought that perhaps did not occur was that with proper forward planning a lot of the problems could have been overcome much more easily and quickly.

On a happier note, the rest of the autumn series of Scottish steam excursions went off very well, though the booking levels on some of the trains were poor. 44767 *George Stephenson* returned south from Fort William to Glasgow on the 30th October with "The Claymore", and steam returned to the Highland Line in November for the first time since July 1981 when 44871 ran a Stirling-Perth-Inverness excursion on the 6th, followed by an Inverness-Aviemore special on the 7th. After a week's stay on the Strathspey Railway, 44871 hauled an Aviemore-Stirling special on the 13th.

An exciting autumn programme of steam excursions in Wales was presented in response to the success of the summer trains, capitalising on the Central Wales line's 125th Anniversary year. After the disappointments earlier in the year, a "Cambrian Coast Limited" was run from Shrewsbury to Aberystwyth on 3rd October with 80079 and 80080 double-heading. The following week, the same two engines returned to the Central Wales line with the "Heart of Wales Anniversary Ltd" from Shrewsbury via Craven Arms to Carmarthen. The 17th October saw both engines work the "South Pembrokeshire" special from Swansea to Pembroke Dock, and on the 23rd 80079 and 80080 completed their short season in Wales by running from Pantyffynnon to Shrewsbury.

Having been excluded from the main line steam routes for most of the year, the "North Wales Coast Express" made its comeback on 10th October with 45596 *Bahamas*, the tour being repeated on 27th November. The "Welsh Marches" saw further action when 46203 *Princess Margaret Rose* ran from Crewe to Worcester via Chester, Shrewsbury, Hereford, Pontypool and Gloucester on the 16th, October.

Christmas saw a lot of activity on the main line. FSS promoted a "Christmas CME" from Carlisle to Farrington Junction double-headed by 44767 *George Stephenson* and 45596 *Bahamas*, the SRPS ran two Christmas "Fife Circle" specials with 44871 on the 5th December and 60009 *Union of South Africa* on the 12th December, and Network SouthEast promoted three Victoria-Brighton trains on the 28/29/30th December which were not only a financial success but generated some much needed good public relations. 75069 worked the trains on the 28th and 30th with 34027 *Taw Valley* heading the 29th departure.

1993 had been a year when reality exceeded expectations. Credit must be given to BR/FSS/SLOA for trying to present a better variety of routes with interesting motive power before its travelling public. Advertising had been much improved, and was one of the main reasons for sustaining the long season of excursions over the S. & C. line. Not least was Network SouthEast's drive and determination to open up new routes in its area.

But all was not well, and the main fear for the future could be summed up in one word, PRIVATISATION. When the Railways Bill first appeared in the House of Commons, ARPS Chairman David Morgan commented "It far exceeds our worst fears". The first concern was the inclusion of preserved railways and other non-BR-owned lines in a bill which in expert opinion had been hastily and carelessly cobbled together. The threat that preserved lines would get caught up in the mesh of the Railways Bill receded after prompt and vociferous reaction by those active in the preservation movement. This still left, however, rail supporters (as opposed to just steam enthusiasts) with concerns that privatisation would bring contractions in its wake. Some argued that open access would exist so that any steam locomotive owner would have the right to operate a train anywhere through any one of the 26 new train operating

companies — but to this statement must be added "if they pay". Fears were expressed that steam running over the main line might find itself priced out of the market if every operator had to cover his direct and indirect costs. In order for a locomotive owner to gain a "Certificate of Acceptance" after April 1994 he would have to provide continuing evidence of the condition of his machine, adopt and adhere to satisfactory maintenance policies and schedules, "audit" his own engineering work, competently maintain workshops and working environments to the BS5750 standard , and provide evidence that staff involved in restoration and repairs were qualified for the work they did. The question of what was going to happen in April 1994 when BR gave way to Railtrack, the Government agency which would control the entire BR network, was in 1993 unanswerable, except to say that the jobs of many dedicated railmen would disappear — such as S. & C. Line Manager Paul Holden, Regional Railways Tom Clift and even InterCity's chief David Ward.

The announcement in August 1993 that Flying Scotsman Enterprises and Waterman Railways (which owned 25 ex-BR diesel and electric locomotives) were to merge into a new company — Flying Scotsman Railways — to spearhead the running of "heritage" steam and diesel traction after denationalisation was greeted with some relief in that the new company would have the resources and skills to deal with a very uncertain future. Whether this new company would occupy a pivotal role in the running of preserved steam on the main line after privatisation remained to be seen.

1994 dawned with the good news that 46203 *Princess Margaret Rose* would run a mini-series of two "Ynys Mon Express" charters on the 3rd and 16th January, when the main line speed limit would be raised to 75 mph. Other excursions in January were limited to a southbound "CML" featuring 44767 *George Stephenson* and 45596 *Bahamas* double-heading on News Year's Day, a northbound "CML" on 29th January with 71000 *Duke of Gloucester*, and 6024 *King Edward I* on a Didcot-Cardiff-Swindon train on 30th January — the first time a 'King' had visited Cardiff for many years.

The winter/spring programme presented by BR/FSS/SLOA cleverly overlapped the change-over period from BR to Railtrack on 1st April, with two runs over the S. & C. line by 5029 *Nunney Castle* perhaps being the highlight. Regional starting points for main line steam excursions introduced in 1993 were an undoubted success and were extended in 1994 to include Brighton, Swindon, Southampton, Norwich, Salisbury and Lincoln. Back again after a 12 months absence were the Steam Locomotive Positioning Trains at a fixed price of £25 a head, mainly re-introduced to facilitate the transfer north of 5029 *Nunney Castle* and 'S15' No 828.

Perhaps the most eagerly awaited event in the winter programme was the 9am departure from Waterloo on 19th February of 34027 "Taw Valley " with the "Taw Valley Swansong" to Yeovil Junction and return — the first such departure since 1967. As an added bonus, the train was timed to the new 75 mph speed limit. The trip was an outstanding success in every way. Four days later, 34027 *Taw Valley* headed north on a Didcot — Bradford Forster Square "Yorkshireman" to be in position for a northbound "CML" on the 26th February and a southbound "CML" on the 5th March. With its boiler certificate expiring in March, these four trips marked the end of a very successful seven years of main line running by 34027, during which time the locomotive had covered in excess of 60,000 miles.

The first to use the new SLPTs was 5029 *Nunney Castle* on the 9th February when it ran a Didcot-Bradford Forster Square "Yorkshireman". For the first time in the history of these trains it was a sell-out, all 446 seats being booked. The trip was not without incident. The engine steamed badly on the latter stages of the trip, thanks to some very poor coal, and twice had to stop for a "blow-up", once outside Derby station and once outside Sheffield. At Sheffield, with the train two hours behind schedule, 5029 was taken off. After working some crew-familiarisation trips on the 10th February on the Keighley & Worth Valley Railway, 5029 *Nunney Castle* headed a CML from Leeds to Howe & Co Sidings on the 12th February (width clearance problems at Shipley precluded a Bradford start, and there was a similar problem with the down platform at Carlisle). This was the first visit by a 'Castle' to the S. & C. line since 7029 *Clun Castle* ran over the route in 1967.

If the 10th February train was unspectacular, the return trip by 5029 *Nunney Castle* on 12th March was a nightmare! Starting 50 minutes late from Carlisle, due to the late arrival of the train from the south, the engine steamed poorly all the way to Appleby, and then on the next leg of the trip slipped to a halt before it reached Kirkby Stephen. A class 47 on stand-by at Blea Moor was dispatched to rescue the train, but by this time stacked up behind the special were a scheduled passenger train, two diesel-hauled charter specials and several diverted West Coast Main Line service trains. The steam special was diesel piloted to Skipton, where 5029 came off the train, and eventually reached Euston at 00.32 — the passengers missing all their connections. BR had to field a great deal of flack not only from the steam special's passengers but also from passengers travelling in all the other trains which were delayed. At a very sensitive time, with Railtrack taking over from BR, the last thing the preservation movement needed was what was described as "One of the blackest days since the Return to Steam in 1971".

To mark steam's farewell to InterCity, the sector which oversaw BR steam for over 20 years, an Easter Extravaganza was arranged along the lines of the "Three Big Red Engines" spectacular in 1993. Five locomotives representing the Big Four and BR's Standards combined to run various legs of an "Ynys Mon Express" (though titled the "InterCity Sunset") on Friday 1st April and Sunday 3rd April, meeting up at Llandudno Junction for a photographic line-up. The five engines were ex-LMS No 46203 *Princess Margaret Rose*, ex-LNER No 4498 *Sir Nigel Gresley*, ex-GWR No 5029 *Nunney Castle*, ex-SR S15 No 828 (which ran north on a Didcot-Sheffield "Midlander" on 23rd March and created all sorts of problems when it dropped a plug at Ambergate), and ex-BR No 71000 *Duke of Gloucester*. Each engine was originally rostered to run one leg of the round trip from Crewe to Holyhead and return, but after the debacle on the S. & C. on 12th March, the rosters were changed so that 828 double-headed with 5029 *Nunney Castle* on the Crewe-Llandudno leg. 71000 *Duke of Gloucester* missed its second day's work due to a collapsed firegrate, 4498 *Sir Nigel Gresley* working the whole of the return Holyhead-Crewe leg. The knock-on effect of this was that 71000 missed its run with a "Welsh Marches Express" on the 14th May — the train being diesel-hauled.

On Saturday 2nd April, 80080 worked a Nottingham-Skegness special. Originally both 'class 4' tanks had been rostered for the trip. The run, however, did not attract the expected support, and a reduced train needed only one of the locomotives.

InterCity marked its demise as a single business sector with a special train on 26th March with 46203 *Princess Margaret Rose* on the first stage from Paddington to Didcot. This was the first steam departure from Paddington since the re-modelling of the track layout started two years earlier, and was 46203's first appearance on the GW main line.

In a nice gesture on 20th April, InterCity paid tribute to its former Special Services Director with a private charter for David Ward's former colleagues and friends. No 4498 hauled the train from York to Carlisle via Leeds carrying the nameplates *David Harold Ward*.

April proved to be a busy month for steam on the main line. It included 6024 *King Edward I* working another pair of trains for the "Bristol Evening Post" — the first from Bristol to Newport via Gloucester, and the second the reverse itinerary. The following day saw an unusual combination with 5029 *Nunney Castle* doubleheading with 80080 on a "Welsh Marches Express" from Crewe to Worcester, with 45596 *Bahamas* working an excursion in the reverse direction on 23rd April. The "William Shakespeare Express" made a welcome return on the 24th April with 6024 *King Edward I* at its head. The route was Paddington, Didcot, Banbury, Stratford-on-Avon, with the 'King' coming off the train at Didcot on the return journey.

Perhaps the most surprising excursion — indicating the erosion of the concept of "steam-approved routes" with the coming of Railtrack — took place on 27th April to facilitate the transfer of 75069 from the Severn Valley Railway to the West Somerset Railway. The locomotive hauled a fully-booked train from Kidderminster to Taunton and then on to West Somerset Railway metals to Bishops Lydeard. Sadly a subsequent epoch-making "first" run from Taunton to Kingswear and back on 3rd July and the return trip to Kidderminster on 25th September had to be cancelled when the engine was found to need all superheater elements replacing and a full retube.

Maunsell S15 No 828 had a most creditable first outing over the S. & C. on the 30th April with a heavy 12-coach train on the northbound "CME", and an equally successful return run on the southbound "CME" of 7th May. Not so successful was the positioning train of the 11th May when 828 was scheduled to run Derby-Sheffield-Derby-Didcot — the locomotive having been dispatched from Butterley facing the wrong way!

With the "All Change" rule applying from 1st April, uncertainty was very much in the air. It was generally assumed that for some time to come the FSS/SLOA Railtours operation would continue, and indeed they produced an imaginative spring and summer programme, helped by buoyant bookings. By mid-February all the "CMEs" and "CMLs" up to and including 21st May were fully booked.

Highlights in the early months of the programme were the return of steam to the Great Western main line west of Bristol, two further daylight runs out of Waterloo — one on to Mid Hants Railway metals, and the return of steam to the Folkestone Harbour branch.

Perhaps the most significant move was steam being allowed on the Great Western main line again after all the trials and tribulations in 1985 with GWR150. The occasion this time was "Exeter 150" — the celebration of the 150th anniversary of the opening of the Bristol and Exeter line. The star attraction at the RailFair was 6024 *King Edward I*, which ran from Didcot to Exeter via Gloucester and Bristol on the 29th April, before heading off to the Torbay Steam Railway on 2nd May. Then on the 1st May 80079 and 80080 doubleheaded a train from Bristol to Exeter, performing a round trip to Barnstaple before the train was diesel-hauled back to Paddington. On the 2nd May, the train arrived at Exeter, diesel-hauled from Paddington. The pair of tanks then ran a round trip to Paignton before taking the train back to Bristol.

The 7th May saw the return of steam to the Folkestone Harbour branch when 80079/80080 ran 13 shuttles under the title "The Harbour Master". On the same day, 70000 *Britannia* — appearing as 70014 *Iron Duke* on the outward run — headed "The Golden Arrow" from London Victoria to Folkestone Central as part of the celebrations marking the opening of the Channel Tunnel. The following day it made its epoch-making daylight run from Waterloo to Alton with the "Mid Hants Daylight" where the train was taken on to Alresford by 9F No 92203. 70000 *Britannia* then took over for the return run from Alresford to Waterloo. One week later 777 *Sir Lamiel* was scheduled to bring the mini-series of daylight steam excursions out of London to an end with "The Solent Limited" — a grand tour of its former Southern Railway territory running from Waterloo to Andover, Salisbury, Redbridge, Southampton Eastleigh and then back to Waterloo. Late in the day it had to be withdrawn because of problems with the superheater elements and 'Goods Arthur' S15 No 828 substituted and put in a very competent performance. It was amazing how often 777 had problems whenever it was due to be let loose on its old stamping grounds.

In Scotland, the West Highland Line celebrated in 1994 its centenary and the 10th anniversary of steam's revival on the line. 50 steam runs were planned with "The Lochaber" at £16 return, and a further 25 runs with the "Royal Scotsman". The rostered engines were 44767 *George Stephenson* and K1 No 2005. No 44767 *George Stephenson* travelled up to Fort William via a positioning special from Derby to Carlisle over the S. & C. on 19th May and an SRPS private charter train from Carlisle to Edinburgh via Dumfries on the 22nd May. It was in position to work the first "Royal Scotsman" of the season on the 23rd May, and the first "The Lochaber" on the 31st May, but with drought conditions and fire-risk the runs did not start until 14th June. The K1 made its way up to Fort William on a mould-breaking NELPG-sponsored railtour on the 29th May when it ran on the East Coast Main Line from Darlington to Newcastle, picking up at Durham, and then across to Newcastle where 60532 *Blue Peter* took over for the Carlisle-Skipton leg. The 12-coach train was fully booked and both locos performed faultlessly. Having reached Carlisle, however, it fell foul of the drought conditions, finally arriving in Fort William on 23rd June.

As if losing the first two weeks of the "Lochaber" season to a fire risk ban was not enough, the new rake of BR Mk1 maroon coaching stock was severely damaged on Sunday 26th June when 37.424 crashed into them whilst running light engine into Fort William station. One coach was described as "beyond economic repair", and the other five coaches were despatched to Springburn Carriage Works for full safety examination. Ten days later, having been limited to using three 'spare' coaches — and suffering a loss of £2,500 in revenue each day the train ran — the rake was brought back to full strength with three TSOs from the SRPS's own set of coaches and two stored TSOs.

The August celebrations of the centenary of the West Highland Line included the K1 No 2005 and K4 No 3442 *The Great Marquess* double-heading the "West Highland Centenary Special" from Cowlairs to Fort William on the 7th August — the first northbound steam working on the West Highland line since 1963. Because of multiple celebratory stops on the way, some unofficial, and radio signalling fail-

ures, the train arrived in Fort William some four hours late. The same pairing worked the "Lochaber" on the 9th and 10th August (running smoke-box first out of Mallaig) and on the 11th August the re-enactment ceremony at Fort William of the arrival of the first train in 1894 took place with 3442 *The Great Marquess*. No 2005 ran smoke-box first out of Mallaig for the rest of the season, only being turned in time to double-head "The Claymore" of 22nd October.

Whilst in Scotland 3442 *The Great Marquess* worked two trips from Edinburgh over the Forth Bridge and round the Fife Circle on the 14th September. The Fort William season closed with 44767 *George Stephenson* and 2005 double-heading "The Claymore" from Fort William to Edinburgh via Glasgow and the Forth Bridge on the 22nd October, and then on to Berwick and Newcastle on the following day.

If one was asked to name the regular steam operation which was the safest bet to continue year after year, the Fort William-Mallaig operation would spring to mind after 10 years of continuing success. However with four weeks lost to the high fire risk and then industrial action with the RMT signalmen's strike, coupled with a spell of three-coach running after the accident to the rolling stock, the financial returns in 1994 caused the Waterman Special Trains unit — which of course was now geared to making the specials pay their own way — to think seriously about the operation in 1995. In spite of all the problems in 1994, the "Lochaber" grossed £149,000 before expenses, carrying 11,000 passengers on 43 trains — an average of 250 passengers per train against a seat capacity of 320. In view of these figures it was surprising that noises were being made towards the end of the year suggesting that the whole programme might be seriously scaled down for 1995.

Southampton Dock Authority celebrated the 50th Anniversary of D-Day over the weekend 4th and 5th June, and amongst the various events 777 *Sir Lamiel* and 828 made three round trips with the "D-Day Invasion Express" from Salisbury to Southampton. Unfortunately the trains were barely even a third full — perhaps the £18.50 ticket for a one-way journey was a bit too steep. Surprisingly it was the 'Arthur's' first run on the main line since October 1992. In the intervening period no fewer than eight consecutive tours which should have had *Sir Lamiel* at their head had been either postponed, cancelled or run with alternative motive power.

Between the 4th June and 1st October, FSS/SLOA produced a comprehensive programme which included 17 "CMEs", three "Cotswold Venturers" on June 19, July 17 and September 11 featuring 5029 *Nunney Castle* and 70000 *Britannia*, and two "Bristolian" runs by 6024 *King Edward I* from Didcot to Bristol and return on June 5 and September 4.

A worrying feature during the early part of the summer was the cancellation of several trains due to poor bookings. These included the 5029 *Nunney Castle* trip on 30th May from Kidderminster via the Cotswold route to Didcot, the "CME" of the 4th June, the first "Bristolian" on the 5th June and the "Britannia Cheshireman" of 10th July.

To celebrate the centenary of the opening of the Sheffield-Manchester Trans-Pennine route through the Hope Valley, two out and back excursions from Manchester Piccadilly to Sheffield were arranged for the 26th June — the first time steam had appeared on this route for five years. Initially 45596 *Bahamas* was the selected engine to haul the trains, but after clearance problems were noted with overbridges at Grindleford and Chinley, plans were made to bring 44767 *George Stephenson* back from Scotland as a substitute.

When no crew could be found for this run, Ivatt Mogul 46441 was hurriedly drafted in, though with 31.421 attached to the rear of the train in case of problems.

No 60532 *Blue Peter* finally reached Aberdeen on the 21st August with an incident-free run, though the tour was cut back to a Stirling-Aberdeen-Stirling run following installation of new up lines on the Forth Bridge.

With its main line seven-year certificate expiring at midnight on the 24th September, 45596 *Bahamas* said farewell on the 18th September by resurrecting the "Scarborough Spa Express", running through from Bradford to Scarborough via York and a York Circle and then on to Scarborough. The return trip did not include the York Circle. An out and back run over the S. & C. had been the preferred option, but this had to be abandoned due to engineering work on the line at Skipton. This was doubly unfortunate as the locomotive missed out on its last two booked turns over the S. & C. on the 27th and 29th August when it was derailed at Keighley on the 27th whilst setting off for that day's "CME" which had to be diesel-hauled. Happily the engine suffered no serious damage, but had to be failed until ultrasonic testing confirmed that the axles were undamaged.

The weather could have been kinder on the 24th September — it poured all day — when the Ivatt Class '2' No 46441 ran with 300 passengers on a six-coach train — "The Westmorlander" — tender-first from Carnforth to Hellifield, then smokebox first over the S. & C. to Appleby. The return from Appleby to Hellifield was tender-first, with the final run back to Carnforth smoke-box first. The engine performed exceptionally well on a trip which even a year earlier would have been considered unthinkable.

On Saturday July 24th 1993, Betty Beet's BR Ivatt 'Class 2MT' Mogul No 46441 returned to the main line, working a special from Carnforth to Keighley and return. Further main line work was undertaken with the "Furness Flyer" shuttle to Barrow-in-Furness on 15th August. In 1994 the pinnacle of achievement was reached with a Carnforth-Appleby and return excursion on a very wet 23rd September. On the 26th June 1994, substituting for first choice locomotive 'Jubilee' No 45596 Bahamas *and second choice locomotive 'Black 5' No 44767* George Stephenson*, the 'Mogul' is illustrated here leaving Chinley en route from Manchester Victoria to Sheffield with "The Hope Valley Centenarian". The 7-coach train ran with a tailing diesel — No 31.421 — in case of problems, but the 'Mogul' coped splendidly.* (Tom Heavyside)

September 24th saw the return to the main line of No 35028 *Clan Line* after extensive overhaul, and the fitting of air brakes. The occasion was the Royal Society for the Blind's big charity run from Victoria to Portsmouth and back with the VSOE Pullman set. The following day saw 70000 *Britannia* in disguise as 70014 *Iron Duke* work the "finale" special from Victoria to Dover Western Docks, formerly Dover Marine. The train marked the end of regular passenger services and actual closure of the famous station.

The downside of September was the poor loadings of the "Cotswold Venturer" with No 70000 *Britannia* on the 11th, and the news that 71000 *Duke of Gloucester* had to be taken off its scheduled runs in September and October because of serious boiler problems with leaking superheater flue tubes.

When Pete Waterman bought BR's Special Trains unit on 11th May 1994 with its fleet of over 200 Mk1, Mk2 and Mk3 coaches, including sleeping cars, and six class 47 diesels, he predicted that the volume of main line steam operations in Britain would increase by 50% in 1995 and double in 1996. The publication of the programme for the last three months of 1994 gave enthusiasts more than a glimpse of what was in store for the future. It was a programme which even six months before would have been described as incredible. Open access had suddenly become reality.

The season started with an NELPG-promoted tour — the "Heart of Midlothian" with 60532 *Blue Peter* working over the ECML from Edinburgh to York via Darlington. The triumph and euphoria of steam being allowed to work over the East Coast Main Line after so many years absence was soon forgotten with the tragedy of the catastrophic full-regulator 36-second wheelslip on Durham viaduct which left the 'A2 Pacific' crippled with £65,000 worth of damage to its wheels, axles, motion and valve gear. Traffic on the main line was delayed by over three hours, and trains had to be diverted over the West Coast Main Line. Immediate reaction was "Would Railtrack promptly ban all steam workings on the main line?", but in fact they were very understanding and played the incident down — likening it to any other locomotive failure, pointing out they would not reconsider using electric traction just because a Class 91 locomotive had a serious failure.

The big news from the S. & C. was that from the 3rd December the "CMEs" would run steam-hauled throughout between Crewe and Carlisle. 60009 *Union of South Africa* was to have been the first to lead off on these trains, but because of the problems it faced in London the first two trains on the 3rd and 10th December were worked by 70000 *Britannia*. Due to engineering work on Shap these were both worked as southbound "CMEs". The A4 was "released" in time to work the first northbound "CME" out of Crewe on the 17th December.

The "William Shakespeare" made a welcome return to the programme with 46229 *Duchess of Hamilton* working out of Paddington via Didcot, Oxford and Banbury on the 6th November. On the 18th December, with trainmen now apparently eligible to undertake guarding duties, 5029 *Nunney Castle* with 12 bogies but only 180 passengers worked to Stratford from Paddington via High Wycombe and the "Chiltern Line" — the first steam over Saunderton since May 1993. Sadly, 5029 *Nunney Castle* again suffered steaming problems and put in a very poor performance on the return journey. Coal consumption was very heavy and with no coaling facilities having been organised at Stratford, the engine ran out of coal and had to be taken off the train at South Ruislip. At that stage it was running 210 minutes late. 5029 was temporarily withdrawn from the active main line list pending an investigation but was subsequently re-instated with a recommendation that future loads should be restricted to 400 tons. As a consequence the "Severn Cotswoldman" of the 1st January which should have featured 5029 out of Paddington to Kidderminster saw 46521 and 80079 doublehead the train instead. They had been scheduled to work a similar train on the 14th January with 5029 on the return leg, but this was now cancelled.

It was in the south and west, however, where the major changes took place. On Sunday 2nd October No 6024 *King Edward I* worked through the Severn Tunnel with the "Torbay Venturer". The route was Newport–Bristol Temple Meads–Weston-super-Mare–Exeter–Paignton, and was the first steam passenger working through the tunnel since

6000 *King George V* in the 'Return to steam' programme in 1971. Surprisingly even though this excursion took in the famous sea wall at Dawlish the loadings were poor. Saturday 8th October saw "The Mendipman" with 5029 *Nunney Castle* from Paddington via Reading, Savernake, Westbury, Frome and terminating at Cranmore — the first of a new series of specials running to the East Somerset Railway via the "Berks & Hants" line. Again the level of loadings was surprisingly poor. The following day saw *Sir Lamiel* return to the main line in the guise of 30777 with BR brunswick green livery with a Victoria-Dover-Canterbury and return special — "The Man of Kent". No 35028 *Clan Line* ran on the Merchant Navy Locomotive Society's first public railtour on 15th October with a 7.45am start from Waterloo to Yeovil Junction, the return working being from Weymouth to Waterloo. The next day saw the return working for 6024 *King Edward I* with the "Devon Venturer" from Newton Abbot via Exeter and Bristol to Didcot. On Sunday 30th October 70000 *Britannia* repeated her successful trip of the 8th May with the Waterloo-Alresford and return excursion.

A delightful series of short main-line trips took place over the weekend of the 8/9th October featuring LSWR 0-4-4T M7 No 30053 (masquerading as No 30129) between Yeovil Junction, Yeovil Pen Mill and Maiden Newton.The event was co-ordinated by the newly formed South West Main Line Steam Group.

Undoubtedly the highlight of the winter programme was the first A4-hauled express from King's Cross in 30 years and the first steam-hauled passenger departure since 4472 *Flying Scotsman* some 25 years previously. It fell to 60009 *Union of South Africa* — the same locomotive worked the SLS/RCTS "Requiem Special" in 1964 — to work this historic train, "The Elizabethan", from King's Cross to Peterborough and return on the 29th October. With the 442 seats selling in two days, a second run was arranged for the 30th Both were trouble free and highly successful. Indeed they had to be as after the tragic demise of 60532 *Blue Peter* four weeks earlier, this was one of the most politically sensitive steam railtours to be run since the return of steam to the main line in 1971.

Controversy followed when the A4 was accused of causing a "near-flashover" whilst running light engine with one coach under the wires at Primrose Hill on October 27th, and not only was the locomotive refused permission to leave Bounds Green Depot, but all steam was banned from running under the wires on both the East and West Coast lines. These actions caused the cancellation of three steam specials — the positioning train for 60009 *Union of South Africa* to return to Crewe ("The Eastern Cheshireman"), and the "Ynys Mon Express" on the 12th and 19th November. The matter was not resolved for 45 days — the A4 finally being absolved from blame, and the ban lifted. However in that time the engine lost five main line trips — the three previously mentioned and the "CMEs" of the 3rd and 10th December which were worked by 70000 *Britannia*.

November saw 46229 *Duchess of Hamilton* work a positioning special from York to Didcot on the 3rd, and after working the "William Shakespeare" on the 5th, the locomotive hauled "The Bristolian" on the following day from Paddington to Bristol via Reading, Basingstoke, Salisbury, Westbury and Bath. Unfortunately the engine was derailed at Bristol Bath Road Depot whilst taking water so the return journey to Paddington via Didcot — the highlight of the tour — had to be completed by Class 47 diesel. After ultrasonic clearance, 46229 *Duchess of Hamilton* completed her season in the south with the "South Western Venturer"

On the 6th March 1993, the NELPG sponsored an excursion over the S. & C. from Bradford Forster Square to Carlisle and return. The special featured Peppercorn 'A2' Pacific No 60532 Blue Peter, *seen here on the return journey crossing Birkett Common.* (John Cooper-Smith)

on the 13th November, running from Waterloo to Salisbury, and return via Southampton Central, before returning to York on a positioning special "The Yorkshire Duchess" on the 17th November.

Saturday 19th November saw 'Standard' tank No 80079 and and Ivatt class 2 No 46521 head a positioning special, "The Capital Envoy", from Worcester via Moreton in Marsh and Oxford to Paddington — a rare steam foray over the "Cotswold Line". The two locomotives were used on a series of four "Santa Special" round trips per day on the weekends of December 3/4, 10/11 and 17/18 from Kensington Olympia via North Pole Junction. After Christmas on December 27-29th, the same two locos ran a series of "Mince Pie Specials" consisting of four round trips daily from Paddington round the Greenford loop.

Steam was scheduled to return to Weardale during December with 46441 hauling two specials a day from Darlington Bank Top to Bishop Auckland, and then along the freight-only branch line to Stanhope where the Weardale Railway Society had its headquarters. The first two runs on

December 3rd and 10th were lost when in the wake of the *Blue Peter* disaster in October, Special Trains ordered that crews had to have both route and locomotive knowledge. Crews could not be found who were sufficiently experienced in handling the locomotive. After trials were run on December 16th for engine and route familiarisation the programme got under way on 17th December — the first trains on the branch since K1 No 2005 ran two excursions in March 1993. A similar situation arose when the "Blythe & Tyne" route (Newcastle-Newsham-Bedlington-Cramlington-Newcastle) was opened up to Santa specials hauled by 44767 *George Stephenson*. The fully booked trips on the 3rd and 4th December — three round trips per day at £10 a head — had to be diesel hauled when no experienced crews were available. Eventually they were found for the trips on 16th and 17th December, and extra trips were made to accommodate disappointed passengers from the earlier trips on 22nd and 28th December. The excursions were promoted by a firm new to steam tours — Days Out Ltd.

December again mainly belonged to steam in the South and West with 35028 *Clan Line* working "The Brunel" from Paddington to Bristol and return on the 4th using the "raspberry ripple" VIP set. Christmas lunch and afternoon tea was served en route. Two other dining trains — "The Sarum Limited" from Waterloo to Salisbury via Southampton and return on the 11th, and "The Man of Kent" from Victoria to Dover via Canterbury on the 18th were cancelled due to poor bookings. After Christmas 35028 *Clan Line* was again out on

On the 9th May 1993, SR Maunsell Class S15 4-6-0 No 828 returned to the main line after restoration with a test run from Westbury to Eastleigh. Then on the 10th September 1993, Network SouthEast pulled out all the stops to welcome the locomotive back on to the main line when it worked an inaugural special from Eastleigh to Salisbury and return. The loco is seen heading away from Salisbury with the 'Queen of Scots' stock.
(Brian Morrison)

Below:
'King Arthur' 4-6-0 No 777 Sir Lamiel *suffered a series of setbacks between October 1992 and May 1994 when no fewer than eight consecutive tours featuring the locomotive were either postponed, aborted or alternative motive power had to be found. The final tour to be disrupted was the "Solent Limited" from Waterloo to Salisbury with return via Southampton on the 15th May 1994, when 777 was sidelined with a recurrence of the superheater problem which surfaced in September 1993. 'S15' No 828 took over the tour and is seen backing the ECS down to Waterloo station on the morning of the excursion.*
(Brian Morrison)

GWR 4-6-0 No 5029 Nunney Castle *made a foray into "foreign territory" early in 1994, the highlight being a northbound run over the S. & C. on the 12th February 1994 — the first run by a 'Castle' over the route since 7029* Clun Castle *visited in 1967. The train is seen here at Blea Moor , heading for Howe & Co. sidings where the steam section ended due to clearance problems at Carlisle station. The main reason for the northern expedition was to ensure GWR representation in the "Farewell to British Rail" pre-privatisation railtour spectacular on the Crewe-Holyhead "North Wales Coast Express" route at Easter.* (John Cooper-Smith)

the main line with "The South Western Explorer" from Waterloo to Exeter on the 28th December, with the return trip running the following day. The grand finale for a *Clan Line* dominated December was the December 31st/January 1st. "The Auld Lang Syne" which ran a circular trip from Paddington via Reading, Westbury, Salisbury and Basingstoke before returning to Paddington. Advertised as the first main line steam-hauled New Year's Eve party-on-rails, there was a five-course dinner with wine and New Year was celebrated during a 25 minute stop at Whitchurch station with a piper and a champagne toast! Someone with a sense of humour priced the ticket at £94.95 (i.e. 94/95).

So ended 1994 — a year which saw an A4 express from King's Cross, a 'King' along the sea wall at Dawlish, and a 'Duchess' from Waterloo to Southampton. For 23 years steam on the main line had struggled with the strait-jacket of hide-bound secondary routes with a massive amount of

restrictions. Suddenly since rail privatisation in April of 1994 the shackles had been removed. Railtrack's brief from Government to sell track space and train paths to all comers had made open access a reality, but would the magic last? Where next for steam on the main line? The run-up to the 25th anniversary of steam's return to the main line in 1996 would be fascinating, but would it be comfortable?

After a major overhaul, and installation of the new air-braking system, Bulleid 'Merchant Navy' Pacific No 35028 Clan Line *returned to the main line on the 17th September 1994 with a "dry run" of its high profile first charter train on the 27th September 1994 for the Royal London Society for the Blind, using the VSOE Pullmans.* Clan Line *is pictured on the 24th with the VSOE Pullmans waiting to depart Victoria station for Portsmouth via Clapham, Virginia Water and Woking. This was the first-ever air-braked steam charter, and happily both* Clan Line *and the air-braking system worked splendidly* (Brian Morrison)

Left:
On the first three weekends of December 1994, a series of "Santa Specials" — four trips per day — were run on a circular route starting and finishing at Kensington Olympia using Severn Valley Railway engines Ivatt Class 2 'Mogul' No 46521 and Standard 'class 4' 2-6-4T No 80079. On the 11th December, No 80079 is caught passing Barnes with the 10.30 "Santa Steam Special".

(Brian Morrison)

Gresley 'A4' Pacific No 60009 Union of South Africa *made several forays into the southern half of Britain in the early part of 1995. On the 18th February, the 'A4' ventured into territory which has rarely seen this class of locomotive, with a Waterloo-Exeter train. The return working was on the following day. It is seen here with a mixed rake of stock at speed near New Malden with the 10.03 Waterloo-Exeter special.*

(Brian Morrison)

Below:
Proposals by Nottingham railtour promoters "Days Out" for a radical programme of 65 long-haul steam charters on high density routes — one every Saturday until March 1996 — caused massive ructions within the main line locomotive owners' establishment SLOA, Special Trains and its successor Waterman Railways. The first train, featuring Stanier 'Black 5' No 44767 George Stephenson, *ran from Newcastle to Manchester Victoria via Copy Pit on 18th March 1995 — an eagerly sought-after route for steam excursions previously denied to railtour operators. The excursion ran without any hitches. On the following week, 'Black 5' No 44767* George Stephenson *hauled the second excursion of "Days Out's" programme — "The Palatine" from Stockport to St. Pancras. Discounting a 1980s promotional run into St. Pancras by the NRM's Rocket, and a filming session with 'Black 5' No 44932, it was the first steam-hauled arrival at the Midland Railway's London terminus since 1962. The train is pictured here approaching Desborough at the summit of the climb from Market Harborough with the Pilkington set of coaches.*

Above:
A feature of the last steam workings before privatisation on 1st April 1995 was the plethora of steam excursions to new destinations. On the 5th March, SR 'King Arthur' No 30777 Sir Lamiel *worked a train from Victoria to Portsmouth via Hove, Bognor and Littlehampton with return to Waterloo, seen here accelerating through Herne Hill.* (Brian Morrison)

Below:
A welcome newcomer to the main line in 1995 was GWR 4-6-0 No 7802 Bradley Manor *which made a loaded test run from Bristol to Paignton on 29th March 1995. The train is seen here on the return leg approaching Newton Abbot at Aller. The 'Manor's' performance with the eight-coach train delighted everyone, and included very competent climbs to Whiteball summit in both directions.* (Brian Morrison)

Another main line "first" in 1995 was Standard Pacific No 71000 Duke of Gloucester*'s first ever run from King's Cross on 'Days Out' "The Comet" to Stockport. The loco climbs Holloway Bank past Belle Isle on the 13th May.* (Brian Morrison)

Whirlpool — 1995

There was a curious paradox which greeted 1995. On the one hand in the 23 years of preserved steam on the main line never had there been so much variety, with new high profile routes and an exciting range of motive power. And yet there was a feeling of unease and uncertainty.

With BR/FSS/SLOA at the helm the programme was never as exciting as it had been in 1994, but even in the darkest days it always seemed secure. Now with Waterman Railways set to buy out the Special Trains charter business on the 1st April 1995, and become the principal main line steam charter operator, the thought that all the responsibility for running a main line steam programme would be in the hands of one company geared to making profits resulted in a feeling of insecurity. The problem was compounded by the rapidly escalating charges for running steam specials. Locomotive owners were now faced with a charge for the six-monthly examination of their engine which had risen from £1,200 to £1,550. In addition a new charge had been introduced for examining an engine each time it ventured on to the main line which varied from £150 to £600 per day! No longer could any cost, however small, be hidden in BR's operating budget. In practical terms this was seen when Waterman Railways announced just before Christmas 1994 that the West Highland line steam operation would not run in 1995, and that there would be no other steam running on the main line north of the border. The reasons given were Railtrack's refusal to budge on rail access charges and the lack of financial support by Scottish tourism and Enterprise agencies.

The nub of the question was, would Pete Waterman go through with the deal without a two-year "exclusivity clause" which he felt was necessary to establish his business? The Government-appointed regulator, John Swift QC, expressed himself as "unhappy" with the exclusivity clause which would permit Waterman Railways in collaboration with Rail Express Systems, the Train Operating Unit, to be the sole operator of main line steam charters, and indeed it appeared to be against the spirit of the Railway Act which stood for open access.

A meeting was held at York on the 20th January at the instigation of Waterman Railways with RES managing director Charles Belcher and organisers and users of the special train services. Over 150 locomotive owners and railtour organisers attended. The key announcement was that Waterman Railways would not in effect work the charter trains but that this had been contracted to Rail Express Systems who had an existing operating structure and was the only operator on BR to currently have operating validity over the whole network. It soon became clear that the "restrictive covenant" which would allow Waterman Railways the sole right to charter steam specials for the first two years was no longer valid, and that Waterman Railways was only offering a "one-stop chartering package". Behind the scenes other operators were talking with the Train Operating Units and Railtrack with a view to running steam specials independently of Waterman Railways.

The initial programme for main line steam in 1995 only ran from the 1st January to 18th March reflecting the general feeling of insecurity before the big change-over on the 1st April, and problems abounded. "The Cotswoldman" running from Paddington to Kidderminster on the 1st January suffered a change of motive power when 5029 *Nunney Castle* was temporarily taken off the main line running list, 46521 and 80079 deputising. The train which was planned for their return to the Severn Valley Railway, and to return 5029 to Paddington on the 14th January was cancelled. On the 2nd January, 46203 *Princess Margaret Rose* was at the head of a marathon Derby-Carlisle train which due to late running had to be terminated at Appleby. The problem arose when the empty stock was late arriving at Kettering, the train's originating point, and the steam section left Derby about two hours late. On the 7th January No 60009 *Union of South Africa* worked a "Welsh Marches Express" with a loss-making payload of only 91 passengers. Problems again arose right at the start of the trip, and the steam section left Crewe some 75 minutes late. Further difficulties and delays arose with watering and turning No 9 at Newport, and eventually the special was diesel-hauled to Gloucester. Because of engineering works, the following day's tour with 30777 *Sir Lamiel* from Victoria to Preston Park, Havant and Fratton, with return via the Portsmouth direct line to Waterloo, was postponed until the 5th March.

The southbound "CME" on the 21st January hauled by 46203 *Princess Margaret Rose* was uneventful and the following day saw 60009 *Union of South Africa* on unfamiliar territory with a Waterloo- Salisbury-Southampton-Waterloo special.

Apart from a Northbound "CME" with 46203 *Princess Margaret Rose* on the 11th February, all the action that month took place in the south and west. On the 4th February, 35028 *Clan Line* headed "The Solent and Sarum

Left: There was considerable doubt early in the year as to whether steam would appear on the Fort William-Mallaig line in 1995. Rescued by Steamtown's new operating arm, the West Coast Railway Co, the service followed a similar pattern to previous years. BR 'Class 4' No 75014 opened the season on 27th June, and was joined by David Smith's LMS 'Class 8F' No 48151 later in the year. On the 20th September the '8F' climbs up from Glenfinnan viaduct to Glenfinnan station.

(John Cooper-Smith)

"The Severn Cotswoldsman" of the 1st January 1995 saw Ivatt 'Mogul' No 46521 pilot Standard 'Class 4' 2-6-4T No 80079 from Paddington to Kidderminster, the train being organised as a means of returning the two engines from their "Santa Special" and "Mince Pie Specials" in London to the Severn Valley Railway. Here the special runs with ECS from Kidderminster, through fresh snow near Stourbridge Junction — the first steam train on the line for over 30 years.

(Brian Morrison)

Express", a Waterloo-Guildford-Havant-Eastleigh-Salisbury-Waterloo train promoted by Hertfordshire Railtours, and on the following day 6024 *King Edward I* ran from Paddington to Paignton via Bristol and then on to the Torbay Steam Railway. The return working from Newton Abbot on the 25th February ran through the Severn Tunnel to Swansea, and was promoted by Pathfinder Tours. The 18th February saw 60009 *Union of South Africa* work a train from Waterloo to Exeter, and on the following day haul a second train back to Paddington.

No 6024 *King Edward I* returned to Didcot on the 1st March with an excursion from Swansea to Paddington via Cardiff and the Severn Tunnel. This was the final run by the 'King' before its seven-year boiler ticket expired during which time it had travelled over 12,000 miles on the main line. Its overhaul with a full retube and new superheater elements was expected to keep the locomotive off the main line for about fifteen months. 46203 *Princess Margaret Rose* continued a busy season with a southbound working over the S. & C. on the 4th March and a Shrewsbury-Newport-Severn Tunnel-Bristol and return run on the 18th. The postponed run with 30777 *Sir Lamiel* from the 8th January finally got underway on the 5th March, with 470 passengers enjoying a storming performance from the 'King Arthur'. No 60009 *Union of South Africa* returned north with a Paddington-Didcot-Derby-Sheffield run on the 9th March — the "South Yorkshireman" — the return train being worked by 35028 *Clan Line*, and then hauled a Classic Days Out charter from Nottingham via Sheffield and Leeds to Carlisle on

the 11th March. No 70000 *Britannia* made her first appearance of the year with a Didcot-Birmingham-Derby-Sheffield-Derby trip on the 12th March.

With a three-train programme of "Golden Arrow" excursions from Victoria to Dover and Folkestone with the VSOE Pullman set being planned for the 27th May, 3rd June and 23rd September, No 35028 *Clan Line* worked a familiarisation trip from Stewarts Lane to Canterbury West and Dover on the 18th March. Because of a broken steam pipe between the engine and the tender's air compressor, a class 47 diesel was attached behind the steam loco to work the train's air brakes. These trips marked a further milestone in the history of preserved steam on the main line, with the last steam-hauled "Golden Arrow" having run 34 years earlier behind No 34100 *Appledore*.

Not surprisingly with the 31st March marking the official end of BR's Special Trains operation and the handover to Waterman Railways, two novel special trains were planned.

Before those, however, there was a new initiative involving the use of the increasingly popular Ivatt '2' No 46441. On the 18th and 19th March it operated a Liverpool-Wigan-Southport-Liverpool circular tour. The five-coach train was an all-dining special for 126 passengers, with the Saturday tour running in the evening and the Sunday train a luncheon special. The programme continued over the following weekend with runs to Chester from Stockport via Northwich and Mouldsworth. All the trains were an outstanding success.

Probably the most innovative steam-hauled workings took place on the 24th March as part of Woking Council's Gala to celebrate the Borough's centenary, when 35028 *Clan Line* ran two "commuter trains" — the 06.35 from Woking to

Waterloo and the 19.09 from Waterloo to Woking. Season ticket holders paid a supplement of £4 to ride on one of these trains, and the 500 seat 10-coach train was packed. During the day the loco and coaches worked a schools special from Woking to Salisbury and return and an afternoon Woking to Clapham Junction run. Saturday the 25th saw 35028 *Clan Line* work a Woking-Portsmouth & Southsea and return trip, whilst on the Sunday, M7 No 30053 ran a series of shuttle trains round the Woking-Ashford-Guildford-Woking triangle. The weekend was marred by BR transport police reporting the worst trespassing on the track seen on Southern routes in years.

In a variation of the "Fifteen Guinea Special" theme of 1968 and 1993, a one-way Carlisle-Liverpool Special ran on the 31st March appropriately titled "The Final Curtain". The route was Carlisle-Settle-Blackburn-St.Helens-Liverpool. As well as breaking new ground for steam specials, the train saw the main line debut of Class 4MT No 75014 which piloted No 70000 *Britannia*. After some good early running, No 75014 suffered a broken crosshead cotter pin leaving No 70000 to both pull the train and push 75014 from Garsdale to Liverpool. A surprising statistic was that there were 20 paying passengers on the train, travelling at a fare of £157. The other 232 passengers were guests of Special Trains.

A series of trains were promoted at the end of March 1995 to mark the official end of BR's "Special Trains" operation. Amongst these were a series of dining train specials in the North West using the popular Ivatt 'Class 2' Mogul No 46441. On the 19th March it operated a Liverpool-Wigan-Southport-Liverpool circular tour with full dining facilities. The 5-coach train was limited to 126 passengers at £59 per head. It is seen here running through St. Helens Shaw Street station en route for Southport. (Brian Dobbs)

BR Pacific 'Class 7P' No 70000 Britannia *worked the Blackburn-Carlisle leg of Rail UK's Spalding-Carlisle-Peterborough railtour on the 25th March, seen here arriving in impressive style at Blea Moor.* (John Cooper-Smith)

In order to achieve a "seamless handover" the first Waterman Railways post-BR special ran on the following day — the 1st April. This saw 30777 *Sir Lamiel* work a train from Waterloo to Southampton Docks where it handed over to S15 No 828 for a trip round to Portsmouth. The two locomotives then doubleheaded the train back to Victoria over the direct Portsmouth main line. It is ironic to note that steam on the main line outlived BR when 26 years ago it looked as though the opposite would happen.

The highlight of the new Waterman Railways spring programme should have been a series of four double-headed excursions featuring 75014 and 70000 *Britannia*. "The North and West Limited" did run from Crewe to Exeter St. Davids via Hereford, the Severn tunnel and Bristol on the 8th April. History was then expected to be made on Good Friday, the 14th March, with the two engines crossing over the Albert Bridge into Cornwall with "The Duchy Explorer" from Exeter St. Davids to Plymouth and Penzance — the first steam excursion into Cornwall in 30 years. The reverse working — "The Cornubian" — had been scheduled for Easter Day. The weather took a hand, however, and with no rain

for three weeks and the foliage tinder-dry, the runs were cancelled much to the disappointment of the 800 passengers. The fourth train on the 18th April from Exeter to Crewe with "The Exe-Severn Limited", was also cancelled. In compensation the two engines ran a Plymouth-Paddington special — "The Mayflower" — on 29th April in poor weather conditions. The trip was planned and executed in less than a fortnight and the take-up of seats at just under 300 was rather less than the possible 382. Because the locomotives were out of position, "The Midlander" on the 29th April (75014 Crewe-Keighley) and "The Salopian" on the 13th May, which was being run to bring 70000 *Britannia* south, were both cancelled. A new train with 70000 *Britannia* and 75014 — "The Thames-Usk Limited" — was hastily arranged for the 13th May but had to be cancelled yet again three days before it ran because of fire-risk.

The eagerly awaited main line summer steam programme produced by Waterman Railways was published late in February. It contained seven "repeat itinerary" steam package tours with a total of 69 trains, some of which were blockbooked to independent railtour companies including LSW Railtours, Pathfinder Tours, Classic Days, Hertfordshire Railtours, and Princess Margaret Rose Tours. These were supplemented by several "one-off" specials. The Fort William-Mallaig "Lochaber" as expected did not feature in the programme.

The prime tour was "The Torbay Limited" with 37 trains running from Bristol to Paignton over the 1 in 80 Whiteball summit on Sundays and Wednesdays starting on the May Bank holiday — the 29th — plus Thursdays in the high season. The rostered locomotives were SVR engines No 7325 and No 7802 *Bradley Manor*. With memories of the "North Wales Coast Express" of a few years ago, some doubts were expressed as to whether the market could sustain these trains particularly when holiday makers would be charged £27 for a standard class return, or £70 for a family ticket. 7802 *Bradley Manor* carried out a successful test run/press run/promotional tour from Bristol to Paignton and return on the 29th March.

Special Trains bade farewell in some style on Friday 31st March when "The Final 15 Guinea Special" was steam-hauled from Carlisle to Liverpool by newly restored BR 'Class 4' No 75014 and Standard Pacific 'Class 7P' No 70000 Britannia. *Unfortunately the trip was dogged by problems, including the discovery at Garsdale that 75014 had suffered a broken left-hand crosshead cotter pin. For the rest of the trip the 'Class 4' did little, if any, work,* Britannia *pushing the pilot as well as hauling the 11-coach train, which arrived one hour late in Liverpool. The train is seen here approaching the summit at Ais Gill viaduct.* (Brian Dobbs)

"The Strong Countryman" was a series of seven trains steam-hauled from Waterloo to Bournemouth and back with pick-up points at Clapham Junction, Woking and Basingstoke, and with the chance of leaving the train at Brokenhurst to visit the Beaulieu Motor Museum. The first train was scheduled to run on 11th June with 70000 *Britannia*, 30777 *Sir Lamiel* and 828 forming the pool of locos. Also in the south and west, a series of five trains, steam-hauled throughout on the Paddington-Bristol GW main line under the evocative title "The Bristolian", would run from June 4th with motive power from a pool of 70000 *Britannia*, 5029 *Nunney Castle* and 35028 *Clan Line*. Like the original train introduced in 1935, the outward run would be via Bath, and the return run via Filton and Badminton.

"The Cotswold Venturer" was planned as a direct link between the Didcot Railway Centre and the Severn Valley Railway, with three of the four trains having provincial start points — Brighton, Ipswich and Ashford. The first train on 17th June started at Paddington. The outward route was via the "Cotswold Line" with the return running through the "Golden Valley". Locomotives would be drawn from a pool of 30777 *Sir Lamiel*, 5029 *Nunney Castle* and 70000 *Britannia*.

Three well-known routes from past years made up the rest of the programme. Ten "Cumbrian Mountain Express"

trains were scheduled to run, commencing with a north-bound run on 3rd June, four having Euston as the starting point with the remainder having regional starting points. Locomotives would be from a pool of four — 71000 *Duke of Gloucester*, 46229 *Duchess of Hamilton*, 60009 *Union of South Africa* and 46203 *Princess Margaret Rose*. "The Ynys Mon Express" was to have four outings starting on June 18th, and the two "Welsh Marches Express", both being hauled by 60009 *Union of South Africa*, would run on July 1st from Worcester to Crewe and 29th in the opposite direction.

Suddenly the pace of developments, which had been quite staggering, became even more frenetic with the entrance of a new player in the shape of Melvyn Chamberlain of Days Out Ltd. In the space of a few weeks he staggered the steam railway community by publishing a programme of 65 long distance steam excursions to run over 12 months, ran on the 18th March a train hauled by 44767 *George Stephenson* over the Copy Pit route from Newcastle to Manchester, and then a week later "The Palatine" with the same engine from Manchester to St. Pancras over the former Midland main line. Both of these routes had been the subject of proposed tours for many years but no promoter had ever before succeeded in organising such runs. Crunch time had come for some locomotive owners with the need to decide whether to stay with Waterman Railways or support the competing operators. Days Out's proposed summer programme was bold, imaginative and used three locomotives — 44767 *George Stephenson* with its excellent record of reliability, 60007 *Sir Nigel Gresley* in its new livery of BR lined blue, and 71000 *Duke of Gloucester*.

Just as it had in the south-west, the weather then took a hand, and April steam rail tours were decimated. During Days Out's "North Eastern" on 8th April from Stockport to Newcastle, featuring 60007 *Sir Nigel Gresley* on its return to the main line, some lineside fires were started in the Chesterfield area. In order to gain access to the fires, firemen had to run hoses over the main line which was closed for some two hours. As a consequence Railtrack NorthEast promptly issued a warning that it would not accept further steam workings over its "core" routes "until further notice", and reserved the right to insist in future on a diesel-pilot for any steam-hauled train in their area. Days Out lost "The Blue Borderer" tour — Newcastle, Carlisle, S. & C., Leeds and back to Newcastle over the ECML — scheduled for the 15th April, and the Hertfordshire Railtours "The Derwent Eden" of the 22nd April from Derby to Carlisle via Leeds, which should have featured the welcome return to the main line after extensive boiler repairs of 71000 *Duke of Gloucester*.

Emotions ran high and there was furore at Carlisle on the 22nd April when A4 No 60009 *Union of South Africa* was failed for its southbound run over the S. & C., for what Alun Rees — SVR's General Manager and acknowledged expert on all things steam — regarded as a "minor steam leak". The SRPS special from Linlithgow to Crewe had to be diesel-hauled. In view of the new daily examinations charges being made, questions were asked about the calibre of the fitters conducting the examination.

With Railtrack NorthEast being the only area to enforce the restrictions on steam running, the 5305 Locomotive Association's "The 1066 Limited" ran on the 23rd April with No 30777 *Sir Lamiel* from London Victoria to Eastbourne. The train was then hauled by modern traction to Hastings with 30777 at the rear. *Sir Lamiel* then took over for the return run to London Victoria via Tonbridge and Redhill, the

highlight being the return of steam to the Tonbridge — Hastings line after a long absence.

The good news to break in April was that steam would be appearing on the Fort William-Mallaig line again for its eleventh year in 1995. Steamtown's Chairman, David Smith, with the help of the Fort William and Lochaber Tourist Board, the local enterprise company Lochaber Limited, the Highlands and Islands Enterprise and Lochaber District Council, put together a package for a four trains a week, 14 week season starting on 27th June. Motive power would be BR 'Class 4' No 75014 and David Smith's own locomotive LMS 8F No 48151, and the train's new title would be "The Jacobite". To overcome the problems of available drivers, Callum MacRaild and Arthur Trimbell who were going to retire, agreed to take severance packages from ScotRail and sign up with David Smith's West Coast Railway Company as driver/fireman. In addition to "The Jacobite" workings, negotiations were in hand to provide steam-haulage for the "Royal Scotsman" on Mondays.

During the months of May and June no less than 59 steam charters were booked to operate. Poor bookings produced calls for a reduction and rationalisation of the main line steam programme. Days Out were badly hit particularly with their steam excursions out of Newcastle. "The Norseman" to Manchester over Copy Pit on March 18th only carried 108 passengers, whilst the "Tyne-Forth Express" of April 29th with 60007 *Sir Nigel Gresley* was even worse with 97 passengers. To add insult to injury, the engine was failed at Berwick with a hot-box on the tender, the remainder of the tour being diesel-hauled. Finally "The Taysider" from Newcastle to Perth and Edinburgh on May 27th was cancelled with only 91 bookings.

On the 6th May steam returned to the North Wales Coast route after a gap of 11 months with 71000 *Duke of Gloucester* at the head of an "Ynys Mon Express". Then the continuing hot dry weather forced a ban on steam because of the high risk of lineside fires. Cancelled were No 828's trip with an Eastleigh-Salisbury-Bristol charter for the Eastleigh Preservation Society, and "The Canterbury Tale" hauled by 35028 *Clan Line*, working a round trip from Victoria to Dover via Tonbridge, Ashford and Canterbury, both on the 7th May.

"The VE Day Jubilee Limited" from Waterloo to Southampton Docks via Lis and Fareham, with return to Waterloo via Basingstoke did manage to run on the 8th May, but Days Out "Royal Borderer" which should have featured 44767 *George Stephenson* working up the Lickey Incline — albeit with a diesel banker — was not so lucky and was cancelled.

71000 *Duke of Gloucester* at the head of the "Royal Palatine", a Days Out charter from Crewe on May 10th, nearly managed to make history by reaching King's Cross, but because a path could not be found to release the engine from the station, the train terminated at Harringay goods loop. The 13th May, however saw another main line "first" when the 'Duke' made its first-ever run from King's Cross on the Days Out "Comet" to Crewe.

The "Bournemouth Belle" on the 13th hauled by 35028 *Clan Line* saw the main line steam-hauled debut of the "Statesman Pullman" train, comprising 12 BR-designed Pullman coaches which had been refurbished with maroon and gold livery.

The loaded test run by Collett 2-6-0 No 7325 on 19th May from Stourbridge Junction to Newport and back was unusual in that fare-paying passengers were carried. The engine performed well on the outward trip, but failed with a hot-box on a white metal tender bearing on the return trip, and was taken off at Worcester. Fortunately 7802 *Bradley Manor* had been put on the train at Gloucester, so it completed the run. In spite of remetalling and running-in on the SVR, the "Torbay Limited" train on the 29th May was cancelled.

Two trips over the S. & C. were run in May, on the 20th and 29th, both hauled by 46203 *Princess Margaret Rose*. Days Out ran "The Humbersider" with 44767 *George Stephenson* on the 20th May from Crewe to Cleethorpes and return via Newark, and on the same day 35028 *Clan Line* hauled "The Canterbury Belle" — a round trip from Victoria through Herne Hill, Orpington, Tonbridge, Ashford, Canterbury West, Minster, Dover Priory and Folkestone before return to Victoria. The 21st saw two trains again out on the main line, No 828 running from Salisbury to Littlehampton and return, and 60007 *Sir Nigel Gresley* with "The Blue Borderer" — postponed due to fire-risk from 15th April. The first of the "Golden Arrow" trains ran behind 35028 *Clan Line* on the 27th.

"Steam on the Met" again proved popular with a series of Watford-Amersham shuttles on the 20/21st May, and Harrow-Amersham and Wembley Park — Uxbridge workings on May 27th to 29th. Motive power was provided by 75014, 80079 and 9466. Passenger loadings increased by between 3% and 4% from 1994, but the much-vaunted "parallel running" spectacle involving 75014 and 80079 was a financial disappointment with the trains running half empty.

By the end of May, with the cancellations caused by the problem of fire-risk producing considerable uncertainty in the minds of prospective travellers, ticket sales showed much lower bookings than had been the case for some years. This was evident in one case in particular. Days Out promoted a tour with 440 miles of steam behind 60007 *Sir Nigel Gresley* from Perth to King's Cross with an overnight stay at a hotel in Newcastle, over the weekend of 3rd/4th June. Granted the cost was £190, including hotel, but what was described as Days Out's "Jewel in the Crown" attracted only 90 bookings when 310 were required to break even. The tour was shortened to a Newcastle-King's Cross itinerary which ran on the 11th June. The train — the first all-steam working over the 268 miles from Newcastle to King's Cross for 30 years — had 297 passengers who had pre-booked, but it was only when a further 32 passengers, each paying £19 a head, joined the train at Retford, that the charter became a profit-making venture.

On the S. & C. — for years the barometer of the health of steam specials — bookings were markedly down with the "CMEs" of the 3rd and 10th June, rostered for 71000 *Duke of Gloucester*, cancelled when there were 100 seats sold on the first trip and less than 150 on the second trip. Worse was to come when the first "Cotswold Venturer" on June 17th was cancelled with only 90 seats booked. Days Out had more problems when they also had to cancel — this time the Paignton-Paddington "Torbay Express" with 71000 *Duke of Gloucester* on the 17th June.

One of the most interesting "one-off" trains of the year saw 30777 *Sir Lamiel* run from Newhaven to London Victoria on the 5th June with "The Liberation Express". This was the final leg of a trans-European steam railtour commemorating the liberation of occupied Europe from the Nazis 50 years ago. LSW Railtours' first "Strong Countryman" on the 11th June was 75% full and had a good run behind 35028 *Clan Line* from Waterloo to Bournemouth — the first daylight steam run over that route for 28 years. On the 14th June 71000 *Duke of Gloucester* headed "The Royal Devonian" from Crewe to Paignton, and in the process produced

some stunning performance figures and the fastest-ever assault on Whiteball. Paradoxically, the return working on the 17th June — the "Torbay Express" from Paignton to Paddington — was cancelled because of poor bookings, yet on the 18th June, the "Duke" ran another "Ynys Mon Express" with over 300 passengers. Also on the 18th June, 48151 made her first appearance of the year on the main line with the "Brief Encounter" (reference being made to the famous film which was partly shot at Carnforth) from Carnforth to Sellafield and return.

The fitting of air brakes to 35028 *Clan Line* during the locomotive's heavy overhaul certainly paid dividends in the first six months of 1995, and with 20 main line charter trains booked between June and December the success story continued. A new initiative appeared on the scene when Superlative Travel chartered 35028 for a series of genuine boat trains between London Victoria and Southampton Docks. Working with the VSOE Pullman set, *Clan Line* carried passengers for the *QE2* and *Oriana*. The trains were scheduled to run on 24th June, 8/16/22/26th July, 30th August and 8th September. The weather, of course, took a hand in the proceedings.

The "Three Counties" Bishops Stortford-Ely steam shuttles ran again on the 25th and 26th June with 60009 *Union of South Africa*, 70000 *Britannia*, and the new-liveried 60007 *Sir Nigel Gresley*. *Britannia* disgraced herself by starting ten lineside fires on the first run on the Saturday so the other two 'Pacifics' worked her remaining trains.

June was a worrying month. Bookings fluctuated widely from train to train, and the weather increasingly caused problems — it was too good! The trackside became tinder-dry. Waterman Railways cancelled several of their trains — often at short notice. More worrying still was the poor level of bookings for the "Torbay Express", and with only 100 bookings for the first run the start date was pushed back to 2nd July. Then on the 21st June came the crunch, with Waterman Railways cancelling the complete Bristol-Paignton "Torbay Limited" series of 37 trains. Worse was to follow when Bernard Staite, Operational Director of Waterman Railways, announced the cancellation of a further 11 steam charters from the "Heritage Days Out" programme. These included several positioning trains, both of the "Welsh Marches Express", three of the "Strong Countryman" series, two "Bristolians" and "The Cotswold Venturer" of the 12th August. The knock-on effects were considerable. For example, the SVR had put both 7802 *Bradley Manor* and Collett Mogul 2-6-0 No 7325 through a costly programme of main line preparation and testing and stood to lose £40,000 of engine hire revenue.

The situation had in fact become ridiculous. With the advent of "Open Access" there had been an explosion of steam charters on the main line. In the month of July more than 60 trains had been advertised, and this at a time when there was the worst passenger recession for a decade. Waterman Railways themselves were reported as having lost £100,000 on main line steam charters since purchasing BR's "Special Trains Unit" in April, and their principal rival, Days Out, had lost a reported £40,000. Following the cancellation of "The Torbay Express" on June 17th, Days Out announced that in future they would not run any train with less than 200 passengers. A sign of the seriousness of the problem came when the owners of the three locomotives working Days Out's excursion trains agreed to take reduced engine hire fees on trains which only broke even.

At a time when it looked as though matters could not get worse, they did! The hot dry weather produced a partial

steam ban from 26th June in Railtrack Great Western and Railtrack NorthEast zones, and this became general on the 30th June. Of the 63 UK main line steam tours advertised for July, the only ones to run were 14 Fort William-Mallaig "Jacobite" tourist trains, which went steam-hauled on July 4th after rain brought to an end a week of diesel-haulage. Perhaps the saddest part was that several of the cancelled trains — such as LSW Railtour's "The Strong Countryman" on the 23rd July and "The Derbyshire Dragon" from Peak Rail to Llandudno — were fully booked, resulting in tour operators losing much needed revenue. Some tour operators were driven to distraction. Days Out, whose Southport-Scarborough "Coast to Coast Express" was planned for 1st

July, re-scheduled for 15th July and rescheduled yet again for 22nd July, but never got the train underway!

Several Anniversary trains were affected , including "The 60th Anniversary Special" with 46203 *Princess Margaret Rose* on the 7th and 8th July, which had been in the planning stage for nine months. Notice of the steam ban was given only 60 hours before the steam special was due to run, so 26 hours of phoning around was required to notify all the passengers of this £270 a head special that it would be diesel-hauled. The Scarborough 150 trains with 44767 *George Stephenson* on the 9th July were also lost. The Merchant Navy Locomotive Preservation Society, owners of Bulleid 'Pacific' No 35028 *Clan Line* were particularly hard

Apart from problems negotiating a severe curve on the turn-out on the run-round loop at Mallaig which caused the balance rods on the driving wheels to catch the side rods, 48151 performed in exemplary fashion.

Over the season a total of ten days were lost to diesel-haulage — two because of a failure by 48151 when the rods had to be sent to Carnforth for re-metalling, and eight because of high fire risk. Expectations at the start of the season were a 75% loading factor, a figure which was comfortably exceeded. As a result, the future of summer steam operations on the Fort William-Mallaig line was secured at least for 1996. Unfortunately no end-of-season return trip over the West Highland Line could be organised. There was a sad ending to 75014's journey home to the NYMR. The engine was preparing to leave the National Railway Museum in York on 18th September when it suffered a minor wheel-slip. There was a loud bang and the right side cylinder end cover was punched off and a large U-shaped hole blown in the engine's right hand cylinder wall.

In England, the dry hot weather continued unabated, and the whole of the August programme of main line steam specials was lost. This included Days Out's most ambitious series of main line steam excursions to date — the running of 46229 *Duchess of Hamilton*, 71000 *Duke of Gloucester* and 60007 *Sir Nigel Gresley* on comparative trials of drawbar horsepower over both Shap and Ais Gill during five days of the August Bank Holiday. Almost the last bastion of the main line denied to steam specials was about to fall — the runs being postponed to 30th September and 2nd and 3rd October. The ban was not relaxed until the 16th September when 46203 *Princess Margaret Rose* worked south with a "CME", and the following day headed "The Shamrock Express" — a Crewe-Holyhead-Crewe train, which was, unfortunately, not without its problems.

With 12 weeks of main line steam charter business lost, railtour companies suffered revenue losses running into thousands of pounds. In mid-August, faced with a rapidly-worsening business situation, Waterman Railways announced a fundamental reorganisation. The restructuring was a cost-cutting exercise which involved some redundancies. Days Out reached the same conclusions and five of their staff were laid off in August and the whole of their steam programme was cancelled until the end of September.

Recognising that the weather was not the only factor to blame for the difficult situation they found themselves in, but that to a large extent a very significant factor was the mad free-for-all resulting in a top heavy programme of steam on the main line which could not be sustained, Waterman Railways promoted a reduced programme of only six steam charters in October, November and December. Other operators and locomotive owners also recognised the danger of massive overload of charter trains, and a group was set up

hit when they lost no fewer than five booked turns in July — four London Victoria-Southampton *QE2* and *Oriana* boat trains, and the prestigious Roy Castle "Train of Hope II" from Brighton to London Victoria on 23rd July.

In Scotland, "The Jacobite" got under way after a week of diesel-haulage because of fire-risk, with the six-coach all maroon Mk1 set with seats for 340 passengers almost full on every trip, and on a few trips with passengers standing in the corridors. Because of "contractual difficulties" the "Royal Scotsman" luxury train was diesel-hauled. The train had to be diesel-hauled on four occasions in August because of increased risk of lineside fires. Over the season a total of 60 days of steam operation were run — 43 of them by No 75014.

after an August 8th meeting called "Steam South" — an affiliation of locomotive owners and tour promoters currently operating charter trains in the south of England — with the objective of co-ordinating a reasonable programme of steam charters in the south for the following twelve months. Co-ordinator was LSW RailTours chief Paul Blowfield.

Worse still was to follow when on August 31st, Waterman Railways announced that it would not be promoting any steam charters in 1996, but would concentrate solely on leasing out its fleet of coaches to other charter train promoters and arranging tours for customers. The reason given for the pull-out was that the company had been savagely exposed to costs which the BR charter business never had to pay because they were simply "absorbed in the system." Pete Waterman accused Rail Express Systems of pricing railtours beyond the limit of reason and affordability. A few days later, Paul Blowfield of LSW Railtours announced that his company were abandoning the remainder of their 1995 programme because of "impossible" charges imposed by Rail Express Systems. He revealed that even with trains packed full, all three of his remaining steam charters would have run at a substantial loss. All these complaints by charter train promoters prompted the Government Rail Regulator, John Swift QC, to investigate RES charging and the company's monopoly in handling charter trains over the Railtrack network.

Two other more constructive moves occurred in September. The familiar Steam Locomotive Operators' Association was replaced by a company limited by guarantee, the Mainline Steam Locomotive Operators Ltd., the corporate basis giving a stronger base for furthering the interests of members and the encouragement of main line steam operation than could SLOA. The vacuum left by Waterman Railways' decision to quit the market was filled, after a meeting at Kidderminster Railway Museum in mid-September, by a new consortium of operators all of whom had experience of main line steam. Key players in the consortium were Pathfinder Railtours, Hertfordshire Railtours, the Princes Margaret Rose group, LSW Railtours, NELPG and Past Time Railtours — a new company formed by the three members of the Staite family made redundant by Waterman Railways. Their role was to act as a single co-ordinating body which would regulate railtours to make sure that charter companies did not compete with each other for the same business on the same day, a railtour trade association which could speak to Railtrack and Rail Express Systems with a unified voice, and an organisation which could pool its tours into one clear programme. Proposals for a programme for 1996 were agreed based on known marketable routes and a study of what the market could bear.

Following the steam ban caused by the very hot, dry weather, several interesting trains ran. On the 23rd September steam returned to the south with 828 hauling the "Itchen-Avon Tourer" on an Eastleigh-Salisbury-Bristol-Eastleigh itinerary. As part of a "gala fun day" in connection with the opening of the "Jewellery Line" from Birmingham Snow Hill to Galton Junction, BR Standard 4MT No 80079 worked a series of Snow Hill-Stourbridge shuttles on 24th September.

Far and away the most exciting series of steam charter trains was the "Shap Time Trials" featuring 60007 Sir Nigel Gresley on 30th September, 71000 Duke of Gloucester on 2nd October, and the favourite 46229 Duchess of Hamilton on the 3rd October, from Crewe to Carlisle over Grayrigg and Shap, and then from Carlisle back over the "Long Drag". Independent observers on each train, which were matched for number of coaches, numbers of passengers and quantity of coal, calculated which locomotive could produce the highest drawbar horsepower rating over four different climbs — Grayrigg Bank, Shap, the "Long Drag" and Wilpshire Bank. In poor weather, which got worse with each succeeding day, the runs produced a marvellous spectacle, with 71000 Duke of Gloucester the clear winner.

It was sad that the undisputed triumph of Days Out three-train 'trials' over Shap and the S. & C. should precipitate more problems, but that is exactly what happened. A dispute which had been simmering in the background between RES and Days Out over alleged unpaid bills by Days Out, variously quoted as being between £30,000 and £100,000, came to a head following a meeting of the two parties at Euston on 6th October. Described as "tempestuous", the meeting concerned the alleged overcharging of Days Out by RES of £12,000 for crewing costs for the three trains. The net result was that RES announced that it had ceased trading with Days Out, the remaining 22 steam charters of Days Out programme being immediately suspended. Days Out made a formal complaint to the Rail Regulator's office on the 23rd October with particular reference to the cancellation of the proposed two "Children in Need" charity trains. As a result the trains, worked by 71000 Duke of Gloucester, ran on the 25th November from Liverpool to Euston via Stafford and Northampton and the 26th from Euston to Manchester. Because RES gave Days Out only seven days notice that the trains could run, sales opportunities were limited and the trains ran more than half empty.

Perhaps the daftest story of the autumn concerned three trips by 46203 Princess Margaret Rose from Crewe to Holyhead and return. On the 17th September, and the 21st October, a class 47 diesel locomotive took over from the 'Princess' at Llandudno Junction for the run to Holyhead, and on the 30th September the train never got past Llandudno Junction. The problem was a broken rail in platform 1 at Holyhead, which was closed. Since platform 2 had not been gauged for the 'Princess' a class 47 diesel had to be used into Holyhead. Meanwhile 46203 travelled light engine to Valley, turned and then backed on to the train in platform 2 at Holyhead for the return journey to Crewe — the engine coupling up outside the end of the platform.

Steam finally made it to Penzance after a gap of 30 years, but only with diesel assistance at the rear of the train. The "Duchy Explorer" from Exeter to Penzance on the 14th October was double-headed by 7802 Bradley Manor and 70000 Britannia only as far as Plymouth where the 'Manor' was taken off the train with a hot box on the leading left hand tender wheel. The train continued with 70000 as sole motive power until it stalled on the 1 in 60 climb up to St. Austell. A class 47 diesel held at Par was called up and helped Britannia over the summit, staying on the rear for the remaining 40 mile run to Penzance. With Bradley Manor still unavailable for the "Cornubian" on the 21st October the return run from Penzance to Bristol saw a class 47 diesel coupled inside Britannia as far as Exeter. Both of these Waterman Railway charters were 442-seat sell-outs. The "Welsh Venturer" of the 4th November was cancelled, but its place was taken by the "Severn Valley Adventurer" from Stourbridge Junction to Swansea and return. The trip was to have featured 7325 and 7802 Bradley Manor doubleheading, but in the 'Manor's' continued absence 70000 Britannia substituted. History repeated itself when 7325 also ran a hot tender axle box and had to be failed.

December saw two trains run over the S. & C. line, on the 2nd northbound and on the 27th southbound with 71000

GWR 4-6-0 No 7802 Bradley Manor *and Standard Pacific No 70000* Britannia *burst out of Parsons tunnel near Teignmouth with the "Duchy Explorer" from Bristol to Penzance on 14th October 1995. A melted tender axlebox bearing forced* Bradley Manor *to leave the train at Plymouth.* Britannia *took the train on alone towards Penzance, but stalled on the 1:60 climb up to St Austell. The first steam-hauled train into Penzance for 30 years, therefore, unfortunately was diesel-assisted at the rear.* (Brian Dobbs)

Duke of Gloucester substituting for No 60009 *Union of South Africa* which was undergoing some boiler work. The other leg of each train ran over the West Coast Main Line powered by Waterman Railway's "heritage" diesel D172 *Ixion*. 828 Railtours ran a "Christmas Shopping Special" from Eastleigh to Waterloo on the 2nd December hauled by No 828. Six hours were allowed in London for shopping before the evening return to Eastleigh. Perhaps the busiest locomotive on the main line was 35028 *Clan Line*. It continued its series of boat trains using the VSOE Pullmans with runs from Victoria to Southampton Docks to connect with either the *QE2* or *Oriana* on the 15th and 25th October, and the 9th, 11th and 20th November. Its busy year ended on the 31st December when it hauled a "New Year's Eve Special" from Victoria to Canterbury and Dover and return to Victoria. Waterman Railways signed off with the "Auld Lang Syne" run behind 70000 *Britannia* from Paddington to Gloucester and return with a stop at Kemble scheduled for midnight.

So ended what was probably the most difficult and complicated year for steam on the main line since its earliest days in 1971. Tossed in the whirlpool of privatisation, the year was at times horrendous. During the darkest days in August and September, the prospects for the rest of 1995 and for 1996 could only be seen with a chilling degree of pessimism. And yet, with the appearance of an experienced co-ordinating group to market steam charters and a realisation that some limits had to be put on the numbers of steam charters marketed, a sense of quiet confidence and optimism once again appeared. Would 1996 prove it to be justified?

Maelstrom — 1996

Though no one expected immediate improvements, there was a general feeling of confidence in the air when the very moderate and sensible programme for the first five months of the year was published by the new "steam tours consortium". This confidence was given a boost when, with signs of a "new realism" in charges, LSW Railtours decided to return to the steam charter market place with an exciting and innovative programme which dovetailed with the programme of the "steam tours consortium". The highlight was undoubtedly a series of operations involving M7 No 30053 with various short-haul excursions. Sadly it was not to be, as the loco was unexpectedly withdrawn from service on the 22nd January due to essential boiler work found necessary during the winter examination.

For another rail tour operator — Days Out — things did not get better in the early days of 1996 in spite of the Regulator's "Consultation Report" into charter train services apparently coming down on the side of the railtour companies and rather against the actions of RES and Railtrack. This did nothing to settle the bitter dispute which rumbled on between RES and Days Out over charges. Indeed, the mediator appointed by RES resigned after six weeks in the job! Good news for those running steam charters on the main line came when the new owners of RES, which was sold to Wisconsin Central International Inc in December 1995, agreed to run steam specials "at cost" echoing former BRB Chairman Sir Peter Parker's view that excursions "warm the market" for railways.

The first steam-hauled excursion to run in 1996 was not from either of the two published programmes, but was a Victoria-Portsmouth excursion by 35028 *Clan Line* run with the VSOE Pullman set on 14th January. This was the first of a series of 27 trains planned by VSOE in 1996 with *Clan Line* which would include runs to Folkestone with the UK leg of the "Orient Express", "Luncheon Circulars" — Victoria-Redhill-Guildford-Victoria, and Southampton Boat Trains. It had been hoped that the newly overhauled and vacuum-braked 34027 *Taw Valley* would share this programme with *Clan Line* but because of initial problems with 'hot' bearings, and then difficulty in running a test train because of the drought conditions, the engine never returned to main line service in 1996.

Past Times Railtours first-ever charter train — the Worcester-Newton Abbot "Teign Valley Wanderer" on the 20th January — was the first steam excursion of the "official" programme. Though making a small loss with 360 passengers travelling against a capacity of 440, the trip was a resounding success with 7802 *Bradley Manor* working well with no bearings' problems. January 25th should have seen the return to the main line of 34027 *Taw Valley* after a major

overhaul that took only 14 months. 200 passengers had booked for the test run from Westbury via Salisbury to Eastleigh, but had to be contacted at short notice when on the 24th the run was cancelled because Interfleet refused to approve the new air brake. The Bristol-Swansea-Bristol train on the 27th January, which was to have been the official comeback special for 34027, was also cancelled.

Though only four steam charters were booked for February, each was important in its own way. The first excursion on the 3rd February was a "posititioning" train transferring 60009 *Union of South Africa* from the Severn Valley Railway to Crewe. "The Lace Sherrif" was steam-hauled from Worcester via Bescot, Sutton Park, Nuneaton, Nottingham, Uttoxeter to Crewe. The commercial performance of the LSW Railtours train, "The Southern Vanguard", on the 11th February was set to play a crucial role in the future plans of several railtour operators. Hauled by S15 No 828, it was the first preserved steam special to start from Portsmouth Harbour, and it also brought back steam to the Mid-Sussex and Horsham-Dorking lines after 30 years. It was specially geared to cater for the passengers, with photographic run-pasts being arranged. The train ran well-loaded and arrangements, including the run-pasts on the Horsham-Dorking section of the line, all went smoothly. The only disappointment was that No 828 was not allowed to bring the train back into Portsmouth Harbour — there were fears about running the loco over the above-water girder section of Portsmouth Harbour station. With memories of the problems with GWR150 in 1985, and No 70000 *Britannia* and 7802 *Bradley Manor* in 1995, fingers were crossed for "The Mayflower" which was steam-hauled from Westbury to Newton Abbot by 5029 *Nunney Castle* and then double-headed from Newton Abbot to Plymouth by 5029 and 7802 *Bradley Manor*. Past Times Railtours were delighted because the 448-seat train was a sell-out, and everyone else was delighted when the train stormed over Dainton without any problems. The day was an outstanding success, enhanced by the unscheduled "looping" of the train through Frome on the outward journey. February 24th saw Pathfinder Tours promote the return working.

Evidence that public confidence was returning was seen in the successful programme of 11 steam specials in March. "The Western Star" on the 2nd March, steam-hauled throughout from Paddington to Minehead with 70000 *Britannia*, was a sell-out. "The Dart-Exe Cursion" on the 16th featuring 7802 *Bradley Manor* from Totnes to Worcester via Bristol was also very successful. No 70000 *Britannia* returned to its old haunts on the 23rd when it worked "The Broadsman" from Finsbury Park to Norwich and return. On the 30th March the southbound "CME" hauled by 60009

Carrying the "Broadsman" headboard, Standard 'Class 7P' Pacific No 70000 Britannia *recreates the look of the 1950s while storming through Sawbridgesworth on its run from Finsbury Park to Norwich via Cambridge on the 23rd March 1996. Shortly after this run,* Britannia *was stopped with small tube problems, Gresley 'A4' No 60009* Union of South Africa *deputising on the 4th and 18th May "Cumbrian Mountain Express" workings.* (Brian Morrison)

Union of South Africa created history when the steam section terminated at Stafford after a run over Whitmore summit. The East Lancs Railway promoted their own steam special on the 30th March when 46229 *Duchess of Hamilton* worked the "Trans Pennine Express" from Preston to Manchester Victoria and then via Standedge to Leeds, York and Scarborough.

On the down-side for the month, the southbound "CME" of the 23rd March ran into problems, firstly when a diesel failed on the outward run, resulting in the train arriving in Carlisle 88 minutes down only to find that 60009 *Union of South Africa* had been failed with a leaking regulator valve, 46203 *Princess Margaret Rose* substituting. Days Out planned to return to the steam charter scene on the 29th March with the "Grand National Express" from London Euston to Liverpool worked by 71000 *Duke of Gloucester*, but this train was cancelled. During March, the good news came that steam would return to the Fort William — Mallaig line for the thirteenth consecutive year in 1996. It was announced that the West Coast Railway Co would run the "Jacobite" over a 13-week season from the 24th June with the introduction of a Monday afternoon train. The rostered locos were 75014 — happily now restored to health with the welding of the damaged right hand cylinder, and 44767

George Stephenson. Plans to run the two locos north on a double-headed train on 15th June — "The Deerstalker Express" — from Preston to Fort William via Shap, Carlisle, Kilmarnock and Glasgow had to be abandoned because of high fire risk over the West Highland line at the time.

April saw the unexpected withdrawal of three main-line steam engines, though only one failed in service. This was the unfortunate 34027 *Taw Valley* on its "come-back" train postponed from 27th January. "The Tawe Taw Tourer" was running from Bristol to Swansea when the loco was pulled up near Bridgend with melted bearings on the driver's side centre and trailing driving axleboxes, the train being taken on to Swansea by a class 60 diesel freight locomotive. On the eve of its April 13th "Citadel Express" run on the S. & C. the *Princess Margaret Rose* support crew found water seeping from the firebox and smokebox tube plates of the engine, which was withdrawn from service. The result was that the "Citadels Express" of the 13th had to be diesel-hauled and the 5th May "Ynys Mon Express" and the 6th May "CME" were both cancelled. The northbound run on the "CME" of the 9th April was therefore the loco's last main line run. Weeping tubes at the firebox end of No 70000 *Britannia* caused this locomotive's withdrawal from its rostered duties on the April 27th "West Mercian" and "CMEs" of 4th and 18th May — all part of Past Times Railtours programme. Retubing at a cost of £7,500 was carried out. A4 No 60009 *Union of South Africa* was the substitute engine for all three runs.

Only eight steam specials were programmed for April, but of these "The Tawe Taw Tourer" was steam-hauled for less than half of its scheduled trip and the "Citadels Express" was diesel-hauled throughout. The eight charters included three hauled by 35028 *Clan Line* in the south of the

No 35028 *Clan Line* appeared on three occasions on the main line in May, twice with the "Golden Arrow" on the 19th and 25th, and once with a VSOE special excursion from Victoria to Portsmouth and return. The other interesting run in the south was "The Maritime Historian" on the 25th from Southampton to Bristol and return behind S15 N0 828. This charter connected with Bristol's "International Festival of the Sea".

"Steam on the Met" ran again with great success on the 18/19th and 25/26/27th May with GWR Mogul No 7325, 75024 and 9466. Highlight of the programme was six miles of parallel running on each of the five mornings.

Events during June added up to "more of the same", with tensions between RES and the promoters of main line steam mounting. Forward bookings, though reasonably encouraging were by no means heavy, and the threat of a "fire-risk" ban was ever present. The month, with 12 trains scheduled, started reasonably well with an interesting run on the 1st when 48151 broke new ground yet again whilst working "The Midland Scot" south from Carnforth to Lancaster and Preston, and then via Hellifield to Carlisle with return over the same route — all for a standard fare of £26! Two other proposed trips for the 1st, however, had already been cancelled, and the continuing hot, dry weather caused the VSOE "Guildford Circular" tour to be diesel-hauled in place of 35028 *Clan Line*.

On the 8th June, the "York Royale" featuring 46229 *Duchess of Hamilton* from York to Crewe, did run but because of watering problems, and pathing difficulties, it arrived at Crewe almost two hours late. Scheduled for the same day, Peak Rail's "Derbyshire Dragon" from Derby to Crewe and Llandudno Junction was cancelled as a result of poor bookings and the possibility of enforced diesel-haulage. "The Golden Arrow" of the 9th with 35028 *Clan Line* ran as scheduled. Over the weekend of 15/16th June, the Ipswich — Bury St. Edmonds shuttles with the N7 0-6-2T No 69621 and 70000 *Britannia* were disrupted by the withdrawal of the N7 with firebox cracks. *Britannia* worked the shuttles, but timekeeping suffered with only one available engine.

Confusion reigned on the 16th when the "Ynys Mon Express" with 46229 *Duchess of Hamilton* was terminated at Llandudno Junction due to a train pathing error and doubts about track height and tunnel clearances at Bangor after engineering work. On the same day 35028 *Clan Line* had to give way to diesel haulage on "The Golden Arrow" — the UK leg of the Venice-Simplon-Orient-Express — because of high fire risk. "The Midsummer Cumbrian Mountain Express" of the 22nd June was cancelled by the tour promoter when diesel-haulage due to fire risk was a possibility, and the eagerly anticipated double run by 71000 *Duke of Gloucester* over Shap on the 29th June — "The Royal Scot" — was postponed by the tour promoter, Days Out, when bookings depressed by "market uncertainty" resulted in only 335 passengers, 100 short of the break-even point.

country — The "Ocean Liner Express" from Victoria to Southampton Docks on the 14th, a VSOE luncheon special on the 19th , and "The Golden Arrow" from Victoria to Folkestone on the 28th April.

May was a month of disappointments. What had started off as a programme of 15 steam excursions, with passenger confidence building and the prospect of a real upturn in the steam tour business, turned into a rapidly spiralling downhill trend. Problems started right away with the first train on the 4th May — the northbound 'CME' hauled by A4 No 60009 *Union of South Africa* — which left in its wake a 13-mile trail of over 30 lineside fires causing local devastation. A diesel pilot was added at Garsdale in an attempt to prevent any more damage. As a consequence three trains were cancelled — the Friends of the Settle — Carlisle Line's Bradford-Carlisle excursion with 60009 *Union of South Africa* on May 11th, Past times Railtour's reverse working from Carlisle to Crewe with the same engine on May 18th, and their greatly anticipated and fully-booked two-way "Shap and Back" tour with 70000 *Britannia* on Bank Holiday Monday May 27th. The "Ynys Mon Express" with No 70000 *Britannia* was, however, allowed to run two days earlier on the 25th May.

Another disappointment was the cancellation of LWS Railtours "Bert Hooker Memorial Trains" scheduled for the 11th May — the highlight of which was to have been the double-heading of the two trains by 34027 *Taw Valley* and 35028 *Clan Line*, from Weymouth to Yeovil Pen Mill. The trains were cancelled as a result of the continuing absence of 34027 *Taw Valley* from the main line scene after its failure on the 4th April.

The West Highland programme did get under way with 44767 *George Stephenson* working the first train on the 24th June. On the 27th June the train had to be diesel hauled because of failure of the RETB radio signalling equipment in the cab, but no trains were lost to fire risk. Indeed on the 10th July the train was pulled up on Beasdale Bank in torrential rain to make sure the ballast had not been washed away! 44767 *George Stephenson* worked all the trains till the week of 29th July when BR 'Class 4' No 75014 took over. Throughout the season seven-coach trains were run with excellent loadings — a tribute to the extensive advance publicity. Only two trains were not steam-hauled, the 27th June and a second day in August when 44767 *George Stephenson* suffered a leak on the pipe to the steam brake. Sadly no return special train worked from Fort William to Glasgow — the price quoted for the train was too high.

With all the problems associated with the running of main line steam specials, the feeling of locomotive owners and promoters at the end of June was one of despondency and depression. With train after train being cancelled at short notice, and the confidence of the travelling public at a very low ebb, many operators were beginning to ask the unthinkable question — "was it all worthwhile?"

Perhaps the most significant action in 1996 came when the 5305 Locomotive Association decided to withdraw 'King Arthur' 4-6-0 No 30777 *Sir Lamiel* from the main line in June prior to the expiry of its main line boiler certificate on 16th October. The decision was made when it was known that 30 firebox tubes would have to come out for examination before a new six-month main line certificate could be issued. Normally with four charter trains booked to run before its October deadline, renewing a batch of "wasted"

tubes would have been no problem, but after 18 months of worry, uncertainty and hassle — not only from the weather but also from all the "service providers" following privatisation — it was decided to move to the friendlier and less stressful environment of a preserved railway, in this case the Great Central Railway.

The Nottingham-based railtour company Days Out personified the problem affecting all railtour companies, though in an extreme degree. The company had not run a single steam train since the "Children in Need" special out of Euston on November 28th, 1995. Countless tours had been advertised but all had for one reason or another been cancelled or postponed. With a slump in passenger confidence, all the tour operators were experiencing difficulty in booking trains at a time when cancellations were rife. Despite the continuing hot weather in July, there were actually as many trains cancelled through poor loadings than because of high fire risk!

Apart from "The Jacobite" trains in the West Highlands, nine excursions were booked to run during July. Three of these promoted by Days Out were due to be worked by 60007 *Sir Nigel Gresley* during its stay on the Mid-Hants Railway. The first on the 6th from Woking to Exeter was cancelled due to high fire risk with all 500 seats sold. The second on the 13th, from Twickenham to Portsmouth, failed to attract enough passengers to be economically viable and was cancelled. The third train on the 20th was an imaginative routing from Woking to Nottingham using the Bletchley-Bedford line. Three weeks before the run and with all seats on the excursion sold, it was announced that the station platform at Bow Brickhill on the Bletchley-Bedford line was out of gauge to 60007. Re-routing via Banbury was

BR Standard 'Class 4' No 75014 has proven itself capable of coping with the fierce gradients on the Fort William-Mallaig line. On the 9th July it makes its way powerfully up the severe gradient at Beasdale with a heavily laden train.

requested but denied because it was too late for authorisation to be given for the altered route. No wonder tour operators were becoming despondent.

Other casualties were the "Ynys Mon Express" on the 13th July which was cancelled due to light bookings, the "Cumbrian Mountain Express" with 46229 *Duchess of Hamilton* on the 20th which was diesel-hauled by D172 *Ixion*, and "The Kent & East Sussex Venturer" with No 828 on 27th July from Kensington Olympia to Hastings and return.

The only two trains to run during July were "The Caley Sou'Wester" on the 6th when 46229 *Duchess of Hamilton* worked from Carlisle to Glasgow via Kilmarnock and then back over Beattock to Carlisle (the first steam working over this section of the West Coast Main Line in 30 years) and the "Tenth Anniversary" on the 12th when 48151 repeated its "bargain basement" out and back run to Carlisle from Carnforth via Preston.

With the long hot summer continuing, only two steam charters actually ran in August. On 17th August, 60009 *Union of South Africa* was allowed to run southbound over the S. & C. with a 13-coach train from Carlisle to Crewe. Not surprisingly the A4 was worked very gingerly and no records were broken, but no fires were started even though the lineside was parched. Past Time Railtours actually paid out £3,000 movement fee to get the out of position A4 from Crewe to Carlisle for the trip. It was disappointing for the company that only 254 passengers were carried — the train's capacity was 488 — and they suffered a £5,000 loss on the operation. The other train to run was "The Severn Valley Explorer" from Clapham Junction to Kidderminster on the 31st August with No 5029 *Nunney Castle* coming on the train at Westbury. Unhappily, the 'Castle' suffered a fallen brick arch en route and ended up being diesel-piloted between Hereford and Kidderminster.

Amongst those trains lost in August were 46229 *Duchess of Hamilton* on the 3rd on a round trip from Carlisle over Ais Gill with return to Carlisle over Shap, and the Nottingham-Lincoln shuttles by 60007 *Sir Nigel Gresley* to celebrate "Lincoln 150" on the same day. LSW Railtours cancelled two trains because of the continuing hot weather, "The Interloper" with 5029 *Nunney Castle* from Westbury to Salisbury, Taunton and back to Westbury on the 4th and yet another comeback train for the unfortunate 34027 *Taw Valley* on the 11th from Croydon to Southampton. Perhaps the most surprising cancellation came when Railtrack Midland stopped "The Merchant Venturer" of 16th August. This train was run to bring 35028 *Clan Line* north for the Crewe Works LNWR 150 Open Day. In spite of the train comprising only six coaches from the "Ocean Liner" set, doubts were placed on the locomotive's competence to climb the 1 in 52 Old Hill bank between Stourbridge Junction and Smethwick! The other notable casualty came on the 26th August when high fire risk prevented Stanier 'Crab' No 2968 from making its debut on the main line with "The Central Welshman" from Shrewsbury to Carmarthen via the Central Wales Line.

After consulting the long-range weather forecast, VSOE Ltd pre-empted any "fire-risk" steam ban by giving advance notice that its 25th August, and 1st/15th September "Golden Arrow" steam runs from Victoria would be diesel-hauled. The wisdom in taking this action was proved when Days Out "Blackpool Fairs Express" from Edinburgh to Blackpool via Beattock on the 6th September, Past Times "The Midland Welshman" with No 2968 from Carmarthen to Shrewsbury on the 14th and "The Royal Return" from Banbury to Kidderminster promoted by the same company with the return

of 6024 *King Edward I* to the main line after major overhaul, were all cancelled due to fire risk. The "Gauge O Guild Anniversary Railtour" on the 21st did run from Carnforth to York via Preston and Copy Pit with 48151, but was diesel-piloted throughout. Steam in the shape of 35028 *Clan Line* managed to make a comeback to the main line on "The Golden Arrow" trains of the 28th and 29th September

For the long-suffering owners of 34027 *Taw Valley* there was more heartbreak when on 23rd September Railtrack cancelled for the third time the engine's main line loaded test run scheduled for the 27th. Once again the high fire risk was blamed. When, finally, 34027 did get out on the track with a test run on the 10th October, the engine was failed with a cracked cylinder liner. As a consequence, Railtrack Southern refused to accept 34027 for the two "Bert Hooker Memorial" trains on the 12th October (postponed from 11th May) which were fully booked with more than 900 passengers and should have featured 34027 double-heading with 35028 out of Weymouth. Two class 33's substituted on the LSW Railtour train — it was too late to cancel the train and contact the passengers — but even then operational problems resulted in the train being terminated at Clapham Junction on the Sunday morning at 1.50am, 142 minutes late.

After all the trials and tribulations of the previous four months, there was an all-round feeling of relief when "The 25th Anniversary Limited" — the re-run of the 1971 "Return to Steam" special — actually ran on October 2nd. The train was hauled by newly restored 6024 *King Edward I* from Hereford to Didcot via Newport, Severn Tunnel and Swindon, and then on to Birmingham Snow Hill via Oxford and Banbury. It was perhaps a sign of the times that even this historic run had empty seats, and the train barely broke-even for tour promoter Past Time Rail. This trip was followed by "The Cities United Express" on the 5th October with the 'King' working the train from Birmingham Snow Hill to Paddington via High Wycombe, with return to Didcot. The 5th October also saw 60009 *Union of South Africa* at the head of "The Silver Jubilee" from Peterborough to York and return via Grantham, Nottingham and Sheffield. This train, which was diesel-piloted under the wires to Grantham, and then on to Nottingham (as an "operational precaution") was the first venture for a new railtour company, Hercules Steamy Affairs Ltd. Unfortunately it ran only two-thirds full.

Thirteen charters were booked for October, including "The Golden Arrow" on the 6th from Victoria to Folkestone, a VSOE Special from Victoria to Portsmouth on the 16th and an "Ocean Liner Express" from Victoria to Southampton on the 26th, all hauled by 35028 *Clan Line*. The loco's less than happy experience with the two "Bert Hooker Memorial" trains has been mentioned earlier. On a happier note, 19th October saw Days Out finally run a main line charter — the first for 11 months — with 46229 *Duchess of Hamilton* hauling "The Caledonian" on a Crewe-Shap-Carlisle-Shap-Preston diagram. The northbound run over Shap was described as "awesome", but problems at Lancaster where the loco slipped to a stand when it was looped on the southbound run caused delays of 38 minutes to other WCML trains. This train, in fact, nearly did not run. On the 25th September during a cold examination at Crewe the inspecting engineer found the beaded tube ends lifting from the firebox tubeplate. Rather than lose its last four workings before the expiry of its main line boiler certificate on December 6th, the Friends of the NRM agreed to underwrite a £4,000 full retube. This was completed in a frantic three

An evocative scene recalling memories of the past as Bulleid 'Merchant Navy' Pacific No 35028 Clan Line *crosses Grosvenor Bridge on its way out of Victoria station with the 10.15 for Portsmouth on the 14th January 1996, complete with the VSOE Pullman stock.*

(Brian Morrison)

weeks. The "Bristolian Duchess" from Shrewsbury to Bristol and return with the 'Duchess' was re-arranged from October 12th to the 26th.

As a result of an incident on the West Highland line on September 17th when the loco owner, Bert Hitchin of 75014, was alleged to have been an unauthorised driver on the Mallaig run, ASLEF "blacked" all main line steam charters between the beginning of November and December 5th. In fact this caused the cancellation of only one train — "The Fenland Streaker" of the 23rd November from Peterborough to Worcester via Spalding with 60009 *Union of South Africa*. Other November trains included the two runs by S15 No 828 on the 9th commemorating railwayman Harry A. Firth who was responsible for rescuing 828, "The Test and Thames" from Southampton to Clapham Junction and return, with a

shorter circular train from Clapham Junction via Guildford, Dorking and Redhill — "The North Downs Rambler", and the two runs involving 7325 and 6024 *King Edward I* to the south west. The first of these on the 9th — "The Flying Dutchman" — saw 6024 *King Edward I* run from Paddington to Newton Abbot where 7325 was attached for the run to Plymouth. The return working on the 30th — "The Devonian" — saw the two engines double-headed from Plymouth to Worcester.

The VSOE special day excursion on the 22nd November with 35028 *Clan Line* from Victoria to Portsmouth and return ran into problems when the eleventh coach on the rake of Pullmans — 'Perseus' — caught fire near Virginia Water. The return working to Victoria arrived over three hours late.

The most spectacular main line steam operation in the first half of 1996 was the "Steam on the Met" staged by London Underground. Here is the parallel steam running of the 26th May involving GWR 'Mogul' No 7325 (on the left of the picture and paired with Class 20 No 20.227) and BR Standard 'Class 4' No 75014, near Pinner. (Brian Morrison)

Proudly carrying its Harry A. Firth *nameplates which it received at a special ceremony at Eastleigh on 5th October 1996, 'S15' 4-6-0 No 828 heads the LSW Railtours Southampton-Kensington Olympia-Clapham Junction train of 9th November, here passing West Drayton.* (Brian Morrison)

November 23rd saw the return to the main line of 60532 *Blue Peter* after a £65,000 "bottom-half" rebuild, almost two years after the horrendous incident at Durham which saw its motion wrecked. "The North Briton" ran from Middlesbrough to Newcastle, and then across to Carlisle before heading south over Ais Gill to Skipton. The engine performed faultlessly, but the excursion ran over three hours late thanks to late running of the empty stock from Bounds Green and a class 47 diesel failure.

November, however, belonged to 46229 *Duchess of Hamilton* running its last three excursions before withdrawal from the main line on December 6th — possibly for good. On the 2nd November, the "Royal Venturer" worked from Watford Junction to Guildford, and on the 16th "The Royal Devonian" worked from Guildford to Exeter and return. The fitting highlight to this very special engine's career on the main line took place on the 30th November and the 1st December when on the first day all records were broken with a momentous run from Euston to Glasgow Central over Shap and Beattock. The final run on the 1st December from Glasgow

Central to Edinburgh, Newcastle and York was beset by a number of problems with some three hours lost at Newcastle, and the diesel 47.772, which was present for train heating and "insurance", was called upon to push the Pacific the last few miles into York.

After the disappointments of the summer, LMS 'Crab' No 2968 finally made its maiden main line run on the 7th December with "The Lyndum Fayre" from Dorridge to Lincoln and return. The engine performed in exemplary fashion. It then made its debut over the S. & C. with a northbound run in place of 60009 *Union of South Africa* on 21st December, giving a good account of itself. "The Breckland Express" ran from Peterborough to Norwich and return behind 70000 *Britannia* on the 14th December. On the 23rd December, 80079 hauled a series of four return workings with a set of five coaches for the Bedford-Bletchley 150 celebrations. Tickets were priced at £9 return (outward by steam and return by service train), and it is worth noting that even with all the 258 seats sold on all the trains the operation still incurred a loss and had to be subsidised.

Stanier 'Princess Coronation' class 8P No 46229 Duchess of Hamilton *worked a mammoth two-day special for "Days Out" to mark its last appearance on the main line in the foreseeable future. On the 30th November it worked from Euston to Glasgow, and is seen here at an occupation crossing just north of Scout Green. The photograph was taken with the help of flash, though it is nowhere near as dark as it appears. The NRM Pacific's seven year boiler certificate expired on the 5th December. The engine can run for another three years on a preserved railway, but the NRM have indicated that there is no money available for a further overhaul to return the locomotive to the main line.* (John Cooper-Smith)

The final two runs of 1996 were in the capable hands of 6024 *King Edward I* with "The Cotswold King" from Worcester to Didcot on the 27th December and "The Bristolian" from Paddington to Bristol and return on the following day.

One absentee from the main line over this stormy period had been 4472 *Flying Scotsman*, which still managed to make news! The engine made its last run on 25th October 1992 from Ealing Broadway to Stratford-on-Avon before the expiry of its seven-year main line certificate on 27th November 1992. It then started a tour of preserved railways which was interrupted on the 4th March when it moved to the Llangollen Railway and was found to have half of its flue tubes leaking. After an overhaul which lasted from April to July, it was out-shopped in its final BR condition — 60103, BR Green livery and German-style smoke deflectors. Two months later, in September 1993, when Flying Scotsman Enterprises and Waterman Railways merged, Peter Waterman became joint owner of the engine. After almost two more very lucrative years on private railways, where it was alleged it earned some £100.000 from Driving Experience Courses (£30,000 after expenses), it was declared a "terminal failure" when cracks were discovered in the firebox, and was withdrawn from service and taken to Southall for a major overhaul estimated to cost about £250,000. Unfortunately this coincided with the downturn in Waterman Railways fortunes in the steam charter business, and it came as no surprise when it was announced that Dr. Tony Marchington — the chief executive of an Oxford pharmaceuticals company — had bought the engine plus the rake of nine former SLOA Pullman coaches for a figure approaching £1.5 million. By May 1996, with money for the overhaul available, work was proceeding at a cracking pace, with the avowed intention of getting *Flying Scotsman* back on the main line in time to celebrate the 70th anniversary of its record-breaking non-stop run from King's Cross to Edinburgh in May 1998.

1996 once again produced a summer which was disastrous for locomotive operators, railtour companies and prospective passengers. Some locomotive owners earned not a penny to pay for the inevitable overhauls. Worst hit were 60007 *Sir Nigel Gresley* which up to the end of the year had not worked a main line train for sixteen months, whilst No 71000 *Duke of Gloucester* by the time its boiler certificate expired on the 3rd October had not worked a train for 11 months. Some owners, and custodians, such as Tom Tighe with 30777, decided that with the present conditions in which main line steam excursions ran, guaranteed work on a preserved line was much more acceptable. In addition, apart from all the worry and hassle with cancelled charters, the tour companies had been pushed to the brink of ruin with cancellation charges.

It came as no surprise when, after the First National Passenger Charter Conference on 19th November, decisions were reached by a newly-formed consortium of principal main line locomotive owners, rolling stock operators and rail tour promoters (the Association of Charter Train Operators — or ACTO) to establish an acceptable framework for the successful running of main line steam specials in the future.

The Bedford-Bletchley steam operation proved to be something of a fiasco when the first of five round trips on 21st December was delayed for two hours before departure by arguments over access to the footplate of BR 'Class 4' 2-6-4T No 80079, seen here working near Ridgmont. (Brian Morrison)

This included the voluntary relinquishing of the right to go anywhere on the railway system but to contain all steam-running in future to no more than a dozen or so specified, low-density routes on which repeat-itinerary charters involving a minimum of planning and approval, could run — steam had opted to return to the mid-eighties David Ward regime. There was also general agreement that the numbers of charters would have to be limited.

The announcement in December by Railtrack that it proposed closing the network to steam over the four summer months without prior consultation with the new consortium hardly helped improve relationships, and grave doubts were expressed over the likelihood of locomotive owners going to the expense of having their engines certified for only a few months work.

There is a sea passage on the West Coast of Scotland between the islands of Jura and Scarba which has a fearsome reputation, known as the Gulf of Corryvreckan. In certain states of the tide and in certain wind conditions, a huge eddy forms on the north side of the east end of the gulf which has been exaggerated in description into a whirlpool that can suck down a trawler. In fact in calm weather it is frightening rather than dangerous, though in even moderate wind over tide conditions the mass of breaking seas can overwhelm a small yacht. Specific instructions are given in the Scottish West Coast Pilot as to how this area should be navigated — prefaced by the warning to give it a wide berth if possible. The whirlpool of 1995 and 1996 had been safely negotiated. The problem for the future was would the tide and current still be running with the steam preservation movement, or had the whirlpool been negotiated at low tide, with the full force of the incoming flood tide still to be faced, which might well drive the movement back into the whirlpool — this time to be sucked down for ever?

Ex Lancashire and Yorkshire Rly. Aspinall 'Class 27' 0-6-0 No 1300, built in 1889, formerly 'Class 3F' No 52322.

EPILOGUE

There's always one, isn't there, in any company who has delusions of grandeur, and certainly the Lancashire & Yorkshire 0-6-0 No 1300, seen here on the 29th May 1982 at Carnforth, must surely come into this category if it imagines itself at the head of the "Cumbrian Mountain Pullman" — even the "bottom leg". And yet, when one stops to think about the history of preserved steam on the main line, isn't this what it has been all about over the past 25 years — the realisation of the impossible? First there was the realisation of the impossible dream — of steam returning to the main line after the imposition of "the ban" in 1968. Then there was the slow but steady progress in the establishing of steam on the main line. Enthusiasm and confidence supplemented effort and determination. Men dreamed dreams, and then by sheer hard work and dogged perseverance made them come true. Rusting wrecks were rescued from Barry, and were worked on — sometimes for years — by small groups of people who performed miracles of engineering to produce shining main line locomotives as good as the day they were first delivered on to the main line. Other groups, with no guarantee that their efforts would be rewarded, took a giant step in the dark and bought locomotives from BR out of service and again lovingly restored them. These people, both men and women, were the optimists, the positive thinkers, and the people who made nebulous ideas take shape and form and become reality.

Dedication and hard work, discipline and enterprise are not perhaps words that spring readily to mind in 1997, but these are the qualities which have resulted in the new steam age, and will, with luck, keep preserved steam on the main line.

The extraordinary world of the handful of first "Return to Steam" railtours vanished long before privatisation and the 1st April 1995. Gone is the "captive" band of enthusiasts who filled those early trains. We have moved on to a time when many different leisure activities vie for our spare time and spare cash, often with the help of professional advisers. The events of the last two years, and particularly the collapse of the steam railtour programme in the summer of 1996 simply highlights the problems preserved steam on the main line faces. Now is the time to pause, reflect and take stock.

Progress in the provision of better and even grander rail tours, developed often in the spirit of "Who can do the next big thing", has been literally unbelievable, and yet the last two years have demonstrated that this approach does not guarantee success. Someone once asked "When is a steam special not special?" The answer surely is "When it happens all the time."

So where do we go from here? I think the future, and long-term survival of main line steam, will depend on a cool, calm, considered and realistic approach. The development of the new consortium, and the moratorium of steam runs on the main line during the summer months are a step in the right direction. The consortium can speak with one voice, from a common standpoint in terms which are clear, sensible and above all achievable.

Whatever happens in the future, I am very grateful for the 25 good years that we have had. I have certainly enjoyed recording the miracle of steam's renaissance.

Stanier 'Jubilee' class 4-6-0 No. 5993 Kolhapur *made its first northbound run over the S&C line since BR days on the 21st March 1987. The locomotive is seen crossing Lunds viaduct after a water stop at Garsdale.*

Please note that all photographs NOT credited are by Bill Sharman.

Other contributors are:- Hugh & Toni Ballantyne, John Cooper-Smith, Brian Dobbs, Tom Heavyside, Brian Morrison.